SHAME

SHAME
Developmental, Cultural, and Clinical Realms

Edited by
Salman Akhtar

KARNAC

First published in 2016 by
Karnac Books Ltd
118 Finchley Road
London NW3 5HT

Copyright © 2016 to Salman Akhtar for the edited collection, and to the individual authors for their contributions.

The rights of the contributors to be identified as the authors of this work have been asserted in accordance with §§ 77 and 78 of the Copyright Design and Patents Act 1988.

All rights reserved. No part of this publication may be reproduced, stored in a retrieval system, or transmitted, in any form or by any means, electronic, mechanical, photocopying, recording, or otherwise, without the prior written permission of the publisher.

British Library Cataloguing in Publication Data

A C.I.P. for this book is available from the British Library

ISBN-13: 978-1-78220-254-7

Typeset by Medlar Publishing Solutions Pvt Ltd, India

Printed in Great Britain by TJ International Ltd, Padstow, Cornwall

www.karnacbooks.com

To
RAJNISH MAGO
in friendship

CONTENTS

ACKNOWLEDGMENTS　　　　　　　　　　　　　　　　ix

ABOUT THE EDITOR AND CONTRIBUTORS　　　　　　xi

INTRODUCTION　　　　　　　　　　　　　　　　　　xix

PART I: DEVELOPMENTAL REALM

CHAPTER ONE
Shame in childhood　　　　　　　　　　　　　　　　3
Ann Smolen

CHAPTER TWO
Puberty, adolescence, and shame　　　　　　　　　　19
Mali Mann

CHAPTER THREE
Shame across the adult lifespan　　　　　　　　　　33
Mark Moore

PART II: CULTURAL REALM

CHAPTER FOUR
The cultural faces of shame   49
Apurva Shah

CHAPTER FIVE
Shame and murder-suicide: Adolf Hitler and the Nazi cult of death   71
Ira Brenner

PART III: CLINICAL REALM

CHAPTER SIX
Shame and shamelessness   93
Salman Akhtar

CHAPTER SEVEN
Laziness and its links to shame   115
Jerome S. Blackman

CHAPTER EIGHT
Shame and the aversion to apologizing   129
Melvin R. Lansky

CHAPTER NINE
The dialectic of shame in cross-cultural therapeutic encounters   141
Christie Platt

CHAPTER TEN
The role of shame in treating maniacal triumph and paranoia   161
Patricia L. Gibbs

CHAPTER ELEVEN
The analyst's sense of shame   185
Anne J. Adelman

REFERENCES   205

INDEX   221

ACKNOWLEDGMENTS

Ten distinguished colleagues devoted much time and effort to writing original works for inclusion in this book. They responded to my editorial suggestions with the utmost grace. My assistant, Jan Wright, prepared the manuscript of this book with her characteristic diligence and good humor. Cecily Blench at Karnac Books provided excellent and patient editorial assistance. To her, and to all the individuals mentioned here, my sincere thanks indeed.

Salman Akhtar
Philadelphia, PA
April 30, 2015

ABOUT THE EDITOR AND CONTRIBUTORS

Anne J. Adelman, PhD, is a clinical psychologist and psychoanalyst with the Contemporary Freudian Society. She completed her doctoral studies in clinical psychology at the City University of New York, and later trained at the Yale Child Study Center in New Haven, CT. She joined the faculty there in 1995, providing training, teaching, and supervision along with her clinical practice. Dr. Adelman relocated to Chevy Chase, MD in 1999, and graduated from the Baltimore Washington Institute for Psychoanalysis in 2004. She has published in the areas of children and violence, trauma and the Holocaust. She is the coauthor of *Wearing My Tutu to Analysis and Other Stories: Learning Psychotherapy from Life* (Columbia University Press, 2011). She has also coedited *The Therapist in Mourning: From the Faraway Nearby* (Columbia University Press, 2013). She graduated from the New Directions Program of the Washington Psychoanalytic Institute in 2010 and is currently a faculty member of the New Directions Writing Program. Dr. Adelman maintains a private practice in Chevy Chase, MD.

Salman Akhtar, MD, is professor of psychiatry at Jefferson Medical College and a training and supervising analyst at the Psychoanalytic Center of Philadelphia. He has served on the editorial boards of the *International*

Journal of Psychoanalysis and the *Journal of the American Psychoanalytic Association*. His more than 300 publications include fifteen books—*Broken Structures* (1992), *Quest for Answers* (1995), *Inner Torment* (1999), *Immigration and Identity* (1999), *New Clinical Realms* (2003), *Objects of Our Desire* (2005), *Regarding Others* (2007), *Turning Points in Dynamic Psychotherapy* (2009), *The Damaged Core* (2009), *Comprehensive Dictionary of Psychoanalysis* (2009), *Immigration and Acculturation* (2011), *Matters of Life and Death* (2011), *Psychoanalytic Listening* (2013), *Good Stuff* (2013) and *Sources of Suffering* (2014)—as well as forty-three edited or coedited volumes in psychiatry and psychoanalysis. Dr. Akhtar has delivered many prestigious addresses and lectures including, most recently, the inaugural address at the first IPA-Asia Congress in Beijing, China (2010). Dr. Akhtar is the recipient of the *Journal of the American Psychoanalytic Association*'s Best Paper of the Year Award (1995), the Margaret Mahler Literature Prize (1996), the American Society of Psychoanalytic Physicians' Sigmund Freud Award (2000), the American College of Psychoanalysts' Laughlin Award (2003), the American Psychoanalytic Association's Edith Sabshin Award (2000), Columbia University's Robert Liebert Award for Distinguished Contributions to Applied Psychoanalysis (2004), the American Psychiatric Association's Kun Po Soo Award (2004), the Irma Bland Award for being the Outstanding Teacher of Psychiatric Residents in the country (2005), and the Nancy Roeske Award (2012). Most recently, he received the Sigourney Award (2013), which is the most prestigious honor in the field of psychoanalysis. Dr. Akhtar is an internationally sought speaker and teacher, and his books have been translated into many languages, including German, Turkish, and Romanian. His interests are wide and he has served as the film review editor for the *International Journal of Psychoanalysis*, and is currently serving as the book review editor for the *International Journal of Applied Psychoanalytic Studies*. He has published eight collections of poetry and serves as a scholar-in-residence at the InterAct Theatre Company in Philadelphia.

Jerome S. Blackman, MD, DFAPA, FIPA, FACPsa is clinical professor of psychiatry at Eastern Virginia Medical School, Norfolk, VA; training and supervising analyst with the Contemporary Freudian Society in Washington, DC; and past designated sexual abuse treatment resource for the State of Louisiana. He has been visiting lecturer at Beijing University, Fu Dan Medical University (Shanghai), and Zhe Jiang

Medical School in Hangzhou, China. The Psychiatry Teaching Award at the Naval Medical Center, Portsmouth, VA was named in his honor in 1992. He is the author of *101 Defenses: How the Mind Shields Itself* (2003), *Get the Diagnosis Right: Assessment and Treatment Selection for Mental Disorders* (2010), and *The Therapist's Answer Book: Solutions to 101 Tricky Problems in Psychotherapy* (2013). The first of these books has been translated into Romanian, Chinese, and Turkish.

Ira Brenner, MD, is a clinical professor of psychiatry at Jefferson Medical College. He is a training and supervising analyst at the Psychoanalytic Center of Philadelphia, where he is the director of the Adult Psychotherapy Training Program. With more than sixty publications, he has written extensively on the topic of psychic trauma, most notably in his books *The Last Witness: The Child Survivor of the Holocaust* (coauthored with Judith Kestenberg, 1986); *Dissociation of Trauma: Theory, Phenomenology, and Technique* (2001); *Psychic Trauma: Dynamics, Symptoms and Treatment* (2004), the Gradiva Award winning *Injured Men: Trauma, Healing, and the Masculine Self* (2009), and *Dark Matters: Exploring the Realm of Psychic Devastation* (2014). He has also edited special issues of the *Journal of Applied Psychoanalytic Studies*, on reverberations of the Holocaust (2002) and on anti-Semitism in Muslim countries (with coeditor Nadia Ramzy, 2007). He has received a number of awards including the Pierre Janet Writing Award from the International Society for the Study of Dissociation for his abovementioned 2001 book and the Simon Gratz Award in 2000 from Jefferson Medical College as a Distinguished Alumnus, having graduated from there with membership in the honorary Alpha Omega Society. He is in private practice in the greater Philadelphia area and continues to share his knowledge nationally and internationally.

Patricia L. Gibbs, PhD, is a faculty member and lecturer at the Michigan Psychoanalytic Institute, and a member of the Michigan Psychoanalytic Council. She was an adjunct faculty member teaching graduate courses at Wayne State University (1989–2001), and at the University of Detroit Mercy, teaching in the APA Approved PhD Clinical Psychology Program (2002–2006). She has been a registered art therapist since 1982, and has provided art therapy at the Detroit Psychiatric Institute and Providence Hospital. She has practiced in the Dearborn/Downriver area for the past thirty-five years. From 1979 through 1986 she worked in a number of community mental health clinics and hospitals, including the Macomb County Substance Abuse Center, the Downriver Guidance Center Adult Services Clinic, and the Providence Hospital Partial Hospital Program. She has been the Michigan Chapter head of the International Society for the Psychological and Psychosocial Treatments of the Schizophrenias and other Psychoses—United States Chapter (ISPS-US) since 2004. She maintains a private practice of psychotherapy and psychoanalysis in Dearborn, MI.

Melvin R. Lansky, MD, is clinical professor of psychiatry at the UCLA Medical School, Los Angeles, CA, and training and supervising analyst at the New Center for Psychoanalysis, Los Angeles. He is the author of more than 150 publications including the books, *Family Therapy and Major Psychopathology* (ed., 1981), *Fathers Who Fail: Shame and Psychopathology in the Family System* (1992), *Essential Papers on Dreams* (ed., 1992), *Family Approaches to Major Psychiatric Disorders* (ed., 1995), *Post-Traumatic Nightmares: Psychodynamic Explorations* (1995), *The Widening Scope of Shame* (coed. with Morrison, 1997), and *The Dream after a Century: 2000 Symposium on Dreams* (ed., 2008). He has reviewed books and refereed papers for the *American Journal of Psychiatry; Humanities in Society; Family Process; Family Systems Medicine; The Los Angeles Psychoanalytic Bulletin; Journal of Marital and Family Therapy; Hospital and Community Psychiatry; Psychoanalytic Quarterly; Theory, Culture, and Society; Psychoanalytic Books; Journal of Dreaming; Journal of the American Psychoanalytic Association; Philosophy, Psychiatry, and Psychology; Journal of the American Psychoanalytic Association*, and the *International Journal of Psychoanalysis*. He has been on the editorial boards of the *Journal of the American Psychoanalytic Association* and the *International Journal of Psychoanalysis* and is an editorial consultant for *The Annual of Psychoanalysis*. He has made numerous presentations locally, nationally, and internationally and has received awards for teaching and writing, including the Best Paper of the Year of the *Journal of the American Psychoanalytic Association* (2005). He resides and practices in Los Angeles, CA.

Mali Mann, PhD, is training and supervising analyst and child analytic supervisor at the San Francisco Center for Psychoanalysis. She is a cochair of the IPA's North American Committee on Child and Adolescent Psychoanalysis. She is adjunct clinical professor of psychiatry at the Stanford University School of Medicine. After completing medical school,

Dr. Mann finished her neurology internship and psychiatry residency at the University of Kansas Medical Center. She completed her fellowship in child and adolescent psychiatry at the University of Rochester, New York and then did a second fellowship in adolescent medicine at Stanford University School of Medicine. She published several papers in the *American Journal of Psychoanalysis*, including "Immigrant Parents and their Emigrant Adolescents: The Tension of Inner and Outer Worlds," and "Shame Veiled and Unveiled." She has written several book chapters including "Aggression in Children: Origins, Manifestation, and Management through Play" and "The Formation and Development of Ethnic Identity." Dr. Mann has recently edited a book, *Psychoanalytic Aspects of Assisted Reproductive Technology* (2014). She is a member of the Pegasus Physician Writing Group at Stanford University. She teaches at the San Francisco Center for Psychoanalysis and Child Psychotherapy Program. She is a faculty member at China Alliance Psychoanalytic Association, and teaches at the Palo Alto Psychoanalytic Psychotherapy Training Program. She supervises residents and child psychiatry trainees at Stanford University and San Mateo Psychiatry Residency Program. She has a special interest in applied psychoanalysis, maternal development and motherhood, as well as ethics in working with children and parents. Dr. Mann's community service takes her to Mexico as a member of *Los Medicos Voladores* ("The Flying Doctors") where she visits orphans and assists the orphanage staff in a small village near Ensenada. She maintains a private practice in child, adolescent, and adult psychiatry and psychoanalysis in Palo Alto and San Francisco.

Mark Moore, PhD, is the director of psychological services at the Joan Karnell Cancer Center at Pennsylvania Hospital in Philadelphia, and an advanced candidate-in-training at the Psychoanalytic Center of Philadelphia. In his clinical work over the past ten years he has developed expertise in the psychodynamic treatment of cancer patients and in the use of hypnosis for palliative care. He teaches and supervises clinical psychology interns and postdoctoral students on issues relating to working with cancer patients. Dr. Moore is frequently invited to lecture to health professionals on the topic of psycho-oncology. His contributions to psychoanalytic literature include many book chapters, among them those on the concept of harmony in Japanese culture and sociocultural aspects of dishonesty. He has also published papers on the topics of domestic violence in cancer populations, outcome research and times-series statistics, preparing patients for therapy, and the empirical status of clinical hypnosis.

Christie Platt, PhD, is a psychoanalyst and clinical psychologist in Washington, DC. Her private practice encompasses a diverse population including university students, adult professionals, and veterans of both the Iraq and Afghanistan wars. Dr. Platt's writings on intersubjectivity, issues of race and ethnicity, and the arts have been published in various publications including the *American Journal of Psychoanalysis*. A teaching analyst at the Baltimore Washington Center for Psychoanalysis, she received her doctorate from the California School of Professional Psychology in Berkeley, CA. Dr. Platt is currently writing a memoir about the year she hitchhiked 9,000 miles on her way from Cape Town, South Africa to Cairo, Egypt.

Apurva Shah, MD, is a child and adolescent psychiatrist, currently working at Kaiser Permanente in Lancaster, CA. After finishing his medical school in Ahmedabad, India, he moved to New York City where he did his residency and fellowship training at the Albert Einstein College of Medicine. He became a candidate at the New York Psychoanalytic Institute, but left it to move back to India. In Ahmedabad, he started a not-for-profit company, *Antarnad*, for teaching psychoanalysis and training psychoanalytic psychotherapists. Under his patronage, *Antarnad* has thrived and he teaches and supervises there on his annual visits and via Skype. Now in Southern California, he is a professional affiliate member and the co-coordinator of the Film and Mind Series at the New Center for Psychoanalysis. In his presentations and publications, he focuses on the intersection of psychoanalysis and culture, often through the analysis of movies.

Ann Smolen, PhD, is a supervising and training analyst in child, adolescent, and adult psychoanalysis at the Psychoanalytic Center of Philadelphia. Dr. Smolen graduated summa cum laude from Bryn Mawr College and received her master's degree in social work from Bryn Mawr College School of Social Work and Social Research. She received her doctorate in philosophy from the Clinical Social Work Institute in Washington, DC. Her first profession was as a member of the New York City Ballet. Dr. Smolen has won several national awards for her clinical work, and has presented her clinical work both nationally and internationally. Dr. Smolen has published several articles including *Boys Only! No Mothers Allowed*, published in the *International Journal of Psychoanalysis* and translated into three languages. Dr. Smolen is the author of *Mothering without a Home: Representations of Attachment Behaviors in Homeless Mothers and Children* (Aronson, 2013). She maintains a private practice in child, adolescent, and adult psychotherapy and psychoanalysis in Ardmore, PA.

INTRODUCTION

Shame is a latecomer to the scene of psychoanalytic discourse which has been preoccupied with the affects of anxiety, guilt, and mourning. It is only recently that investigators have turned their attention to the painful experience of shame. The rise of narcissism in Western culture has perhaps necessitated the examination of hubris's underbelly where we encounter insecurity, inferiority, and shame. This "culture of shamelessness," to use Henry Lowenfeld's (1976) phrase, has thus, paradoxically, stimulated the study of shame. Another impetus has come from the spread of psychoanalysis to what Osamu Kitayama (2009) has called "cultures of shame," referring mostly to the societies in the Far East. A third factor contributing to the enhanced interest in shame is that psychoanalytic clinicians are treating more patients whose personality organization, emanating from devastating injuries and humiliations during childhood, is not along the tripartite model of the mind (id-ego-superego) and whose anxieties are less related to instinct-morality conflicts than to the dread of exposure and narcissistic mortification.

One way or the other, shame has succeeded in drawing our attention, and this book represents the trend. Seeking to advance clinicians' empathy and therapeutic skills in this realm, ten distinguished analysts offer their insights here on shame from various perspectives. These include its developmental substrate, its vicissitudes during adolescence, and its manifestations in the course of aging and infirmity. They also discuss shame from a cross-cultural viewpoint and note how a shame-driven search for power and glory can turn malignant and societally destructive. Within the clinical realm *per se*, these authors delineate the rarely commented-upon phenomena of shamelessness, the link between shame and laziness, and the shame that underlies the inability to apologize. They also devote attention to shame in the transference-countertransference axis and highlight the technical challenges in dealing with shame—the analysand's or the analyst's—in clinical encounters. Together, these essays provide an opportunity for readers to enrich their knowledge, sharpen their attunement, and enhance their technical skills when it comes to dealing with issues of shame.

PART I

DEVELOPMENTAL REALM

CHAPTER ONE

Shame in childhood

Ann Smolen

Shame is an affect that has been largely ignored and misunderstood within the psychoanalytic literature. Psychoanalytic scholars have emphasized the affect of *guilt*, which represents internal conflict between the ego and superego. Shame was understood as a reaction to disapproval from the environment and carried little consequence compared to its counterpoint of guilt (Morrison, 1983). Freud (1923b, 1924d) viewed the development of guilt as a by-product of oedipal struggles and superego retribution. He said very little about shame though he did propose (1930a) that it was a derivative of exposure to others through genital conspicuousness and vulnerability. In a later contribution, Freud (1933a) postulated that shame was a feminine characteristic and a defect in women.

Subsequent psychoanalytic scholars modified Freud's views and stated that shame results from a conflict between the ego and the ego ideal (Piers & Singer, 1953). Shame is established when "a goal of the ego ideal is not attained, and therefore is the result of failure" (Morrison, 1983, p. 296). Shame encapsulates the whole self and is a narcissistic response to not living up to the goals of the ego ideal. H. B. Lewis (1971) states that the defense against shame is to hide or run away. The paradox here is when one feels shame, the impulse is to run or cover up, but this creates the danger that one will be abandoned (Levin, 1967; Piers & Singer, 1953). The ego ideal denotes internalization of values, morals, and the idealized object, therefore when the goals of the ego ideal fall short the individual's identity comes into question and narcissistic vulnerabilities are exposed (Levin, 1967). When there is a defect in the sense of self, "the resultant shame carries with it a decrease in narcissistic self-esteem" (Morrison, 1983, p. 299). When an individual experiences the loss of an idealized self-image, she experiences shame. According to Severino, McNutt, & Feder (1987),

> Shame is closely related to anxiety about the loss of the love of the object that can be associated with each developmental stage. It can be associated with the experience of the self as greedy, dependent, and in need of mother, the self as not in control or unable to perform, the self as genitally deficient, the self as humiliated and mortified by Oedipal defeat, and the self as bad in relationship to superego expectations. (p. 94)

Erik Erikson (1950) created his developmental stages and spoke about the stage that he titled: *Autonomy vs. Shame and Doubt*. He recognized that shame and guilt were interwoven and inadequately understood. Erikson stated: "Shame is an emotion insufficiently studied, because in our civilization it is so early and easily absorbed by guilt" (p. 252). He connected shame to the anal stage of development when the toddler's task is to develop autonomy without being inundated by feelings of shame or self-doubt. In order to achieve this, the child must first have acquired a secure sense of trust. Without trust, the young child internalizes a sense of self as *bad* or defective. For Erikson (1963), shame accompanies exposure of an inner sense of inadequacy or self as defective.

Defective sense of self

Freud (1923b) stated that the ego "is first and foremost a body ego" (p. 27). In order to begin to understand the concept of a defective sense of self that then leads to the affect of shame, we must first understand the preverbal, pre-oedipal stage of development when the image of one's body and self are idealized (Severino, McNutt, & Feder, 1987). When a person has the sense of her self as defective, shame is often the affect that is experienced, and with this comes a lowering of self-esteem and a sense of being flawed (Morrison, 1983). These individuals often experience a "distorted, vague, and incomplete body image [that] exerts its pathological influence on ego development" (Blos, 1960, p. 427). When a child experiences her self as defective it becomes a narcissistic injury and is "symbolically equated with badness, and becomes intermingled with disintegration anxiety, [and] castration anxiety" (Yanof, 1986, p. 578). Freud pointed out the significance of the mother-child relationship in helping the child to not feel defective. Freud wrote (1933) that Emperor Wilhelm II's narcissistic vulnerabilities were not about his physical defect (i.e., his withered arm), but were a result of his mother's withdrawal of her love because she could not bear his physical defect. When a person feels that their whole sense of self is defective, there is often a feeling of hopelessness that she will never be good enough or lovable. The "… sense of defect is experienced concretely, as a fact, which is emotionally deeply etched. At the same time the sense of defect is usually vague, poorly defined, not easily verbalized as to what is wrong" (Coen, 1986, p. 54). Coen understands the sense of self as defective as a compromise formation that attempts to resolve the conflict between the ego and the superego or ego ideal. Young children who see themselves as damaged often exhibit learning differences and memory disturbances (Yanof, 1986).

I will demonstrate in the case of "Jane," how this young girl developed a sense of her whole self as defective. Because of this sense of self as defective, she experienced overwhelming shame that was a reflection of feeling like a failure. Jane was unable to live up to her ego ideal and developed narcissistic defenses that covered up a sense of worthlessness. She attempted over and over to conceal her unacceptable self to no avail.

A detailed illustration from child analysis

Jane

Jane was nine years old when she began her analysis. Her mother's analyst had referred Jane to me because she was paralyzed with a multitude of fears. Jane was afraid of dogs, cats, and bugs. She refused to walk past a house if she knew a dog lived there. She could not go into a movie theater or a museum. She was afraid to go to another child's home for a play date and could not sleep away from her mother. In fact, she could not go to bed without her mother sitting by her side every night. Jane insisted that her mother sit with her or lay down with her far into the night. She would cry and have tantrums if mother did not adhere to these desires. Jane was fearful of seeing "mean faces" in the hallway and worried about "bad men" entering the home in the night to kill her and her family. She did not trust the burglar alarm and would not allow her parents to activate it, fearful that it would go off and scare her. This nighttime behavior caused friction within the marriage as the father was inpatient and angry that Jane was exhibiting "ridiculous" fears and causing such trouble. Most difficult of all, Jane's separation anxiety had culminated into a school phobia. She was very good at fooling her mother with fake illness. Jane refused to go to school many mornings and had tantrums and crying episodes where her mother would give in and allow her to stay home. Jane developed a vomit phobia and refused to go to school because she was afraid that she or another child might vomit. In addition, Jane was not doing well in school and had difficulty completing homework and other school-type work even though she was gifted and in the gifted program in her school. Jane was tested for learning difficulties and was diagnosed with a learning disability.

Jane's early history

Mother described Jane's first three months of life as *torture*. Jane was a colicky infant, screaming for hours, unable to be comforted. Jane experienced episodes of apnea and was monitored for several weeks. Her mother watched over her, never leaving her, to make sure she was breathing, worried she would die from SIDS. After these difficult, anxiety-filled first three months, Jane seemed to settle and developed normally. Her mother described her as a sweet baby who captivated everyone by her toothy smiles and belly laughs. She accomplished her developmental milestones early, walking by ten months and speaking in sentences by eighteen months.

When Jane was three, everything seemed to get derailed. Her speech, which had been advanced, deteriorated. She garbled her words and became difficult to understand. Toilet training had become a battleground. She was bladder trained for both day and nighttime by three years of age but continued to wear a diaper for bowels. She became extremely constipated. Her bowel movements were painful and she refused to use the bathroom. Her mother stated that she became "afraid" of the bathroom. This problem persisted and when Jane was six years old her mother attempted desperate measures to help her child use the toilet. She gave her enemas, put a TV in the bathroom, and sat with her for hours, reading to her while Jane sat on the toilet. Jane was given fiber pills at night and there were angry interactions between mother and daughter over bowel movements. Jane's undiagnosed and untreated encopresis became a social problem. Jane's mother had her wear a large sanitary napkin to catch the leakage. This continued until one year before Jane began her analysis. This condition dictated changes in family life; for example, trips caused constipation so the family did not go away. She also refused summer camp and other social situations where other children would become aware of her problem. Through the fourth grade she isolated herself from peers and remained very close with her mother.

When Jane was seven years old she became morose and obsessed about death after being read *Charlotte's Web* (White, 1952). Her mother described her as being obsessed with death. She refused to allow her parents to bring flowers into the home because they would die and it made her too sad. She spoke obsessively about two deceased grandmothers (one died before she was born, the other when she was two) and worried that her parents would die and that she too would die.

Mother reported that Jane did not like kindergarten. In first grade, she was unhappy because her teacher was too strict and the teacher would not allow the children to use the bathroom. Jane was afraid of this teacher. Second grade was a better year. She had a "sweet, loving teacher" but Jane's separation anxiety became worse as she became concerned about dying. She began to complain of "funny feelings" in her chest and stayed home from school a lot. In third grade, Jane became nauseated all the time and was fearful that she would vomit. She developed a phobia about vomiting and was afraid to go to school because she might vomit on the other children. Her mother described this as a "fixation on vomit." In third grade, she became "very clingy" and bedtime problems were exacerbated. Fourth grade was described as a very bad year. She had a "sarcastic, mean teacher" who made life difficult for Jane. A school phobia took hold and Jane spent many days *sick* at home.

Shameful secret

It was not until we were well into our second year when Jane's parents told me the family secret: Jane's mother had a degenerative hereditary disorder that, in time, would cause blindness. The mother was diagnosed with this disease when Jane was three years old. At this time, the parents left Jane and her sisters on several occasions for days at a time, to travel to another state where the mother received the devastating diagnosis. Jane's early history began to make sense, as that was the time when Jane regressed in speech, and behaviors. The parents were adamant in not telling their children because they did not want them to worry about their mother's health or their own future risk of developing the disease; however they did know that their mother was unable to drive at night and had difficulty seeing when dusk set in. Jane's mother told me that, at that time, she was extremely depressed, and received short-term therapy. At this point, it seemed that the mother was operating mostly in denial while underneath she was furious and profoundly sad. I explained that I felt that children on some level knew everything that goes on in the family. Secrets are dangerous and now I held the secret too. It took several more years before Jane's parents shared the secret with their four daughters.

Jane's analysis

Jane, a tall thin child with dark, luminous, sunken eyes, seemed ill at ease in her body. She often tripped as she walked up my stairs, her arms awkwardly dangling. She rarely smiled, and seemed to be an extremely sensitive and serious young girl. She chatted incessantly while anxiously touching items with her hands, rarely making eye contact. In these early sessions, list making was her favorite activity. Jane would sit at the easel in my playroom as she carefully listed each subject that she wanted to cover that day, crossing each item off as we spoke. In addition, as she talked, she wrote every third or fourth word that she was saying. Sometimes she drew next to the list, though always erasing her artwork immediately. Jane exhibited an extensive and sophisticated vocabulary as she regaled me with elaborate fantastical stories.

Jane spoke of many friends, but in reality her friendships were fragile. Her list of topics always contained a retelling of painful interactions with other children. It seemed as if she often misinterpreted others' intentions and missed important social cues. As I got to know her, I found her to have a milk-toast veneer underneath which she harbored intense anger and aggression. Her relationships with her three older sisters and her father were fraught with intense sexual excitement and aggression. Jane was quite efficacious in keeping her mother's attention focused on her worries and phobias, causing intense jealousies and antagonistic feelings to surface among her siblings and father. Jane was especially angry with her father, but did not know why. She was often disrespectful toward him and rebuffed his attempts to be affectionate with her.

At times, Jane had difficulty differentiating between fantasy and reality. She became involved in fantasy play with a girlfriend where her imagination took over and her fantasies became real and frightening. For example, she believed she could teach herself how to fly and she believed she had a protecting goddess who would save her from evil. She would describe video games that she was able to watch as a friend played, but she was terrified that the evil characters and bad and scary things that took place within the game would actually happen. She was involved with Wicca and believed that she had special powers, claiming that when she showered, a beautiful goddess joined her as her protector.

My first impression was that she was a sweet girl who appeared young for her age. She held herself in a stiff way and she seemed nervous and anxious as I showed her my office layout. She began to relax as I explained how I work and she built a "Jane city" in my sand box. She was very verbal, telling me all about her city where there was much fear of fire and villains and war. She spoke of her girlfriend who only sees the bad parts of her. When I asked her what those bad parts are, she explained that she "worries too much." I enjoyed her very much as she became very talkative and animated as she expressed fears of going off to middle school and worries about boys and being liked. In her subsequent early sessions, she was less nervous and spoke about her oldest sister who terrorized her. She began to speak of her nighttime fears and the faces she saw in the hallway.

Jane settled right into her analysis, attending her sessions with a sense of relief as she told me her stories and troubles with girlfriends and sisters and parents. She had a difficult time in her summer camp with many social problems, always feeling left out and isolated. The major themes in her stories were about growing up, separating from parents, and traveling toward death. In one particular session, Jane became agitated, left her list-making activity, and relocated to the floor of my playroom, sitting in a contorted position with the heel of one foot pressed against her anus. I wondered about this, which allowed Jane to tell me her encopresis story. Jane related how painful her bowel movements were and had always been, and how difficult it was in school to be worried about leaking and smelling. Her sisters teased her and her humiliation was so great she had to hide these feelings at all costs. In a proud and enthusiastic tone, she relayed the following: "One day I just figured it out. If I push my heel into my bottom, I can control my poops! I can either make myself poop by doing this, or stop the poop from coming, and best of all nobody knows what I am doing!" I told her that I thought she was a genius as she figured out how to control her body all on her own.

Jane's school phobia improved and when she entered middle school, at eleven years old, she became obsessed with a boy and spoke incessantly about him at home. This caused discomfort in her parents. Jane complained bitterly to me: "My mom doesn't want me to grow up and dad forbids me to have a boyfriend." She exclaimed: "It is all I can think about." I felt that she was exhausting herself from these overwhelming sexual feelings. It was in this session that she first spoke of her fear of menstruation and we began to try to understand this. Jane became very depressed weeks later when her crush, a boy who did not even know she existed, declared his love for another girl.

Jane was entering puberty and was terrified to menstruate. She wanted to shave her legs and armpits, and felt peer pressure to do so, but was unable to use the razor, afraid she would cut herself. Her mother shaved her. She began to speak of feeling very stupid. Other children in the gifted program questioned why she was there and her grades plummeted. Jane remained very depressed for several weeks, having difficulties completing homework, and experiencing social problems. It became apparent that the parents were experiencing significant problems in their relationship. Monthly parent meetings were difficult as each blamed the other and tattled on the other. Mother had the tendency to use her daughters to retaliate against her husband. Her daughters seemed all too eager to gang up on father with their mother. Father responded by withdrawing even further from his family and at times exploding in rage.

Jane's obsession with Wicca became all-consuming. Jane explained to me that her goddess had become her best friend, someone she could depend on twenty-four hours a day. "I only see you four times a week for a short time. You aren't available. I can trust my goddess with things that I can't even trust you with." I wondered with Jane why she needed to have someone available to her at all times, that in real life this is impossible. Nobody can have that. Not fathers, nor mothers, nor sisters, nor best friends, nor therapists can be there *always* for someone else. She replied: "But that's too hard." I agreed with her that it was very difficult and a painful part of growing up. I understood her dependence on this imaginary goddess (who became all too real) first as a replacement for her mother, who was trying very hard to separate from her daughter, and second as a replacement for me who also let her down. I think she became furious with me for helping her mother to leave her bedroom, and when I was not a sufficient replacement she needed to make up an imaginary goddess who was all-powerful. Jane was able to express anger toward me by telling me she needed to replace me with her goddess, and when she shared a fantasy where she threw water in my face and I threw her out my window. I think she was terrified that I would not be able to withstand her intense rage and murderous wishes. The fantasy life of children who perceive themselves as defective and who are filled with shame are often grandiose and unrealistic, and may interfere with reality testing and developing healthy object relations (Jacobson, 1959; Lussier, 1960; Niederland, 1965). Jane's parents became alarmed with her Wicca involvement, which at first infuriated Jane, but also scared her. Slowly over many months she gradually lost interest in Wicca and was able to let go of her goddess.

When Jane was thirteen years old, she began to menstruate and refused to acknowledge what was happening in her body. With her first period, Jane refused to wear a sanitary pad but instead stuffed her underwear with tissues. She insisted that what was coming out of her body was not blood and was adamant that she had not gotten her period. I wondered with her if she was scared because she had no control over the menstrual blood flowing from her body. I thought that this must have brought back shameful memories of when she could not control her bowel movements and had to wear a sanitary pad when she was in first, second, third, and fourth grades. She worried about feces leaking and its associated smells. Now she had menstrual blood leaking and it also had an odor. The next session Jane wanted to draw the female genitalia. She said she was confused about all the holes and did not know what was supposed to come out of what hole. For Jane, puberty was an enormous danger to her existing identity and body ego. However, the beginning of menstruation for Jane has helped to begin to promote a resolution of existing misconceptions and ambiguities about her vaginal structure and function. This has been demonstrated in her improved problem-solving capabilities and her newfound ability to make use of abstraction. "The onset of menstruation makes it possible for the girl to differentiate reality from fantasy. Menarche helps to structuralize her inner and outer experiences, and to communicate and to perceive in an organized fashion" (Plaut & Hutchinson, 1986, p. 419). When her next period arrived, she complained about cramps, the inconvenience of keeping herself clean, and the embarrassment of staining her pants. Normal worries for a young girl.

Just before Jane entered high school, her mother shared the family secret with her four daughters. Jane was livid, mostly angry that the secret had been kept from her and that her mother lied to her about where she was going when she had to travel to another state for doctor's appointments. Jane also verbalized to me that she always worried why her mother tripped over items in the house and could never drive her places at night. She felt her mother's sight was worsening and it would be her job as the youngest to stay home and care for her mother.

When Jane entered high school she expressed how different she was and always felt from her peers. She magnified and made these feelings visible by dressing in a Goth style, all in black, painting her nails black, and wearing very dark makeup on her eyes. Jane had grown from an awkward, somewhat mousey elementary school girl into a beautiful adolescent. She could not disguise her beauty in her black attire. She had her first romantic experience, but was conflicted and overwhelmed by her sexual feelings. After hiding in the woods and kissing after school, which was a secret from her mother who thought she was visiting a girlfriend, Jane began to dislike her boyfriend and find many faults in him. She was not able to break up, but instead behaved in such a way that he was forced to break up with her. This devastated her and her school phobia returned with a vengeance. Jane became depressed and morose, making dramatic statements that life is not worth living. Jane also refused to take an antidepressant, claiming that to do so would be cheating. Jane's mother now had her *sick* child back and Jane became her full-time job. Jane left school and had home tutors for the remainder of the school year.

Jane returned to school the following fall and fell in love with a boy in his twenties. Jane remained in this relationship for four years. Jane attempted intercourse, but found it too painful and was unable to be enjoyably sexual. Jane attended college in the area because she was unable to leave home, and due to her schedule we dropped down to a once per week treatment. Jane chose a major that would require advanced math, which was a difficult subject for her, and she would need to go on for a PhD in order to pursue this field professionally. She continually sabotaged herself so she could not do well in school. This was an intolerable narcissistic wound that she could not cope with. She dropped out of college and for the next three years, Jane traveled from doctor to doctor, diagnosing herself with various illnesses. If the current doctor did not agree with her, she simply found another doctor who would. Jane was eventually treated for a pain disorder, and stated that she could not go back to college or work because she was too sick. Her parents supported her and paid for all of her expenses including her living arrangements.

After three years of traveling from doctor to doctor and undergoing painful diagnostic procedures, Jane asked to add more sessions and began the arduous work (now that she was in her twenties) of exploring and coming to terms with her own limitations and inadequacies. She described her feelings of defectiveness and the burden of carrying that shameful secret with her for as long as she could remember. She confessed to making up her illness, but also saw how she lost the sense of reality because her illness and its associated pain became so real. Jane is getting back on her feet, has gone back to college, and has set more realistic goals for herself. She has entered into a romantic relationship with a young man her own age and for the first time, enjoyed sexual intercourse without pain.

Linking the clinical and the theoretical

From the history and from the little I know of the mother's own history, I speculate that the first three months of Jane's life were stressful. She was not an easy baby to pacify and had long crying jags. Mother seemed to worry about medical problems and had Jane monitored for SIDS early on. Jane developed well after that, reaching milestones early and speaking very early. Toilet training was a battle between Jane and her mother. I speculate that rapprochement and the anal stage of development was fraught with difficulties for Jane and her mother. Shame "in the anal phase may involve an overwhelming feeling that the newly individuating self is falling apart or crumbling" (Elise, 2008, p. 234). It seems that when the mother received her own devastating medical prognosis about her impending blindness and became depressed, development got stymied for Jane and she regressed. This is when Jane became difficult to understand and often did not make sense; it was also at this time that severe constipation set in and severe sleep problems occurred. Perhaps Jane was traumatized by her mother's sudden depression as if the mother she had known had died. I wonder if this has anything to do with her obsession with and grave fear of death, including flowers dying after they have been cut and put in water. The fact that the mother's illness was kept secret added to Jane's problems. I wondered how much she knew but would not allow herself to know. She was furious about the burden of caring for her mother.

When Jane entered kindergarten, she was unable to separate from her mother as evidenced in her need to be sick and stay home and in her inability to go to bed at night. She was experiencing the humiliation of leaking feces, and wearing a sanitary pad. It quickly became evident that Jane had difficulties learning even though she was gifted intellectually. At this young age, Jane had developed a sense of her self as damaged, and needed to hide this defect from everyone. When Jane was in fourth grade she underwent psychological testing and was told she was learning disabled. This diagnosis resulted in Jane experiencing her brain as defective. Early in her analysis, she drew a picture of the inside of her head, which looked like an armoire with many small drawers. For several years, she referred to which drawer held a particular feeling or thought. She told me the drawers often got jammed or were locked shut so she was unable to think properly.

I speculate that Jane experienced a sense of hopelessness about ever being good enough, and felt unlovable. She defended against these shameful feelings by making use of grandiose fantasies such as believing she could fly and keeping a protective goddess by her side at all times. Jane used her phobias and fears to keep her mother worried, as she was in her infancy. Coen (1986) states: "Once a person is convinced of his defectiveness, fears of permanent abandonment, rejection, ridicule or criticism are too frightening" (p. 55). Jane was terrified of being abandoned by her mother.

There is an intensified vulnerability to shame during adolescence. Puberty was especially difficult for Jane and she dealt with her maturing body by using denial, externalization, and projection. "The adolescent must deal with the transformation of puberty, disengage from childhood objects, and establish a sense of separate and distinct identity. Difficulties and failures in each of these tasks may be associated with shame and a sense of inadequacy" (Severino, McNutt, & Feder, 1987, p. 95). Jane relived her earlier humiliation when she was encopretic for so many years. When she began to menstruate she hid her body by wearing a large sweatshirt around her waist. She was terrified that others would see her menstrual blood and was enveloped by shameful memories. Morrison states: "Shame is a reflection of body functions and comparison of self to other, with resultant feelings of inferiority. [This] leads to hiding and compensating activity to camouflage a defect" (1983, p. 296). Jane's separation anxiety heightened at this time and she kept her mother tending to her as if she were a baby by shaving her legs and armpits.

After her first romantic encounter, which she could not tolerate, Jane became depressed, left school, and was tutored at home for several months. Jane felt great shame and humiliation that her boyfriend dumped her, and had a narcissistic reaction; she ran away and hid. Her depression was a passive hostility against her self (Lewis, 1971).

When Jane entered college, she undertook a field of study that she was unable to be successful in. She dropped out of college because she was overwhelmed by shameful feelings of failure. She was unable to explore her grandiose defenses and responded to shame with "ego regression, defensive grandiosity, and impaired reality testing" (Severino, McNutt, & Feder, 1987, p. 98). Jane had developed a grandiose personality structure that allowed her to avoid self-awareness. She became *sick*, which enabled her to deny her sexual and aggressive feelings. She was unable to be sexually active and her anger was directed toward her body as she went from doctor to doctor undergoing painful medical procedures. Jane was unable to develop a capacity for shame, which resulted in "the inhibition of sexual and aggressive drive expression and precludes a person's learning from life failures because each failure confirms his sense of himself as defective" (Severino, McNutt, & Feder, 1987, p. 104). Jane's sense of self as defective also had an adaptive function. As a sick little girl, then a sick adolescent, and then a sick young adult, she succeeded in getting some very early regressive needs met, while at the same time avoiding her anger toward her parents. In addition, when she was a sick girl she could also avoid her competitive urges toward her mother and sisters, and her analyst.

Concluding remarks

Jane had developed an all-encompassing sense of shame from very early, perhaps during her anal phase and rapprochement subphase of separation-individuation (Mahler, Pine, & Bergman, 1975). She felt inferior, incompetent, inadequate, and experienced her sense of self as defective. Her inability to explore and accept her limitations and flaws led to "a pervasive sense of failure, unworthiness, and to an experience of being scorned, unloved, and forsaken" (Elise, 2008, p. 76). Jane needed to run away and hide over and over throughout her childhood and adolescence in order to keep her sense of self as defective a secret for fear that she would be abandoned and rejected if her shameful secret were revealed. Secrets about physical defects were a major chapter of Jane's family's story.

When Jane was in her early twenties, she added sessions and returned to her analysis with a newfound conviction and ability to be more self-reflective. She was better able to be in touch with her feelings of shame and could tolerate these feelings without retreating into narcissistic, grandiose behaviors. Within this analytic frame, Jane began to develop the capacity to tolerate shame and began to experience her self as good despite flaws and imperfections. Jane needed to be able to find love for her flawed and imperfect self. With her newfound ability to tolerate feelings of shame, her self-esteem began to regulate and she was able to make more realistic choices and return to college.

In the first several years of Jane's analysis, I often felt as if Jane had little attachment to me, demonstrating her troubled object relations within the transference. Over the many years of her analysis, she achieved a more cohesive sense of self that, in time, allowed for self-acceptance of her limitations and flaws without falling into an ego regression. Simultaneously, Jane's relationship with me grew intimate and warm. Clearly the traumatic experience of living with a feeling of chronic shame interfered with Jane's emotional growth and her ability to develop autonomy and to separate and differentiate.

While it is difficult, if not impossible, to generalize dynamic observations and technical interventions from one case to a larger clinical sample, it is my sense that *two conclusions* can be safely drawn from what I have offered here. The first applies to the ontogenesis and multilayered organization of shame experience, especially as the child grows into an adolescent and later into an adult. The second pertains to the technical handling of children struggling with shame and secondary symptoms around it. *Regarding the first conclusion*, I believe that shame is intimately related to the fear of abandonment by the primary love object and may accompany each developmental stage. As demonstrated in the case of Jane, shame was experienced as a young child when she demonstrated greed and total dependence on her mother, as a latency child when she was unable to perform well in school and experienced a loss of control over bodily functions, as an adolescent when she began to menstruate and worried that her genitals were defective, and as an older adolescent when she was unable to join her partner in sexual intercourse. *Regarding the second conclusion*, the child who experiences chronic shame develops a narcissistic character structure in the attempt to ward off overwhelming feelings of badness. As in any child treatment, the analyst must be sensitive to the patient's narcissistic vulnerabilities, and slowly over time help the child, using displacement and interpretations, to address her aggression that is often turned toward the self as somatic symptoms, depression, and suicidal ideation. It is helpful to identify overwhelming feelings and put words to them. In this way, the feelings can be contained and experienced as less threatening. Interpretations may be experienced as shaming, which may result in an angry reaction from the patient, which need to be addressed and understood. It is also imperative to work with the parents, who are most probably suffering with their own complicated feelings of shame as they may experience a sense of failure as parents.

As a child analyst, I often make use of fairy tales in my work with children. Cinderella is a story about shame and humiliation. Cinderella experiences oedipal defeat when her father marries the evil stepmother. After the father's death, Cinderella faces increased humiliation as she is denigrated and shamed. Cinderella makes use of grandiose magical fantasies and goes to the ball where she falls madly in love with the prince. In the end, she can only find happiness when she comes to terms with her humble life and her shortcomings. Likewise, after many years of analysis, patients begin to face their limitations and within the context of such enhanced contact with their inner and outer realities, find some happiness.

CHAPTER TWO

Puberty, adolescence, and shame

Mali Mann

Adolescence is a time of physical, cognitive, and emotional changes. The onset of adolescence by and large coincides with puberty. Puberty designates the marked physical maturation that occurs in almost every system of the body. In girls, this occurs on average around age ten and in boys around age twelve, although the actual age of o nset varies greatly between individuals (Tanner, 1962, 1971; Young, 1971). The changes that girls go through at puberty are increase in height and weight, breast development, increase of hair in underarm, pubic hair, and onset of menstruation. The changes that occur in puberty-aged boys happen over a period of several years. The changes that one can expect are increase in the size of penis and testicles, pubic hair, facial hair, voice changes, growth spurt, and wet dreams.

The child's chronological age is too non-specific a guide to his or her maturational level. Mussen and Jones (1957) found that late-maturing boys were more likely than normally maturing boys to have feelings of personal inadequacy, feelings of rejection and domination by others, and prolonged dependency needs toward their parents. Early maturing boys were more likely to feel self-confident and independent, and seem to be more capable of playing a mature role in their social relationships.

In addition to physical maturation in adolescents, psychological maturation and self-development are rooted in the attribution of mental states to self and others, which emerges through interaction with a caregiver, in the context of an attachment relationship, via a process of mirroring (Fonagy, Gergely, Jurist, & Target, 2002). Internal coherence and mental separation of self and object require the physical presence of the other. Otherwise, the adolescent fears that the residual core self will be swamped, he will lose contact with it, and his sense of identity and self will be lost.

The young adolescent is still very much a child at this stage, who depends on family, is concerned about body changes, and is prone to anxiety. The adolescent boy or girl brings to this process his or her earlier stages of childhood's unfinished separation-individuation issues and acquired sense of self, confidence, and trust. Physical changes during puberty cause anxiety, and if the adolescent's expectations of these changes are different from the ideal sense of self, they bring about a feeling of shame, which is a developmentally rooted emotion.

The intensity of the strong affect of shame can be manifested in clinically observable ways. At the weaker end of the continuum, there is the feeling of embarrassment, referring to a less painful experience, that is—one associated with action or exposure, often of a social nature. Humiliation is usually felt more strongly, a feeling of embarrassment at being humbled in the estimation of others, often a specific act. Chagrin is humiliation mingled with vexation or anger. Shame, the strongest of these feelings, often involves unconscious elements, associations of factors coming from infancy, childhood, or adolescence. The role of culture as well as knowledge from infant observation can offer a better understanding about this important affect. Shame includes a searing, painful affect accompanied by gaze aversion, a wish to disappear (Kilborne, 2002), a disconnection from the prevailing interpersonal process, maybe from the social order entirely. Adolescents are especially more vulnerable to the threat of falling from their expected peer social order.

Adolescent girls who mature early are at greater risk of depressive and anxiety symptoms than are girls who mature at the "normal" time, and get into more behavioral problems. On the other hand, later maturing girls are more likely than "normal" maturing girls to be more competent and responsible, and more likely to adapt well and function at a higher level in school (Schwab-Stone, Cohen, & Garcia, 1985). In female adolescents, menarche is usually associated with enhanced self-esteem, a heightened awareness of one's body, and an increase in social maturity (Simmons, Blyth, & McKinney, 1983). Mixed feelings, such as excitement, pleasure, fears, and anxiety are also present (Petersen, 1983). An adolescent girl with a delayed menarche may feel flawed and ashamed of her body functions, meaning her body is not functioning like those of others in her peer group. Delayed breast development also triggers a feeling of inferiority and a sense of shame in girls. The concept of the "somatic self" as a characteristic captures the female adolescent's sense of herself and her body. The shape, size, and functioning of the body contributes to her psychic reality.

The counterpart is also true among adolescent males. An adolescent is especially sensitive to the reemergence of an earlier childhood shame experience while the body is going through dramatic changes. These changes are so rapid that the emotional adjustment is discordant to the newly shaped body that is going through physical development. We, as clinicians in our clinical observations, are aware of the prevalent emergence of shame affect in our adolescent patients.

Some theoretical considerations

For over a century, there have been psychoanalytic studies regarding shame. Comparisons have been made with social and philosophical theories and contemporary views on affect. The relation of self and object in the early developmental life of infants has been studied in order to better understand shame (Caparrotta, 1989; Lansky & Morrison, 1997; Yorke, Balogh, Cohen, Davids, Garshon, & McCutcheon, 1990). Newborns can grasp the equivalence between facial patterns of movement they see and patterns of movement they make on their own (Field, Woodson, Greenberg, & Cohen, 1982). Infants can recognize correspondence across perceptual modalities innately because they can recognize the equivalences between the acts they themselves perform and those performed by adults; they have a mechanism by which to begin identifying with other human beings, to recognize them as "like me" (Tronick, Wise, & Brazelton, 1978).

Shame is closely linked with intentionality and intersubjectivity. As Lichtenberg (1988) points out, the infant is an accomplished action initiator and responder before he can achieve psychic representation of the purpose of the action or of himself as the originator of the action. Competence in being involved in infants' early efforts with the caregiver makes it possible to elicit responses in the intersubjective field. Infants' innate understanding of the affective code, the earliest developmental trigger for shame, is a sense of inefficacy (Brazelton & Als, 1979). A perceived failure in infancy, a failure to initiate, maintain, or extend a desired emotional engagement with a caregiver is emphasized. A disruption in the "flow" of affective exchange could be looked upon as the trigger for shame (Broucek, 1982, 1991). This sudden disruption of affective flow would bring about what Kaufman (1985) called the rupture of the interpersonal bridge. This interpersonal bridge is established through good-enough affective attunement on the part of caregivers so that an affective dialogue can take place between the infant and caregiver based on reciprocity and complimentarity in affective exchange (sometimes called flow) that promotes the development of the sense of self. By sense of self, I mean a self-awareness of an immediate, preconceptual type; it is the basis of our most profound identification with our body, and it is what provides us with the experience of "indwelling"—the experience of the "lived body" rather than the body as a part of the object world.

Emde (1983) refers to the sense of self as the "pre-representational self" that he sees forming around an affective core, which guarantees our continuity of experience despite developmental change. Tomkins (1963), an affect theorist, writes that experiences of shame are preceded by affective states of interest-excitement or enjoyment-joy rather than by negative affect states. Yet our clinical experience informs us that the experience of shame is frequent and pervasive in those persons whose affective states are primarily negative. Tomkins's writing on shame reflects, however, a great sensitivity and understanding of the intersubjective context in which it is apt to occur. Morrison's (1994) view is that shame is elicited by an intersubjective disjunction resulting in a sense of rejected desire and rejected affectivity, failed intentionality, and inefficacy and the result of mis-attunement. Schore (1994) tries to tie the earliest experiences of shame to Mahler's practicing of separation-individuation (twelve to eighteen months). He notes the function of shame as an inhibitor of hyper-aroused states when a practicing toddler, in an expansive, grandiose, hyper-stimulated state of arousal, reunites with the caregiver expecting shared excitement and affective attunement but experiences instead a mis-attunement.

To create an integrative understanding of neurological development and psychoanalytic concepts is undoubtedly a challenging task.

However, we need to be aware of the importance of shame and its connection with objective self-awareness. Objective self-awareness appears to be the result of the interplay of developmental maturation of the central nervous system and social contextual factors such as conflicting points of view and disjunctive affectivity. Amsterdam (1972), in her study of mirror self-image reactions in infants and toddlers before age two, concluded that every subject who showed recognition behavior also manifested either avoidance or self-consciousness or all three. Those reactions point to a shame experience. Many of the behaviors that Mahler, Pine, and Bergman (1975) described as characteristic of the individuating child during the rapprochement subphase of separation-individuation may reflect the shame and ontological insecurity associated with the acquisition of objective self-awareness.

Objective self-awareness (OSA) makes possible the formation of a self-image, and later, with increasing cognitive maturation, a self-concept. At this point, standards, rules, and goals begin to become increasingly important. M. Lewis (1992a) notes that failure with respect to standards, rules, and goals may bring affective disjunction interpersonally as well as difficulty in maintaining a favorable self-image. It may be helpful to think of the earliest self-representation as a representation of a relationship, a representation more affective than conceptual in nature, which, once firmly installed in the unconscious, may be very resistant to change. Shame induction is prevalent globally. Parents, teachers, and peers deliberately induce shame in children by the use of power, overt verbal expressions of disgust or contempt, sadistic teasing, various forms of ostracism such as "the silent treatment," and love withdrawal. Lewis believes love withdrawal elicits global self-evaluation of failure. It is also the most painful form of severance of the interpersonal bridge. Moreover, shame is heavily influenced by cultural context and linguistic convention. Indeed, it has been suggested (Benedict, 1946) that there are cultures based on shame in the same way that Western cultures, at least in the past, have been based on guilt.

Clinical illustrations

The following are cases about adolescent kids who are particularly vulnerable during their maturational development to the affect of shame. These cases demonstrate how the affect of shame is intensively experienced by them and how their minds become disorganized by the intensity of this affect, until a reorganization ensues. Till then, the adolescent individual tends to engage in withdrawal, avoidance, or to attack self or others, as well as experiencing mortification.

Clinical vignette: 1

Ted, an eleven year old, came to see me for analytic treatment because he suffered from depression, hair and eyelash pulling (trichotillomania), and self-harming behavior. He was a bright, articulate youngster who worried about his baldness. Despite initial parental resistance and psychopathology, Ted's innate capacity to reflect and his wonderment about his own mind, his desire to make deep and empathic connection with people, especially the maternal figures, helped him to make good use of his analyst as a new developmental object. His high intelligence along with his obsessive character structure made his analysis effective and successful. His articulateness and intelligence were positive protective factors that helped him to be heard and facilitated through my interpretive work containing his anxiety through use of words. He was unaware of his intense angry feelings especially toward his mother. (He learned how he could use his anger as a signal to stop himself from being self-destructive.) Ted developed a good working alliance with me. We were a good fit and he liked seeing me. I was his wished-for mother in the transference. Mother's attachment to Ted was ambivalent and insecure. She lacked emotional attunement.

Ted's hair pulling was the presenting problem which elucidated his repressed anger and his underlying depression. Ted was quite eager to see me and he had shown enthusiastically his wide range of interests in political, social, and cultural matters, and sports and literature. There was an intense desire to want to impress me by telling me about his computer games. Through his play and drawings, he was able to express his conflict about his anger, body image, identity, and overall self-concept.

His sense of bodily shame manifested in his choice of attires. He would wear baggy clothes and a do-rag topped by a baseball cap. Somatic conversion and self-injurious behavior in the form of self-hitting was an important theme that initially became a core aspect of his analysis which gradually abated as his analysis deepened. The feeling of shame was intense and he frequently showed up with his gaze down and hiding his bald patches under his do-rag which covered his whole head and neck. The meaning of his hair pulling could be a displacement upward of genital masturbation as well as relief of his inner tension. He might have been ridding himself unconsciously of his unacceptable impulses. It looked like an unconscious masochistic wish perhaps just like when he hit himself in the head. It also had a castration fear component as an aspect of long-standing paternal transgenerational transmission of castration anxiety.

I believe that the experience of tension relief was multi-determined; perhaps it goes back to his early mother-infant non-attunement state, when the infant's bodily care was not fused with adequate love. Thus, it resulted in symptom formation. His eczema also can be viewed analytically, seen as an expression of lack of good enough maternal holding. After a considerable amount of analytic work with him, and parent work, his hair grew back, he was no longer ashamed of himself, and he was not the target of school bullies because of his bald spots or made fun of. He saw me as a wished-for mother and we worked well together.

The analysis continued to explore Ted's conflicts about aggression, and observing his gradual compromise solution for his unconscious conflicts in the analytic process seemed to be transformative. His analysis has been complex and lively. As his hair pulling symptoms abated, he played chess and became sadistically excited as he killed one of my pieces and was unable to hide his pleasure by sounding so buoyant. He was unconsciously inducing in me a feeling of embarrassment when he beat me in chess. He resorted to cheating to win the game. When I interpreted how important winning was at the cost of being discovered, he agreed that he was taking a chance to avoid his own sense of shame for losing.

He also feared that I would get upset with him if he was the winner. Later on, there were some changes in his attitude about winning and losing. He became able to observe himself in such situations. He also agreed with my interpretation that now he did not want to win due to the fear of upsetting me. I told him that he was trying to find out if I was going to help him with his intense and urgent feeling of wanting to please me very badly.

As his anxiety lessened, he was able to see that I understood his difficulty, tolerating his intense feelings, and that I would not retaliate when he would get angry with me. These themes were repeatedly interpreted; the sadistic elements of his play lessened, as did his intense competitiveness. Ted kept reassuring me that he was no longer having bad dreams. He did not have to feel badly about his hair, since his hair grew out with no patches of baldness. He said that his grades were all very good and that he did not need to continue therapy. He weathered our breaks in the treatment without the recurrence of his anxiety symptoms. He was grateful for his full head of hair.

He told me about all the girls he was meeting and how much they liked him. He liked his friend Anna's mom who was pregnant with her second child. He showed excitement about her being pregnant and that his friend was going to have a brother. He compared his mother with Anna's. An oedipal theme was activated and his curiosity was aroused watching pregnant women and he asked how grown-ups have sex and have babies. There was a clear oedipal theme at this point in his analysis. I interpreted that he wondered if his friend's mother was going to like the baby boy better and Anna would feel as he did when his mother thought his brother was the "good one."

The steady interpretation of defense, interpretation of his underlying conflicts, and my continued strengthening of our working alliance, helped him to develop a self-observing capacity and self-reflection. His maternal transference and negative oedipal transference emerged fully in the form of longing for his father and getting rid of his controlling mother as he felt I too was trying to keep him in analysis and was not allowing him to have a life outside of our work together.

I believe the building of a more robust ego structure, affect development, and formation of the capacity to build a mentalization process had been making good progress. Whether he would return for further analytical work in the future or not remained to be seen.

My second case is a female adolescent whose affect of shame emerged in association with the medical investigation about her lack of menarche.

Clinical vignette: 2

Ann was sixteen years old when her parents brought her to see me because of her depressive symptomatology. She had become depressed when her doctor discovered she was born with no uterus and no ovaries. She grew anxious when she did not have menarche like many of her friends. She felt inferior and was ashamed of her body that betrayed her. She suffered from dis-regulation and inhibition of her mental activities.

As an infant and during most of her childhood, her mother had suffered chronic depression, and her father, an alcoholic, had episodic temper outbursts. While growing up, Ann felt her mother was emotionally non-expressive and frozen. She felt she had to be a chatterbox to get her attention or be super compliant and "perfect" to win her love. She felt she had to be vigilant to secure a possible eye contact from her preoccupied mother. Her early sense of pseudo-maturity cost her a normal happy childhood playfulness and pleasure. The former state was mixed with an overdeveloped sense of self-sufficiency. She grew up struggling with poverty and emotional deprivation.

In one of her sessions, as she was playing with her hair, she talked about her difficulty relating to other children in her class. She then added that she was not sure what she could do to feel included in the circle of her friends. She suddenly looked as if she remembered something very important and wanted me to know urgently. She said, "I was loitering at a slew near the shore line with my two friends. I guess I must have been six years old or so. We threw rocks along the highway. The teacher saw us and reprimanded me. I hurried and told the teacher the name of a boy in our class and told her he did it. I knew I was lying. I went home and could not sleep. The next day, I went up and told the teacher that it was not the boy who did it and that it was me. The teacher praised me in front of the class by telling everyone that at first Ann lied but she now came forward and told the truth." At this point, Ann's tone of voice changed to self-mockery. "I was not a truthful kid! I was there to save my own skin. It was me who wanted to do it, and I started the whole rock-throwing scene. I was supposed to get home right after school, but instead I was loitering along the shore. My mom would not have noticed it anyway, for I was not noticeable at home. She would not have known when I got home; she was in her own world!"

I said, "You worried that you would be exposed and have to bear humiliation, if the truth were found out. You felt an urgent need to save yourself." She responded, "Yeah, I was horrified at the thought of being embarrassed in front of my classmates. I was not thinking about the boy who I was getting in trouble. It was myself I had to save. Just like what I am going through with my body. No one knows that I am defective."

She told me that she also felt embarrassed to tell me about her little "secret." She felt as if she was in a jail if she did not tell me. I said she worried I would not like her when I found out she did hide the truth. And maybe she held on to her secret for such a long time for fear of me not liking her, just like she feared her teacher would not like her. Here, it is not guilt as the motivating factor for stepping forward to tell the truth. It is a shame mechanism that was operating. She was horrified, anticipating the risk of her affectionate tie to her teacher, a woman who cared for her greatly to make sure she had had a proper meal or had clothes when she came to school. Ann was very fond of her teacher and had a conscious wish to have her as her mother. She then said, "It was not like I was such a good girl to go and confess to her. It was me I was saving in her eyes."

Ann was able to talk about her teacher in an extra-transferential way and the unconscious projective communications was corresponding to her level of ego development and affective state of mind. My countertransference was intense: I was feeling her pressuring projections and needing to stay in the transference as reliable container. My understanding of her internal and external object representation as well as my representation in her mind as a "new analytic object" had an impact on my technical approach with her. Her inadequate and unavailable internal object representation did not equip her to modulate her painful affect of shame. However, in our interaction, an emergence of a positive sense of trust and reliability for the analyst, and tolerance of her negative, aggressive, and shameful affect was noted. She survived the risk of reliving the shame affect and I was there to help her develop her self-reflective function (Fonagy, Steele, Moran, & Higgitt, 1991). Ann's association to an earlier shame experience made her prepared to talk about her traumatic experience of realising she had been born with no reproductive organs. There was an anticipated awareness of infertility with a developing feeling of an "inferiority complex." The latter term referred to a feeling of shame on the sense of inadequacy of body parts (Adler, 1927).

Her sense of self-worth was intertwined with her lack of reproductive capacity. Her confidence in her body-self was eroded and she fell into a deep depression. She felt defeated and humiliated. At the height of Ann's expected normative psychosexual development, she experienced even more of an intense sense of shame, since there was an absence of maternal mirroring and misattunement from very early infancy and toddlerhood. The bearing of the sense of shame was overwhelming to her and, bit-by-bit, she withdrew from her peer group for fear of her envious feeling of her female friends. She was worried that her friends would find out about her secret. She could not talk about her menstrual cycle like her friends openly talked about their tampons or premenstrual mood change.

Our work together on her intrapsychic disturbance in the sense of self as well as reexamination of her social peer context helped her to come to terms with her shame affect and sense of being flawed over the course of her analysis. Gradually her sense of failure was transformed into an affirmation of her strength and acceptance of her limits.

Unlike this case of bodily shame largely emerging during adolescence, the following case demonstrates an early affective developmental failure. The disruption of self-regulation due to the failure of reciprocity between caregiver and child in this case gave rise to the early emergence of shame affect.

Clinical vignette: 3

John, an eleven-year-old white Anglo American boy, was referred by his pediatrician at the age of six, because his parents were concerned about his physical threat to other children. He kicked and hit his classmates for no apparent reason. School authorities were very unhappy about his aggression and contemplated dismissing him. He had already been expelled from two other schools for similar behavior. He was disruptive and ganged up with other boys to hit girls during recess time. He bullied older students when he was in kindergarten. He also hit his only friend on the swing set. He had superior intelligence and was highly articulate. He was in a GATE program. A considerable amount of analytical and parent work was done as part of his early phase of analysis. He achieved a relatively good sense of self-containment in spite of his mother's failure in mirroring and her inability to contain his aggressive impulses.

There was a history of maternal mis-attunement and the birth of his younger brother when he was only eighteen months was a major developmental trauma. He was a colicky baby and his mother thought there was nothing she could do because "he was just wired that way." She could not handle infants by her own admission. She thought she could only deal with children who spoke and not crying babies!

After some period of analytical work, his aggressive symptoms disappeared. We worked through many important themes of his intrapsychic conflicts until one day he announced that he was one of three students in his class who was picked for a spelling bee contest. He was terrified about the next step that required him to stand in front of the whole student body and participate in the contest. He became preoccupied with the terror of being gazed at, and could not sleep the night before the big day. He also had the return of his original symptom of aggression and developed a skin rash. He was mortified at the thought of not being able to spell words correctly in front of the whole student body. He could verbalize his strong wish of not wanting to be humiliated for guessing incorrectly. At the same time, he did not know how to excuse himself from participation.

His capacity to regulate his affect, especially his shame, was deficient. His primary narcissistic defenses were not going to be sufficient to save him from an anticipatory massive, disastrous failure. He imagined he was going to die in front of everyone, should he misspell a word. His anticipated failure to be a spelling bee star in relation to a failure to attain an ideal phallic power made him feel ashamed and mortified.

The first and third cases demonstrate when there is an absence of validation or an unempathic early mother-infant relationship; the resulting shame can lead to despair, anxiety, and rage reaction. With respect to the second case, the development of shame affect developed in the adolescent phase of development. The process of coming to terms with the shame of absent reproductive organs with a sense of bodily deformity and the subsequent infertility required a most sensitive attunement from the analyst.

Conclusion

Adolescence is a period of rapid growth and marked change in body structure as well as increase in drive development. Anxiety results from the increase in aggressive impulses, and the ego is subjected to internal pressure. There is a simultaneous upsurge in libidinal drive which is anxiety producing. The conflict between progression and regression continues. In both male and female adolescents, there is concern over self-identity, masculine and feminine identity, sexual adequacy, and body integrity.

In the case of Ted, there is a concern over his masculinity and his somatic sense of self. His castration fears and his resistance of masturbatory impulses lead to his obsessive-compulsive neurotic formations. His sense of shame is considered a defense against oedipal conflict. Even though his symptom of hair and eyelash pulling subsided, he feared that it could come back and he had to fight his embarrassment. This was very threatening to his perfectionism defense and to his adolescent pride. The experience of tension relief was multi-determined which has its historical root in his earliest mother-infant non-attunement stage. He was shame sensitive and feared that his symptoms would return, and it made him susceptible to bullies.

In the case of Ann, there is an intense affect of shame connected to her sense of flawed biological reproductive organs. Her body is a representation of her somatic sense of self, her overall self-concept, and its function. This in turn contributed to her sense of warped psychic reality. Her expression of her early memories and affect of shame was expressed through her "somatic self." Her anxiety accompanied the discovery of her traumatic experience of having been born with an absence of female reproductive equipment. She was not prepared to deal with the shock of an inevitable reality. Additionally, the lack of maternal libidinal availability with its pre-genital conflicts influenced adversely her affect development. She had difficulty accepting her somatic limitation and was vulnerable to the affect of shame. She was able to recover the earlier memory of a shame incidence reemerging in the transference (Mann, 2010), but talking about her body was not emotionally tolerable at this juncture of her analysis. Gradually, with the help of our analytic work, she was able to confront her bodily limitation and reach a reasonable level of acceptance and humility.

In the case of John, his mother-infant non-attunement state led to his sensitivity to develop the shame affect as a signal anxiety. His infantile body care was not fused with maternal love, and resulted in the symptom that became a compromise formation, which made him avoid his anger toward his object. At an important anticipated moment, as his spelling bee contest approached, his skin rash reappeared as a reminder of his skin problem in the form of eczema throughout his life, and his acne as he entered into adolescence. This was his bodily expression of inadequate holding with his maternal object. His sense of shame is bound to his problem of narcissism lovability, acceptability, and self-identity. The experience of mutual affective attunement with his earlier maternal object was missing, which made him prone to the threat of collapse of self-coherence in situations where he was in the public eye.

The process of integrating shame of different origins is a long and gradual one that takes a well-attuned analyst to be able to tolerate the difficult evoked countertransference feelings in the analysis of similar cases. The analyst's neutrality is crucial in order to maintain a safe holding environment. Management of one's emotional reactions prevents further generation of shame for the shame-prone patients. H. B. Lewis (1971) discovered that shame in the therapeutic relationship between patient and analyst was a special contributor to the negative therapeutic reaction. If the therapist can tolerate his or her own shame, as well as that of the patient, holding and interpretive movement can lead to mutative change and growth.

CHAPTER THREE

Shame across the adult lifespan

Mark Moore

To grasp the concept of shame and its dynamic form over the adult lifespan, allow me to begin with a fundamental question: What constitutes shame? Unbearable self-consciousness, pained affect, a sense of exposure, inadequacy, a failure to measure up, and a desire to hide or vanish are among the ways in which analysts have given form in their writings to the experience of shame. However, often a singular feature has been used to construct a theoretical perspective on the nature and causes of shame, muffling the concept in a splendid simplicity and thus limiting any effort to understand the intricacies of how shame and adult development impact upon one another.

To clarify the complexity of the adult experience of shame, consider the act of writing this chapter on shame and adulthood. The very act of writing is one that can evoke anxieties related to both exhibitionism and exposure. For an early career analyst, there is likely to be a fear of exposing what may be a superficial and limited knowledge of psychoanalytical theory in general and of shame in particular. Here the sense of vulnerability is centered on a sense of worthiness and inadequacy, pre-oedipal concerns of being valued and loved by one's parents, and oedipal concerns of measuring up. Were the author older and possessed of fifteen more years of analytic practice, perhaps he would have greater confidence in his knowledge but still fear that his peers might judge his writing in a more exacting fashion. Over the years would the ego ideal have softened in response to accepting the limits of what can be achieved in life, or from the realistic yet supportive affirmations of colleagues? Jump a further fifteen years ahead, and would the prospect of retirement, with its attendant associations to ending and mortality, heighten the importance of viewing oneself as accomplished? Would the act of writing constitute an effort to leave an indelible sign of one's unique selfhood as expressed in lifelong work as an analyst? Would such an act provoke ancient childhood fears of individuation, fueled by the encroaching prospect of a final separation, and the potential shame of standing alone in one's understanding of the theory that has shaped so much of one's work-life and sense of identity?

A quick survey of literature

No single theorist provides a sufficiently developed concept to guide us in a consideration of the experience of shame across the adult lifespan. Therefore, before proceeding further, a brief overview of some relevant theories of shame is warranted. Freud (1905d, 1926d) emphasized the relationship between disgust and shame and its connection to expression of the sexual drive. He stated that:

> The sexual instinct has to struggle against certain mental forces which act as resistances, and of which shame and disgust are the most prominent. It is permissible to suppose that these forces play a part in restraining that instinct within the limits that are regarded as normal; and if they develop in the individual before the sexual instinct has reached its full strength, it is no doubt that they will determine the course of its development. (1905d, p. 162)

In delineating the ontogenetic unfolding of development, Freud (1905d) recognized three "mental dams" (p. 178)—disgust, shame, and morality—that govern the outcome of infantile sexuality. Fenichel (1945) agreed with this but emphasized that shame was mostly a repressive defense against exhibitionism. Piers and Singer (1953) made an important contribution to the concept of shame by conceptualizing it as the result of tension arising between the ego and the ego ideal, and they noted its association with the threat of abandonment and rejection.

Morrison (1983) noted that shame has been relegated to second order importance within psychoanalytic literature due to the late development within theory of an adequate concept of the self. He cited the work of H. B. Lewis (1971) who wrote that shame was "about the whole self, and its failure to live up to an ideal; as such it is a narcissistic reaction" (Morrison, 1983, p. 297). Morrison also highlighted the centrality of shame in understanding the concept of the self as put forward by Heinz Kohut (1977).

Erikson (1950) connects shame to the experience of being exposed and looked at, which gives rise to a wish to be invisible or "to destroy the eyes of the world" (pp. 252–253). Erikson notes that a sense of "rightful dignity and lawful independence on the parts of the adults around him" enables a child to expect that the "autonomy fostered in childhood will not lead to undue doubt or shame in later life" (p. 254). Related to the concept of autonomy is Kinston's (1983) paper on shame in which he conceptualizes shame as "the signal, affective and cognitive, that a move from 'self-narcissism' to 'object narcissism' is imminent" (p. 213). He explains that object narcissism derives from early experiences of the child attempting to solicit love from parents by being what the parent wants, which may be effective especially in the face of a parental wish to maintain symbiosis but it also comes at the cost of negating the spontaneous self-experience of the child. Self-narcissism is grounded in experiences that are spontaneous responses to internal needs and conflicts, rather than mechanical responses to impingement from the external environment.

Kinston (1983) writes that activity arising out of object narcissism, for example attempts to generate a desired response in the other, "can be mechanical and highly efficient, but it is essentially unfeeling and inhuman … because it avoids the crucial issues of: Who am I? What do I want? What do I think?" (p. 217). These are crucial questions that need to be re-asked and reworked at every stage of life and an avoidance of them creates escalating problems centered on identity and purpose in life. Kinston stresses the role of shame in signaling an individual's wish to avoid a state of painful self-awareness by shifting into a state that denies human need and meaning, which is accomplished by focusing on the other rather than the self. This dynamic is a useful way to consider shame in adulthood, as an important arc in the life-long development of the adult is characterized by a movement, often uneven and circling back and forth, between merger with others and individuation.

A central feature of adult development involves the ongoing attempt to consolidate one's identity and to determine how to retain a unique sense of identity while also ensuring that one is capable of intimate relationships and of being part of the wider world of friends, peers, and society. Erikson's (1950) stages of identity versus role diffusion (ages 11 to 20) and intimacy versus isolation from ages 21 to 40 reflect these concerns. Kinston (1983) emphasizes how shame is the consequence of an emerging awareness of separateness, and reflects the individual's discomfort with discarding or destroying parental objects and with the sense of loss inherent in reevaluating one's identity. For example, he cites Lynd's (1958) observation that shame involves exposure of vulnerable aspects of oneself, primarily to one's own eyes, to argue that it is related to the experience of discovering one's unique identity. Kinston notes that Lynd emphasized how shame involves an "element of unexpectedness, a feeling of inappropriateness or incongruity" and related this to the discrepancy between what is felt from within and what is apparent from without (p. 216).

Kinston (1983) also describes how a retreat to object-narcissism, that is, negating one's sense of separateness, acts defensively to reduce the awareness of shame. However, as mentioned above, such a defensive shift is costly and deprives one of an opportunity to face and accept the uniqueness of oneself. In contrast, an "unashamed" individual, likely one whose parents responded well to early acts of assertion and individuation, can tolerate self-awareness without a need for fusion with the other. Such an individual responds to self-exposure with "a sense of modesty, humility and reticence because of an awareness, at a tolerable level, of sensitivity and vulnerability" and develops "a perspective of one's significance and place in the order of things" (p. 218).

Shame in the context of adult development

Colarusso and Nemiroff (1979), in a paper on the psychoanalytic theory of adult development, proposed several hypotheses about adult development that will serve as a model for considering shame across adulthood. Their first hypothesis was that in achieving new developmental tasks of adulthood the adult, despite increased autonomy and adaptive capacity, is as subject to the influence of the environment as the child is, even though that environment changes over time. For example, one's college career may be a cause for celebration or shame depending on how well one does, and the audience to whom one is exposed now extends beyond one's family to include peers and prospective employers.

Clinical vignette: 1

Mitch was a twenty-four-year-old male who presented for symptoms of anxiety related to difficulties he was experiencing at work in becoming accepted and included by his peers. His childhood history was notable for early obesity that caused him to be frequently taunted and bullied by peers, and on occasion by teachers. This created a pervasive self-consciousness and sense of shame about his body. Furthermore, the lack of protection afforded by some teachers undermined his faith in the capacity of the environment and adult world to ensure fair treatment and safety. As he entered adolescence, his larger size provided him relief from physical bullying and his sharp wit and intelligence afforded him some means to deflect cruel teasing and jokes. He also developed validating friendships, often with the "misfits" and he prided himself on his ability to connect with a range of people. However, he never lost his sense of embarrassment about his body and gym was an emotionally torturous experience for him.

His college years were both successful and emotionally satisfying as he developed a supportive network of friends and he started dating a classmate who eventually became his long-term partner. He excelled in his field of study and took appropriate pride in his accomplishments. He was also sexually active, yet despite the clear expression of desire and attraction from his girlfriend, he remained awkward about being naked with her and he often felt compelled to minimize foreplay and to rush through the experience. Throughout his college years, he also continued to experience a contentious relationship with his parents—he enjoyed a close relationship with his father but he felt that he was a disappointment to his mother who favored his younger, more athletic brother. She often criticized him for being overly sensitive, immature, and provocative. As therapy progressed, it became clear that she had always fought against his expressions of independence as a child, labeling him as difficult and unruly. His sense of being a disappointment was intensified by his continued financial dependence on his parents, although this was softened by the fact that his father was the principal earner and that his father was an advocate for the importance of a college education.

Mitch's success in college and his increased acceptance by peers enabled him to develop a veneer of self-confidence but he remained vulnerable to slights and he was ever vigilant about the possibility of rejection, often causing him to overly extend himself to others in order to ensure their continued friendship. He felt pressure to maintain a friendly and affable persona, which often belied resentment and envy for friends who did not seem to struggle with esteem issues as he did. Upon graduation, he and his girlfriend obtained work in a different city. His new job entailed working as part of a large team, and while he was very capable of mastering the skills necessary for his work he quickly felt excluded from subgroups that were forming among the most recent hires.

He became convinced that he was viewed as brash and outspoken, and he feared that his peers viewed him as "difficult" due to his willingness to offer differing opinions on how to approach problems. Over time, he came to accept the reality of how certain coworkers were indeed not including him in newly forming friendships but he also recognized his contribution to this dynamic by way of his defensive distancing from them in order to elude the possibility of rejection. In this regard, Levin (1971) describes the following defenses employed by the ego to avoid shame: limiting self-exposure so that shameful thoughts or feelings are hidden from others, and limiting libidinal investment in others so as to be less vulnerable to criticism or rejection. He also describes the defensive discharge of aggression whereby shame is avoided by blaming others, and I clarified passive aggressive strategies that Mitch engaged in that enabled him to turn what felt like unbearable criticism and shaming rejection onto others.

Over time, we were able to clarify how leaders in his organization offered a counterpoint to his conviction that he was not valued by others. His reviews were consistently positive and supervisors often stressed how they valued his willingness to think outside the box. This experience stood in contrast to the lack of support he had experienced from teachers and his mother as a child, and he began to question views he held of himself as troublesome, unlikeable, and inferior to others. Increased distance and financial independence from his parents also fostered greater comfort with expressing different opinions and values from them, without collapsing into depressive self-recrimination.

Colarusso and Nemiroff (1979) offer a second hypothesis that adult development is an ongoing dynamic process, countering the notion that the adult is a finished product and that development stops once adolescence is passed through. Thus, while we must concern ourselves with the origins of shame in early life and remain alert to the influence of childhood experiences on later experiences of shame, as analysts we are tasked to uphold the complexity of how the dynamics of shame shift and mutate in response to later life events and in turn shape and are shaped by the developing psyche of the individual. Their third hypothesis elaborates on this view but stresses how adult development is focused on the evolution of existing structure, rather than the formation of new structure as in childhood. Thus, change in adulthood may be subtle and not easily discerned in our work with patients. They also hypothesize that adult development is influenced by the adult past as well as the childhood past.

Clinical vignette: 2

Jill was a thirty-four-year-old single female who presented for help with self-assertion in relationships. In our early sessions, she spoke at length of her sense of exposure and self-consciousness over how tall she was as a child, and how her mother warned her to slouch in order to not draw attention to herself. She felt gawky and awkward, and later convinced herself that she was not as attractive as "cuter" girls, but there was no viable means of hiding this aspect of herself. This self-consciously critical view of herself influenced how she chose partners, often settling for dismissive, narcissistically absorbed men whose need for admiration enabled her to focus outward and to feel that their love of her attention was equivalent to a love of her. She struggled to ask for more in such relationships as she felt she was fortunate to have any man's interest.

However, in her early career, her sharp intelligence combined well with her imposing height as she came into her own as an assertive and dominating figure in a high pressure workplace. She began to feel respected for who she was and to value her herself, tall frame and all, as someone of worth. Over time, this enabled her to expect more from romantic partners and to experience herself as attractive and deserving of more.

It would be tempting to hear her continued struggles with self-acceptance as primarily—and perhaps only—a continuation of childhood concerns. Indeed, it took careful attention to her avoidance of the topic of her career successes and curiosity on my behalf about the trajectory of her work-life to bring to light the contrast with her childhood wish to hide herself. Her source of shame, her height, now holds more nuanced significance for how she feels about herself—if one listens carefully, it still continues to contain echoes from early life of discomfort and exposure, and yet it also serves as a source of strength and confidence, an experience that only became available in adulthood.

Colarusso and Nemiroff (1979) also stress that while the fundamental developmental issues of childhood continue as central issues in adulthood, they do so in altered form. They offer as an example Steinschein's (1973) observation that self and object ties are altered at "critical affect-laden junctures such as marriage, parenthood, grandparenthood, the climacteric, retirement and senescence" (Colarusso & Nemiroff, 1979, p. 63). They also note how oedipal phenomena are at play in how parents react to their adolescent children's emerging sexuality—in the form of envy, competition, and protectiveness—but that adults' responses to these phenomena differ from that of a young child as they now have an outlet for release in that they are sexually mature, and furthermore they can modulate and express oedipal feelings more effectively due to more mature ego functioning. Finally, there are wider opportunities for sublimation in the form of work and adult creativity.

Marriage, parenthood, and the establishment of a career give rise to opportunities to reexperience and either reinforce or resolve earlier issues connected to shame. A partner who is beloved by his (or her) in-laws can seem to refute years of disparagement within his family of origin, but fears that a partner is disliked may deepen a personal sense of not being good enough. Divorce, though common, may be experienced as a personal failing, and a frequent initial concern among those considering divorce is what others will think. Marriage also brings about the merger of two family cultures, and what was considered a norm within one partner's family of origin may now seem embarrassing. Shameful family secrets may also be revealed to a partner who is now witness to the private tensions and conflicts that had before occurred behind closed doors, which often purges them of their furtive intensity.

Careers can be a source of pride but also a means of comparison that may leave an individual, who otherwise enjoys his work, feeling that he fails to measure up to peers (or sibling and parents) in terms of income and prestige. Lack of career success is at its most exposed when an individual is unemployed, and the difficulty of hiding this state from others can create inescapable feelings of shame. Conversely, success in work and associated financial independence can free an individual from the evaluative constraints of his family and begin to loosen the grip of earlier shame dynamics.

Clinical vignette: 3

> Paula was a thirty-eight-year-old female academic who taught at a small college where she had tenure, yet she had failed to achieve much success in her career and she felt that she was lazy and relatively untalented. She recounted a wide array of research topics she had thought of pursuing but she would talk herself out of them by imagining how she would be unable to muster sufficient commitment to do the necessary work. As I inquired further about her work experience, I noticed that she felt great disappointment over the lack of mentorship and support she had received from more senior faculty members in her department. I noted a connection to an earlier experience when her father tried to teach her how to sail but he quickly became frustrated with her clumsiness and lack of alacrity in following his instructions. She felt chagrined and pulled away from the activity to let her older brothers take over the tasks. This incident was representative of their relationship in which she often felt herself to be a disappointment to him, and which led to her finding ways to "fly under his radar."
>
> Further consideration of this dynamic enabled her to recognize an ongoing fear of shame in her adult life that compelled her to avoid attention from others, for fear she would be criticized for her ideas. Her core self-image was that of someone who was of mediocre intelligence, unworthy of her job, boring, and undeserving of others' attention. She feared that if she allowed herself to be seen for who she was, she would be rejected in a humiliating manner. Over time in therapy, it became clear that her denigrating assessment of

herself as lazy and dull were a defense against expected shame, which enabled her to avoid achieving success, and thus unwanted attention, in her career. She came to realize that her disappointment in her mentors was largely of her own making as she had actively avoided a close relationship that would entail close scrutiny of her work. By emphasizing the contrast between her experience of shameful ineptitude as a child and her greater capacities for success, especially in the academic realm, she gradually became able to surrender her defensive underachievement and to infuse her career with newfound enthusiasm and hope.

Finally, in considering Colarusso and Nemiroff's paper on adult development and its relevance to the topic of shame, it is important to note their emphasis on how adult development is "deeply influenced by the body and physical change" (1979, p. 65), and their claim that "a central, phase-specific theme of adult development is the normative crisis precipitated by the recognition and acceptance of the finiteness of time and the inevitably of personal death" (p. 68). Spero (1984) writes of how during old age or terminal illness shame is "evoked by the perception that one's infirmities, loss of control, and body excrements are exposed ... the body becomes deindividuated, evoking a sense of loss of self" (p. 270). He notes that aging often produces a defensive withdrawal from others, that serves to reduce shame in the presence of others but at the cost of increasing shame felt before one's self. Furthermore he suggests that the "combined effects of control and privacy, and increased attention to self and bodily needs, bring the ego back to painful, shameful experiences of childhood" (p. 270). Lax (2008) in writing about becoming "really old" writes of how loss of physiological control, such as urinary function, can be "deeply embarrassing and invades the self-concept and self-image" (p. 840). The following case example illustrates several of these issues.

Clinical vignette: 4

George was a sixty-one-year-old chief financial officer at a large and successful firm who sought help with anxiety he was experiencing related to chronic back pain and arthritis. Our exploration of the form of his anxiety and related fantasies revealed that he had spent his life maintaining control over his body through disciplined exercise and that he now feared losing his ability to deny his body's needs. As he had grown older he had prided himself on his ability to ignore arthritic pain and fatigue that was exacerbated by excessive work hours, and he worried that any visible sign of age-related difficulties would undermine the respect and admiration that his coworkers felt for him. However, as I inquired about the culture of his workplace it became evident that his expertise and knowledge of the company was highly valued, and that his coworkers were motivated to accommodate him and to ensure that he could continue working beyond the typical retirement age of sixty-five.

During our treatment he required back surgery that necessitated a two-month leave for recovery, and his colleagues were very supportive, giving the lie to his concern that they would be critical of him for being ill. However, George felt "exposed" and "vulnerable" and his response to missing time at work was to throw himself back into it with a single-minded dedication and corresponding neglect of himself by way of long workdays, working weekends and not taking vacations. My confrontation about the imbalance between work and play in his life was initially met with protestations that his work was intense and his role as CFO had always required long hours, but that work provided him with an important sense of purpose in his life, especially since the death of his older partner five years prior.

It became clear, however, that a pattern of extreme self-sacrifice characterized most areas of his life and had long preceded the death of his partner. Over time I was able to help him view some of his choices as extreme and often self-harmful and he became more curious about his lifelong need to appear self-sufficient and without need. As I encouraged him to reflect on feelings related to this issue and his fantasies about how others would think of him if he expressed needs or vulnerability, he began to talk in greater detail about childhood experiences. Central to this issue was his sense that he was most loved by his parents when he was "not being a bother" and he recalled that he was praised and recognized for being "good" and keeping out of their way by busying himself with schoolwork.

He had also felt that he was a disappointment to his father, who had been a college baseball player, because he was not a natural athlete. This was further complicated by his growing awareness of being homosexual as adolescence progressed, and feeling a need to hide this from others. He threw himself into "pursuits of the mind" and excelled academically but at the cost of minimizing his physical experience of self, including physical desires. His body came to represent what was weak, disappointing, and effeminate. He avoided sexual relationships until his late twenties and throughout his life he related to his body as "something to be maintained" rather than to be lived in.

He met his partner in his early thirties and through his support, George developed a greater comfort with his sexual identity and a capacity to enjoy sex. However, this comfort and joy was predicated on feeling that he looked attractive and fit, and he threw himself into working out in a manner similar to how he dedicated himself to work. Despite reassurances from his partner, he believed that their continued relationship depended on him "looking good." This conviction that others would only be interested in him if he looked young and attractive contributed to his unwillingness to date anyone, despite profound loneliness, after his partner's death. He felt ashamed of how his "sixty-one-year-old body" would look to others, even though he was interested in dating others who were his age or older.

We continued to talk about his shameful experience of his body and how it reflected an earlier sense of shameful inadequacy that could only be countered by being seen by his parents as good, hard-working, and academically successful. In adult life, his work accomplishments served to divert others' potentially shaming attention from his core sense of never being good enough. The thought of being accepted and loved "warts and all" seemed incomprehensible and as he grew older the prospect of aging and its attendant dependency on others gave rise to a profound sense of exposed vulnerability that he felt ill-prepared to show.

Conclusion

Both the experience and expression of shame evolves over the lifespan. Early childhood instances of shame can be expected to derive their form from the inherent vulnerability of being young, small, and dependent. Counter defenses against the sense of feeling exposed are underdeveloped, and the stakes feel impossibly high when caught up with struggles of individuation with adult caregivers. Early triggers for shame are also often associated with bodily experiences: lack of motor control, accidents involving bladder and bowel function, limited strength and stamina, and feeling too big or too small. School, with its attendant emphasis on academic performance and the immersion into the world of peer relationships, allows for new arenas in which to feel like a success or failure.

These early experiences follow us into adulthood and shape how we feel about our self. In some instances they influence our choice of friends and partners, while for others the good fortune of a supportive mentor, a loving partner, or gracious friend can push in the opposite direction and undo the influence of the past, or at least change the nature of its influence. Work can become a new measure of one's worth, and parenthood provides a different perspective on childhood struggles, as the new parent now becomes the source of praise, recognition, and love or of criticism, negation, and rejection. Older age, and the experience of illness and the prospect of death return us to the reality of the body's limits. With it come old and new fears of inadequacy, frailty, and helplessness.

The arc of life would be tragic indeed if it begins and ends with a heightened vulnerability to shame. I do not hold to this tragic view of the trajectory of shame. While shame may be a given in life, it is capable of amelioration. Kindly parents, compassionate teachers and mentors, caring friends, and loving partners all contribute to shifting the trajectory of shame over the lifespan. And a yet greater hope resides in the individual's capacity to relate to him- or herself in a humane and non-shaming fashion—this is certainly a hope offered by psychoanalytic therapy and by life itself.

PART II

CULTURAL REALM

CHAPTER FOUR

The cultural faces of shame

Apurva Shah*

While growing up in India, it was not an uncommon occurrence for us children to sing the ditty:

Shame, shame, puppy shame
All the monkeys know your name.

I myself was the "puppy" on more than a few occasions. The moment I remember with the most intense shame was when I lost control of my bowels in my kindergarten classroom. If the ground had opened up and swallowed me then and there, I would have been the most relieved person on earth, or in earth, as it were. Even the retelling of the incident was so shameful that I could not talk about it in my analysis for years. While my analyst handled the "confession" well and we worked on how it affected me, I feel that there was (is) a lot more to be mined from the experience.

Being shamed is a powerful and profound experience, and a uniquely human one. As Mark Twain (1897) wrote, "Man is the Only Animal

---

*I am grateful to Sudhir Kakar for the magical evening on the beach and the ideas generated from same. I would also like to thank Maansi Shah for all her helpful suggestions.

that Blushes. Or needs to" (p. 256). Shame, and the defenses employed against shame, can have far-reaching consequences that psychoanalysis has only recently started exploring in depth.[1] This is surprising as shame has been very frequently and quite vividly described and discussed in literature and philosophy from the beginning of recorded history. It has also been studied extensively by sociologists and anthropologists, and called the "master emotion" by Thomas Scheff (Scheff & Retzinger, 1997). The spike in the interest in the psychology of shame appears to have coincided with the diminishing of shame in Western culture. Perhaps because of this, shame is being increasingly seen as negative or pathological, something that needs to be overcome or treated—in short, as something shameful.[2] In my psychiatry residency[3] and in the psychoanalytic seminars I attended[4] during that period, shame was generally contrasted with guilt and considered to be the more primitive of the two, and as the one that was more prevalent in other, non-Western cultures.

Why study shame across cultures? If, as Ian Parker (2008) states, all psychoanalysis is cultural, then historically psychoanalysis has not interacted well with other cultures. Being a quintessentially Western[5] and "white" discipline, it has tended to measure other cultures using its own yardstick, and then found them wanting (Altman, 2006).[6] But perhaps it cannot be otherwise, as psychoanalysis is, by its very nature, subversive. Then again, psychoanalytic (and anthropological) studies of cultures outside of the West have often only served to reinforce the normative nature of development in the West (Parker, 2008). My hope for cross-cultural studies is that the "Other" can act as a mirror for the Western observer, a marker of difference between the inside and outside of the Western culture. And, equally important, vice versa.

As I review theories of shame in and from different cultures, the most noticeable motif is the division of the world into shame-cultures and guilt-cultures (Benedict, 1946; Dodds, 1951; Lewis, 1992a; Piers & Singer, 1953; Wu, 2014). This has been accepted and elaborated on by some of the psychoanalytic thinkers of the shame-cultures (Kitayama, 2010; Obeyesekere, 1984), though not all (Doi, 1973). I will attempt to look at the phenomenon of shame both culturally, that is, across various cultures, as a relativist; and cross-culturally, thinking through the cultural differences, as a universalist. At the same time, I will try to avoid the trap of privileging either culture, by totally accepting or outright rejecting the hierarchy inherent in the notion of shame-cultures and guilt-cultures.

Before I can begin to look at the cultural aspects of shame, I will look at the different definitions and descriptions of shame and its etymology. I will propose a multi-axial schema to help categorize the various descriptions. After reviewing the phenomenon of shame within and across cultures, I will end by cataloguing the implications of the study on theories of development of shame and the treatment of patients from a different culture.

Definition and description

Shame is a word that is so much easier to describe than to define. It is a universally shared experience with many facets and nuances. Even a cursory review of what has been written about shame reveals several subtle, and some not-so subtle, differences in how people conceptualize it. It is more difficult to say whether these differences correspond with real differences in the *actual* experience of shame, and if they do, whether those differences (in the experience of shame) are due to differences in culture, the individual, or observed psychopathology? At times, it feels as if we are reading descriptions of an elephant written by five blind men.[7]

For now, we can do no better than start with the definition of shame in the *Comprehensive Dictionary of Psychoanalysis* (Akhtar, 2009a):

> Shame refers to a painful experience which can be broken down into five components: (1) collapse of self-esteem; (2) feeling of humiliation; (3) rupture of self-continuity, whereby what one was, in one's mind, a moment ago is experientially lost; (4) sense of isolation and standing apart from the group, and (5) feeling of being watched by critical others. (p. 264)

In a later work, Salman Akhtar (2012b) goes on to emphasize the sense of self-exposure, the visual element, and the increase in self-consciousness/self-awareness in shame. In *Guilt* (2013), he contrasts it with guilt and adds that shame is often accompanied by visual markers such as blushing, that it results from falling far behind one's ego ideal, that it pushes for hiding, and that it is more primitive than guilt. He lists a few defenses against shame: narcissistic self-inflation, withdrawal, turning passive into active, and shaming others.

As noted by many authors (Kilborne, 2002; Scheff & Retzinger, 1997; Twitchell, 1997), shame is derived from the Indo-European root *skam* or *skem*, meaning to hide, to cover. The English words *skin, camera*, and *chamber* (through the Greek word *kamara*) and the Hindi words *kamara* (room) and *kambal* (blanket) share the same root, thus linking shame with its action tendency—to hide or cover—as well as highlighting the visual and protective aspects of shame. While a comprehensive review of the literature on shame is beyond the scope of this chapter, I will focus on some authors who have talked about various types of shame. As Twitchell (1997), Ayers (2003), and others have noted, several European languages have two words for shame. The Germans and the French differentiate between what can be translated approximately as modesty (*scham, pudeur*) and disgrace (*schande, honte*). The Greeks used *Aidos* for the quality that restrains man from doing wrong and *Aischron* for disgrace. Hindi has three words for shame that can be translated as shame (*sharam*), modesty (*lajja*), and dishonor (*apmaan*). While English does not have two words for shame, it does, interestingly, have two opposites for it: shameless and unashamed. The differences in the meanings and usages of the two give us a hint about the dual nature of shame. *Shameless* has a negative connotation, that is, brazen and devoid of ordinary social graces; while *unashamed* often, though not always, has a positive connotation, unapologetic, unabashed. Also, as Twitchell (1997) points out, *shameless* and *shameful* mean practically the same thing, thus implying that having no shame is a thing to be ashamed of in itself.

Helen Lewis (1971) writes about consciously experienced shame, bypassed shame (when shame is experienced but not focused on), and unconscious shame (when shame is experienced without an awareness of it). Andrew Morrison (1989) talks about disavowed shame, shame that is defended against and kept out of awareness. Jane Middleton-Moz (1990) differentiates between the shame experienced by us all, the "temporary" shame, and "debilitating" shame, which is intense and much longer lasting, in which the individuals feel as if they did not just *make* mistakes but they *are* mistakes and failures. Michael Lewis (1992a) considers shame to be ubiquitous and distinguishes it sharply from shyness, modesty, and embarrassment on one hand and humiliation and guilt on the other, although he accepts that it is not always easy to figure them out objectively. Mary Ayers (2003) talks of absolute shame, which leads to fragmentation and an emptiness of the self, and distinguishes this from our everyday experience of shame, which is transient. Leon Wurmser (2013) differentiates between shame-anxiety (the fear of being looked at and being exposed and humiliated); shame-affect (the contempt felt by self or others after being exposed as a failure); and the preventive/protective shame (a character trait that prevents disgraceful exposure; an attitude of modesty and respect).

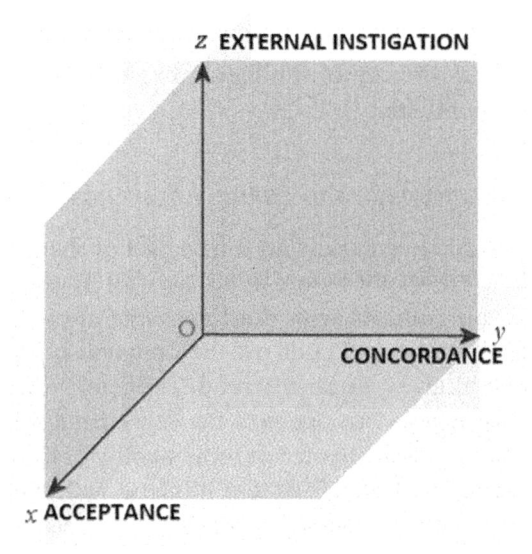

z **EXTERNAL INSTIGATION**

CONCORDANCE *y*

x **ACCEPTANCE**

To encompass all the aspects of shame and for heuristic purposes, I propose a schematization of the experience around three axes. The manifest behavior is noted on the x-axis. This axis denotes whether the individual accepts (and feels) the shame or defends against it, usually by pride, but also by anger, anxiety, turning passive into active, and so on. This is on a continuum; an individual can feel some shame, whilst also defending against deeper shame. This corresponds to Glen Gabbard's (1989) concept of the "oblivious" and "hypervigilant" subtypes of narcissistic personality disorder.

The concordance of the values between the individual shamed and the individual (or group) in front of whom the individual is shamed is noted on the y-axis. This is a major factor in determining both the threshold at which the shame is experienced and its intensity. This does not mean that shame cannot be felt when an individual is alone; the concordance would then be with internalized object representations and ego ideals. Later in the chapter I will illustrate this point with clinical vignettes.

The z-axis plots the "location" of the experience of shame—whether the experience is of keeping up appearances and "fitting" into the group, or of following principles integral to one's self-image. This corresponds to Agnes Heller's (1985) description of skin-shame and deep-shame, in her work with the New Guinea tribes.

Now, to complete the description of the experience of shame, we only need to add whether the experience of shame occurs prophylactically as an anticipatory anxiety or inhibition, or post-hoc, as an emotional experience or humiliation.

Shame, guilt, and culture in psychoanalysis

Several authors have remarked on the neglect of shame in psychoanalytic literature, especially before 1980, as well as the accompanying overemphasis on guilt. As with most concepts in psychoanalysis, the first mentions of shame and guilt and their relationship with culture are found in the writings of Sigmund Freud. These references are scattered throughout his oeuvre, but one gets the sense from his later writings that he does not feel that shame is a topic worthy of the depth psychology he has formulated.[8] He feels that it (along with morality) leads to "cultural hypocrisy." However, at one point he somewhat begrudgingly acknowledges the role of shame (and morality) in creating civilization, and states: "It is debatable whether a certain degree of cultural hypocrisy is not indispensable for the maintenance of civilization" (1915b, p. 284). Interestingly while Freud (1913c) himself never included any specific mention of shame or similar emotions while articulating his "fundamental rule of psychoanalysis," others (Gill, 2000; Schafer, 1981) have added the word "embarrassing" to "irrelevant" and "trivial," as objections that the patient must set aside while talking to the analyst. I feel that, far from being a mistake, this was a recognition of Freud's attitude toward shame—something that can, and should, be overcome consciously and easily. Curiously, Freud's relative neglect of shame did not prevent him from being partly credited for the decrease in shame (amongst other things) in the American culture (Menninger, 1973).

A close reading of Sophocles' *Oedipus* trilogy can provide an example of how Freud privileges the concept of guilt over shame. Freud bases his concept of the Oedipus complex, whose resolution leads to the formation of superego and guilt, on the first play of the trilogy, *Oedipus the King*. However, I would argue that the feeling Oedipus experiences is much closer to our current concept of shame than guilt. When Oedipus finds out that he is the murderer of his father, and that he has married his mother, Jocasta, his first reaction is rage and he asks for a sword and goes to her room, presumably to kill *her*. However, he finds her dead, having hanged herself. He proceeds to untie the rope around her and stretches her corpse in front of him. Then he "tore the golden brooches that upheld her queenly robes" (p. 52), presumably disrobing her, and "smote" the eyeballs with the brooches, saying, "Those ye should ne'er have seen; now blind to those" (p. 52). Later, he pleads, "O, I adjure you, *hide me* anywhere, Far from this land" (p. 55, emphasis added). The second play, *Oedipus at Colonus*, indicates that Oedipus felt little remorse. He says, "Deeds of a man more sinned against than sinning … Yet am I then A villain born because in self-defense, Stricken, I struck the striker back again? E'en had I known, no villainy 'twould prove: But all unwitting whither I went, I went—To ruin" (p. 72), and later, "I slew who else would me have slain; I slew without intent, A wretch, but innocent In the law's eye, I stand, without a stain" (p. 85).

Franz Alexander (1938) considers shame to be a broader category that includes both guilt, which he feels is a result of social adjustments, and "feelings of inferiority" (p. 45), which he considers to be "pre-social" (p. 45) and capable of stimulating aggression and violence. He accepts that in societies where individualism is not as valued, the feelings of inferiority may be more easily accepted. In their seminal work on shame and guilt, Gerhart Piers and Milton Singer (1953) start out with a sharp differentiation between the two, but then go on to contend that one can lead to or conceal the other. They add that the presence of an audience, actual or imaginary, does not differentiate between shame and guilt, as both can be felt in either situation. They find it more useful to talk of a shame-ridden person and a guilt-ridden person, than shame-cultures or guilt-cultures, although they caution against the idea of a person exclusively driven by shame or guilt. After studying the psycho-anthropological data on shame and guilt, particularly in the Native American cultures, they question the distinction between shame-cultures and guilt-cultures and the assumption that guilt-cultures are correlated with moral and technical progress. Based on Robert Redfield's works (e.g., 1952), they problematize Freud's notion that feelings of guilt increase as civilization progresses and conclude by saying that the current evidence supports the idea that the sense of guilt *and* the sense of shame are found in most cultures, and that their relative distribution has little to do with how progressive or backward the culture is.

Erik Erikson (1950) feels that shame is insufficiently studied because "… in our civilization it is so early and easily absorbed by guilt" (p. 110).[9] He talks about the "destructiveness of shaming" (p. 111), which is attenuated in some cultures by customs that allow people to save face. In any event, he feels that guilt can be more destructive than shame. H. B. Lewis (1971) adds that "Guilt is used to bypass shame, since it is a less acute emotion. … But the opposite transformation is not likely to occur, again reflecting the intensity difference between the two" (p. 121).

Henry Lowenfeld (1976) gives considerable importance to shame and its civilizing property. He writes, "Shame has been an ingredient of paramount importance in shaping character structure in harmony with the standards of civilization since the beginning of man's history" (p. 62). Lansky and Morrison (1997) feel that the explosion in the writings on shame, after 1980, was made possible by Heinz Kohut's (1977) theory of self psychology, formulated in the '70s. Certainly the concept of the self, including notions of the private I-self and the more social We-self can be found in many psychoanalytic writers in their encounters with Asian cultures (Kitayama, 2010; Roland, 2011). Finally, Mary Ayers (2003) starts off her work on shame by stating that "… people are ashamed of even experiencing shame" (p. 7), a thought which I will return to later.

Shame in the West

The roots of much of Western culture has been traced back to the ancient Greek civilization. According to E. R. Dodds (1951), guilt was absent in the pre-Homeric and Homeric Greece, and the pre-Homeric man was preoccupied with shame and public esteem. He considers Greece to be a shame-culture in this period. Shame is then slowly replaced by guilt, and by the time of Sophocles and Socrates, approximately 400 to 600 years later, morality has been internalized. This, Dodds says, is the beginning of guilt-culture. However, this division has been problematized by Jessica Moss (2005). She points out that Socrates uses shame very effectively to refute each of his three detractors in *Gorgias* because it can differentiate between what is pleasant from what is morally good.

Bernard Williams (1993) reexamines some of the Greek texts and argues that shame was a much more complex emotion during ancient Greece than has generally been acknowledged. He goes on to demonstrate that a number of qualities usually associated with guilt, like an internalized other, indignation, reparation, and attenuation by forgiveness were associated with Homeric shame. He feels that shame is, in many ways, superior to guilt: it can be amoral and understand guilt, while guilt cannot understand shame; shame can help rebuild the self after one has done wrong to someone else. Finally, Williams talks of how shame can give rise to "shared sentiments" which "serve to bind people together in a community of feeling" (p. 80).

Within Christian theology, guilt is generally associated with "original sin" and the fall of man. Prior to that, Adam and Eve lived in the Garden of Eden with God, in perfect harmony, knowing neither shame nor guilt. When they disobey God, by eating the apple, they gain the knowledge of good and evil. This is generally considered to be the start of guilt, which subsequently became part of our inheritance. And yet, what Genesis describes first is the onset of shame, not guilt (Velleman, 2001). J. David Velleman points out that evidence of their shame, by virtue of covering their genitalia, *preceded* their punishment, or even God's discovery of their disobedience. In fact, it is their shame that leads to the discovery of their disobedience and, ultimately, their punishment. Thus shame, not guilt, lead to remorse.

Jean-Paul Sartre in his seminal work, *Being and Nothingness* (1943) posits a relationship between shame and the sense of Self. Whenever we encounter the Other, we are forced to share our world with them. Also, we become acutely aware of the fact that they can see us, and objectify us. With this awareness comes the understanding that we can *always* be seen and be judged. This is, for Sartre, the essence of shame. Through shame we come to know ourselves as an object created by the Other's look. We are then forced to judge ourselves. Shame thus creates a sense of Self, but a Self centered outside of ourselves.

Commenting on the more current era (since the 1960s), James Twitchell (1997) laments the relative lack of shame in the American consumer culture. He gives several examples of how individual acts have gone from being stigmatic to becoming a trend, for example, living together out of wedlock, political scandals, etc. He believes that shame codes work to limit the behavior of the individual within the group, but are no longer a socializing device, instead are seen as a hindrance to individual fulfilment. Twitchell calls shame the "invisible electric fence" that works to stabilize the culture.[10] He warns against the excesses of shame, and believes that acceptance by others, and a sense of self-irony, can act as "vaccinations" against shame, preventing its most harmful effects.

In a recently published book, Jon Ronson (2015) catalogs the shaming of public figures in social media and online. He believes that there is a resurgence of public humiliation in this digital age, where shaming is an anonymous but powerful force. Jennifer Jacquet (2015) acknowledges that such online public shaming can often be disproportionate to the act, and that the anonymity has a disinhibiting effect. However, she feels that, properly used, it can be a powerful tool to challenge corporations and even governments.

Shame in the East

Although psychoanalytic movements have recently started in China and South Korea, as of now, only two Asian countries (excluding the former republics of the USSR and Israel) have well-established psychoanalytic movements—India and Japan (Akhtar, 2009b). In order to get a fuller picture of the experience of shame in these countries, I will supplement the available psychoanalytic writings with anthropological observations and works, and works of literature and mythology.

India

India has generally been labelled a shame-culture. Indeed, there is plenty of evidence for this. Both the great Indian epics, *Ramayana* (c. 450 BCE) and *Mahabharata* (c. 400 BCE) have significant episodes concerning the shaming of women. In *Ramayana*, Lord Rama doubts his wife Sita's fidelity after he rescues her from King Ravana who had kidnapped her, and makes her enter a fire to prove her purity. Though he claims to be satisfied with the results, when some of his subjects are not, he banishes her to the forest, even though she is pregnant with their twin children. Reunited after years, he once again demands that she prove her purity, again for the sake of his people. At that point, Sita's shame becomes overwhelming and she begs her mother, Earth, to open up and swallow her, which is indeed what happens. In *Mahabharata*, when the oldest of the five Pandava brothers, Yuddhisthira, loses everything in gambling with his Kaurava cousins, he gambles his wife, Draupadi. When he loses her too, the Kauravas start disrobing her in public. However, because Draupadi has always followed her *dharma* (right way of life),[11] her sari[12] extends itself endlessly and she averts humiliation.

Both of these stories show a close association between shame and the superego. In Sita's case, because of her guilt-free conscience, she does not "burn" from shame, not once, but twice. However, when she realizes that her husband was too weak to stand up for her in front of his subjects and is still ashamed of her, this is when she is overwhelmed with shame and returns to her mother's womb.[13] In Draupadi's case, she is able to ward off her humiliation because of the fact that she has always done the right thing, and hence, has a clean conscience.

Modern India also does not lack evidence of shame as a dominant social principle. For example, until fairly recently, it was unheard of to see a lip-to-lip kiss in an Indian movie. Even now frontal nudity is very rare in a mainstream movie. While things are changing in the metropolitan cities, most Indians still cringe from any public display of affection. Similarly, India has a very complex and rigid social hierarchy, based on an interplay between one's caste, age, gender, socio-economic status, etc., which is enforced quite effectively, mostly through the threat of shame. Shame is the fabric that both interweaves *and* protects the society. As Salman Rushdie (1984) says, "*Sharam*, that's the word. For which this paltry word 'shame' is a wholly inadequate translation" (p. 34).

However the casual visitor to India may be surprised at the apparent *lack* of shame in certain areas. As an example, it is a fairly common sight to see men urinating in public, against a wall or a tree. In villages and poorer areas of cities, it is not unusual to see children, men, and even the occasional woman[14] defecating in open fields. While the paucity of appropriate facilities is partly responsible for this, it does not explain the lack of shame associated with it. Similarly, farting, burping, picking one's nose, etc. are not usually associated with shame. In fact, in many parts of India, it is customary, almost obligatory, for the guest to give out a loud burp after a meal to show approval of the food.

Lawrence Kubie (1937) writes about the fantasy of dirt, and connects it to bodily fluids and wastes. He also speculates on the role that they play in the stratification of society. Sudhir Kakar (S. Kakar & K. Kakar, 2007) builds on this and talks about how the caste system in India may be partially connected to the fantasy of the feces. He also talks about how Indians have an intolerance of keeping bodily waste products inside, and are obsessed with expelling all waste products, with no shame associated with the act of expulsion itself. He contrasts this with the Western attitude, in which the act of expulsion itself has become shameful, resulting in a greater emphasis on controlling the moment of expulsion and more tolerance for the retained waste products. Building on Kubie's idea of the taboo around bodily apertures, I feel that both the social norms are extensions, albeit in different directions, of the same taboo. It could help us understand the difference in the locus of discomfort. Indians are more uncomfortable with the idea of something bad being retained inside of them and would prefer to let it be exposed to the public and feel the resultant shame, while Westerners have a greater degree of discomfort with the idea of being exposed in the act of expelling the dirtiness, and the resulting inclination is to retain the bad inside, perhaps leading to a greater comfort with the sense of guilt.

Guilt is not an emotion that most Indians articulate. As part of my research for this chapter, I asked about a dozen of my friends and family to translate the word into an Indian language. To my surprise, no one could come up with an appropriate word![15] Online and traditional dictionaries fared no better. Nevertheless, as is evident from the examples from the epics above, and my own personal experience, Indians do feel guilt. To paraphrase Erikson, guilt is insufficiently articulated in India because it is so early and easily absorbed by shame.

Japan

In his book on *amae*, Takeo Doi (1973) has a delightful section on sin and shame in the Japanese culture. He first gently critiques Benedict (1946) for considering guilt-cultures to be superior to shame-cultures. He posits that the two emotions are closely related and many people feel both simultaneously. He admits that guilt is not apparent in Japanese society but states that it is very much there, not as an inner problem but as a sense of betrayal of the group. He then goes on to trace the origin of guilt within Western society and feels that it too originated with a sense of betrayal of the group. Under the influence of the Judeo-Christian religions, this group was gradually replaced by God. When the influence of God diminished, the individual was left to carry it on by himself. He feels that traces of the sense of betrayal of the group can still be detected, although this is no longer experienced as shame. Thus shame starts from the awareness of the outside world, but is directed inward, whereas guilt starts from the inside and is directed outward.

He states that both shame and guilt are felt most intensely in relation to the group in which one belongs—guilt for betraying it and shame at being ostracized from it. At the same time, as long as neither occurs, one experiences very little of either within one's group. He goes on to give examples of how the sense of guilt leads to an apology and a plea for forgiveness. He points out that it is the Japanese who apologize more profusely, even though the West is supposed to be the guilt-culture.

George A. DeVos (1973) finds evidence of guilt as being a stronger basic determinant of behaviors in Japanese society, although less easily recognizable as it requires a more intense analysis than shame, which is readily apparent.

In his brilliant book, *Prohibition of Don't Look*, Osamu Kitayama (2010) has written extensively and elegantly about shame, guilt, and the mother-child bond in Japanese culture, analyzing myths and folk tales and illustrating liberally with clinical examples. In the first chapter, he analyzes several folk tales, most of which have as a central plot point a "prohibition of don't look" by a wounded wife/mother, who is masochistically taking care of the hero. Per Kitayama, this prohibition is different from a taboo in that it is a pre-oedipal maternal proscription and *meant* to be broken, as opposed to the oedipal taboo of incest, which is absolute. Indeed it is broken in all of the folk tales, with tragic consequences. Typically the women are left feeling extremely ashamed or angry and the men feeling guilty (at their transgression) and depressed (at the resultant loss of their wife). In chapter three Kitayama focuses on the guilt and masochism of the caregiver. After briefly mentioning the Ajase complex,[16] Kitayama goes on to talk about "forced guilt": guilt induced by the extreme self-sacrifice of the caregiver. Linking it to Winnicott's concept of "implanted guilt," Kitayama deduces that this is a moral form of masochism as a way to win love, not a part of the sadism-masochism dyad. He states that masochism and altruism often go together, as is evident in the folk tales described, and form the basis of the cultural ideal of the Japanese mother. He also finds it to be a common phenomenon within helping professions, and speculates on whether Florence Nightingale had this dynamic of masochism and altruism. In chapter five Kitayama writes about the resistance created by *both* the shame *and* the ambivalence around dependency. In his experience, once the patient enters into a stable therapeutic relationship, his identification with and guilt toward his altruistic and damaged mother is activated. Kitayama postulates that the shame-complex: the fear of intrusion and rejection, expectation of acceptance and love, and anal impulse of dirtying and retention, is often projected onto the analyst, in the transference. He cautions against attempting to penetrate into the shame-complex, instead advocating that the therapist accept it nonjudgmentally. In chapter seven he again brings up the deep sense of shame that the Japanese may feel for having hurt someone significant, in the present or as a child. However, he feels that the Japanese hide these feelings deeply in their shameful true self and create an "ideal self" for their public persona. Kitayama uses dramatic metaphors to differentiate between the "back stage" where there is the "I" of the true, shameful self, and "front stage," to which the true self must never be allowed to come, even when the analyst is non-judgmental and accepting. That is, the patient should never feel humiliated in therapy. Throughout the book, he does not distinguish between shame and guilt, using them more or less interchangeably.

Relatively little psychoanalytic material is available from other countries in the East. However, we do have some tantalizing bits of data from a few other cultures.

Sri Lanka

Gananath Obeyesekere is a psychoanalytically informed anthropologist from Sri Lanka who has carefully studied the Sinhalese society over decades. In *Medusa's Hair* (1981), he differentiates between primary guilt, which is related to the Oedipus complex, and secondary guilt, which is "the later utilization of primary guilt to establish normative control of drives and conformity to society" (p. 76). Obeyesekere finds evidence of primary guilt in all societies, including that of Sri Lankan Sinhala and pre-Homeric Greeks, and views symptoms, dreams, and visions as three signs of it being externalized. He calls primary guilt a personal emotion rooted in unconscious experiences, and hence, all cultures and languages may not have words to communicate it. By contrast, secondary guilt and shame are social emotions that do similar work. He states that different cultures privilege one over the other. Therefore, the so-called guilt-cultures, like today's West and post-Homeric Greece, have both primary and secondary guilt, while shame-cultures, like that of Sri Lanka, have primary guilt, which remains uncommunicated verbally and is often only recognized by its externalization, and shame. In *The Cult of the Goddess Pattini* (1984), Obeyesekere talks about the *lajja-baya* (literally, modesty and the fear of social disapproval) as a central, organizing principle in Sinhalese society, especially with women. Women who have *lajja-baya* dress modestly, never speak loudly, and are restrained and respectful. *Lajja-baya* is instilled from an early age and shaming through ridicule is employed as a disciplinary measure and to control behaviors.

Turkey

Shame-cultures are sometimes further subdivided into honor-cultures (like Spain, Greece, and Turkey) and face-cultures, like Japan. Within this terminology, the West is seen as a dignity-culture (Cohen & Nisbett, 1994). In honor-cultures, shame, accompanied by or converted to anger, can result from a loss of honor. However, it remains an important modulator of social behavior. As Alan Roland (2011) notes, a Turkish psychologist, Zeynep Catay, found in her research that the shaming of children by Turkish parenting was much more oriented toward correcting the child's behavior than toward conveying that the child is a bad person, a practice more common in European and American societies.[17]

Clinical examples

Having reviewed some of the theory and literature around culture and shame, I will share two clinical vignettes from my practice. I hope to illustrate how the expression of shame in therapy is influenced by the cultures of the patient and the therapist.

Clinical vignette: 1

> During my residency training, I was referred a young Indian man, who I soon found out was approximately my age. He came from the same part of India as I do and had emigrated to the US only a few months after I did. We connected instantly and rapport was established easily. He talked freely and articulately about the problems that had brought him into therapy. After detailing a few minor problems, he informed me that he was a homosexual. While he professed no ambivalence, he was terrified of his family's response. We talked a bit more about this in that first session. I was baffled when he did not return for a second session. My supervisor at the

time interpreted this as a homoerotic transference that developed too fast. While this is probably true, I now realize that he also left to avoid shame. For him our basic values were concordant, and hence, the danger of him experiencing intense shame too high.

In contrast to the rapid development of transference and the threat of the emergence of intense shame, I will now give an example when shame took a long time to appear, and when it did finally, it did not have the same destructive effect on therapy.

Clinical vignette: 2

A middle-aged Caucasian male was about a year away from early retirement. While he had been looking forward to his retirement for years, as the time grew closer, he realized that he was very conflicted about what to do after that. For a variety of reasons he did not want to stay at home with his wife of forty years, who had a few more years of work left before she could retire. However, leaving her for a few years, no matter where he decided to go and for what reason, was becoming more and more of an uncomfortable idea as the time drew nearer, in spite of the fact that their marriage had had major problems for the last thirty years. For a few months he talked about his guilt at the idea of leaving her. We explored its roots in his relationship with his parents and parental figures. However, he kept coming back to this discomfort. One day, tipped off by a free association, I asked him about the group of younger men from his church that he occasionally socialized with. He had always emphasized how happily married each and every member of that group was and how he envied them for *that*, not for any of their wives. Then it all came out—his shame in confronting the group of men who had, by his own estimate, always looked up to him and his feeling defective when they would discover that his own marriage was broken. I was quite taken aback, as this was the first time he had talked about shame. Of course, there were other emotions mixed in there—envy, jealousy, and masochism.

In the first vignette, the coincidental concordance in our cultures induced rapid development of intense shame in my patient, which became more than he could bear. Hence, this shame was defended against and became a resistance. In the second vignette, the *dis*cordance in our cultures acted as a resistance to the appearance and recognition of shame, which was defended by, amongst other things, guilt.

Discussion

For decades, shame was largely ignored by psychoanalysts—it was the "Cinderella of emotions" (Nathanson, 1992, p. 15). Not so by others. Historically, shame has been referred to, explicitly and implicitly, in works ranging from the ancient Indian text *Rig Veda* (c. 1500 BCE) to works of Confucius, from St. Augustine to Shakespearean plays, from Darwin to Mirza Ghalib. What is clear is that the phenomenon of shame is universally prevalent, possibly biologically programmed, profound, powerful, and pervasive, and that we are only now waking up to the full impact that shame, and the defense mechanisms to avoid it, have on our actions and affects. As Susan Miller (1996) states, several recent psychoanalytic works have compensated, perhaps even overcompensated, for the early dearth of exploration of the topic. I agree with her that shame now needs to be viewed in context, and my attempt here has been to study shame in the context of culture.

While shame is undoubtedly a universal, human experience,[18] there are significant differences in how different cultures have articulated and emphasized it, especially vis-à-vis guilt. I do believe that shame and guilt can and should be distinguished theoretically, but it is not always easy to do clinically, especially in translation. Here I agree with S. Kakar[19] that, clinically, "… the differences between shame and guilt have been exaggerated. They are experienced on a continuum and only at the extremes do we get examples of pure shame or pure guilt. Most often we get admixtures of the two. What one labels as shame versus guilt depends largely on the individual, the culture and the context." And indeed, as we have seen, several authors have noted this admixture of guilt and shame, the co-occurrence of the two, and the difficulties in teasing them apart, phenomenologically, experientially, and even theoretically. Others have noted the common origins and aims of the two. Is it possible, then, that the difference between them is no more than the difference between introjection and identification?[20]

Many people continue to demarcate sharply between the two and create a pecking order. For example, reacting to the immolation of the Jordanian pilot by the ISIS[21] in Syria, Nancy Kobrin (2015) tries to explain the *jihadi* psychology on the basis of shame. She writes:

> Unconsciously and concretely, they have recreated their own group self-perception of being "caged in" emotionally and mentally because of the debilitation of growing up in a shame-honor culture: they realize that, in the eyes of the world, Islam has been shamed. Fire, too, in the context of psychoanalysis, has many aspects worth considering. It might express projected rage. It might also purify an obsession with feeling dirty, deeply linked to this shame, which is supported by a religious conviction that normal human needs are unclean. They must therefore find a scapegoat and then kill off the contaminated one.

This creation of a hierarchy between shame and guilt is what S. Kakar calls "psychological colonization".[22] It is also interesting to juxtapose this with what Twitchell (1997) tells us about the Victorians, who equated shame with blushing. They felt that only people who felt shame could be trusted, and as Africans and Indians do not blush, they were considered to be shameless, and hence, subhuman. These contrasting examples show not just the politics of power, but also the 180-degree change in the value of shame within Western society in a little over a century. Shame may have decreased in the West, but it has also become largely invisible, unacknowledged, and something people are ashamed of (Middleton-Moz, 1990). In Gershen Kaufman's (1989) words, "Shame has become a taboo in contemporary society" (p. 3). Or as Donald Nathanson (1992) puts it, "The very *idea* of shame is embarrassing to most people" (p. 15, italics in original). Why does the West now have such a hard time accepting shame?

Perhaps the answer lies in what Roland Barthes (1970) calls the "Western mythology" of privileging the inside over the outside, whether it be the greater authenticity of Freudian unconscious motivations over conscious ones or the value inherent in the Winnicottian terms, the "false self" and the "true self."

Perhaps the feeling of shame is affected by the increasing loss of privacy. The omnipresent cameras, both still and video, are turning the West into a *Panopticon*.[23] If there is no place to hide, then shame has to be eschewed.

Perhaps it is related to the gendered nature of shame. Shame is very often considered a feminine reaction. Freud, in his lecture on Femininity

(1933a) states "Shame ... is considered to be a feminine character *par excellence*," although he goes on to add "but (that) is far more a matter of convention than might be supposed" (p. 132). He connects shame with women's sense of "genital deficiency" and their need to conceal same. Sidney Levin (1967) talks about how men who blush and show strong reactions of shame "often consider themselves unmanly and may harbor intense fears of whatever homosexual tendencies they do possess" (p. 272). Aneta Stepien (2014) hypothesizes that shame has the power "to undermine and emasculate men" (p. 7), and hence it has to be "masked and repressed" (p. 7). The Kakars (2007) talk about how the Indian man is more feminine, which is in accordance with his greater acceptance of shame.

Or perhaps the answer lies in the history of the Judeo-Christian religions, as suggested by Takeo Doi (1973), with the replacing of the group with God and the more recent decrease in faith.

This leads us to another important question: Is shame necessary? Plato feels it is absolutely essential for society. In *Symposium*, (c. 450—400 BCE) he writes, "... shame for what is disgraceful and ambition for what is noble; without these feelings neither a state nor an individual can accomplish anything great or fine" (42). Even Mark Twain (1897), who writes cynically about the human's need to blush, adds in the very next line "... the universal brotherhood of Man is our most precious possession" (p. 256). Kakar calls shame "a more evolved version of guilt as it is much more social and interpersonal".[24] Nathanson (1992) concurs, calling shame the most recent affect to develop through the process of evolution.

Shame is an interpersonal emotion; it needs the presence of an Other, real or imagined. This Other has to share the values that lead to shame for one to feel shame.[25] As Doi (1973) has noted, shame is felt most intensely in relation to the group to which one belongs. Aristotle (c. 350 BCE) says that people also feel shame for those with whom they are closely connected. Thus, shame is felt both individually and collectively. It both creates and maintains social bonds. It should then come as no surprise that shame-cultures are close-knit and interdependent societies. However, this quality of shame appears to be contradicted by the need to hide when feeling shamed, at least until we consider that this need includes a wish to unite. Dietrich Bonhoeffer (1955) states, "Shame is man's ineffaceable recollection of his estrangement from the origin; it is grief from this estrangement, and the powerless longing to return to unity with the origin ... Shame is more original than remorse" (p. 24).

He goes on to add that the public confession of our sins, and tolerating the resultant shame, is necessary in order to be one with God again. Ayers (2003) notes that shame is connected to a pre-mature separation of the infant from the mother, which she interprets as the symbolic meaning behind the expulsion of Adam and Eve from the Garden of Eden. Shame seeks reunion with the mother, a return to the womb, symbolized by the various descriptions of shame in which there is a wish to be swallowed up by the Mother Earth (as in the tale of Sita, above). Thus we hide in order to be found, in order to be reunited with our mother.

Notes

1. On PEP-Web, a search for "shame" in the title revealed 242 entries. Of these, all but forty-eight were after 1990, and there were a mere fourteen before 1970. "Shame" does not even merit an entry in the otherwise excellent vocabulary guide, *The Language of Psycho-Analysis*, by Laplanche and Pontalis (1973).
2. On amazon.com, a search in the book section for "shame" brings up thousands of books. Of the first ten nonfiction books, eight considered shame negatively, at least in the title, with names like "Healing the Shame that Binds You," "Letting Go of Shame," "Healing the Shame You Don't Deserve," and "It Wasn't Your Fault."
3. At the Albert Einstein College of Medicine, Psychiatry Program, in the late 1980s and early '90s.
4. Mostly at the New York Psychoanalytic Institute and Society, but also at various other places in the Tri-State area.
5. Here, and throughout this chapter, I use the words "West" and "East" as denoting cultural rather than geographical places. While this is painting in very broad brushstrokes, anything finer is beyond the scope of this chapter. But I do agree with Ananda Coomaraswamy (1945) that the East and West are separated geographically only accidentally. As was explained to me by his son, Rama Coomaraswamy, in a personal communication c. 1994, what his father means by that somewhat cryptic statement is that there is nothing inherent in either of the two civilizations to account for the differences other than accidental historical events.
6. While Altman is specifically referring to the experience of the African-Americans, I believe what he has written can be generalized to most ethnic minorities. I certainly can relate to his experience of going to a

psychoanalytic seminar and realizing that I am the only nonwhite individual in the room.
7. Donald Nathanson (1992) comments on how every writer has a slightly different view on shame and that it is very subjective and includes individual prejudice.
8. Almost all of the mentions of shame in Freud's writings occur before he formulated the concept of the superego. Prior to that, he does not really differentiate between shame and morality, and feels that *both* are heavily influenced by the social upbringing.
9. Within the context of the book it is clear that Erikson is referring to Western culture when he talks of "our civilization."
10. I think that an "invisible electric fence" is a great phrase to describe how shame works in any culture—how it remains hidden, in spite of being a major force in shaping the character of both the individual and the culture.
11. The concept of *dharma* is a complex one and difficult to translate adequately. It includes notions of an inner morality, a cosmic balance and a degree of free will. As S. Kakar (personal communication, 16 December, 2014) has pointed out, the Indian (Hindu) concept of the superego is a contextual and individual one. To know what is right at any given moment, one has to know one's *dharma*. And the only way to do so is by introspection or through discourses with the learned sages.
12. The sari is the traditional garment of the Hindu woman, which is basically a long wrap.
13. Sita's story includes the two most extreme metaphors for shame—to "burn" with shame and to be "swallowed" up by the ground with shame. Is it just a coincidence that most cultures either cremate their dead or bury them? Could it point to a deeper connection between shame and the death instinct? The metaphor of "burning with shame" is probably also related to blushing.
14. Interestingly, you will sometimes find women who have bared their nether regions in order to do the deed, but still have their heads covered, as per the tradition.
15. Most words for guilt in Indian languages translate into its legal meaning—one responsible for an illegal act.
16. The Ajase complex was first postulated by Heisaku Kosawa in 1931 (but not published until 1954). The name comes from an ancient Buddhist tale of Prince Ajase whose mother nurses him even after he tries to kill her. This act of forgiveness evokes a sense of guilt and penitence in him and he goes on to kill his father. Kosawa postulates two kinds of guilt

feelings—one arising from the matricidal wishes (Ajase), the other from patricidal wishes (Oedipus).
17. Roland feels that this is true of other non-Western societies also and attributes the better behavior of Indian children in public to such tactics by their parents.
18. Are there things of which human beings are universally ashamed? Or is shame entirely determined by values within a culture? While I do not pretend to have a definite answer, it does appear that, unlike guilt with its universal taboos of parricide and incest, shame does not appear to have any universal triggers. Or perhaps, given how the workings of shame are often invisible, they are well hidden from us.
19. Personal communication at Benaulim beach, Goa, in January 6, 2015, while sharing a dazzling sunset.
20. Introjection and identification are both types of internalization processes, wherein the psychological contents of significant others are brought inside one's mind and made a part of it. In introjection, the process of assimilation is incomplete, and hence, there remains a feeling of "Otherness" to the introjects. In identification, the process of assimilation is complete and hence, is more ego-syntonic (Akhtar, 2009).
21. Also called the "Islamic State," "ISIL," or "Da'ish."
22. Personal communication, January 6, 2015.
23. A Panopticon is a hypothetical institutional building first designed by the eighteenth-century British social reformer Jeremy Bentham. The design allows for one watchman to observe all inmates, who are unable to tell whether they are being watched at any given time or not. Michel Foucault (1975) used it as a metaphor for modern society and social institutions, even before cameras became ubiquitous, and considered it as an exemplar of how a situation of an unequal gaze (cf. Sartre) is created between the people in power and the rest, and discipline enforced.
24. Personal communication, January 6, 2015.
25. X can make Y feel guilty without having to share the values of Y. But X can make Y feel ashamed *only* if X shares some of the values, or at least, Y believes that to be the case. While I believe this intuitively, the only reference I could find was in Eleanor Wu (2014).

CHAPTER FIVE

Shame and murder-suicide: Adolf Hitler and the Nazi cult of death

Ira Brenner

The crimes against humanity perpetrated between 1933 and 1945 were largely due to the murderous regimes of Adolf Hitler in Germany and Joseph Stalin in Russia. Historians have concluded that the policies of each contributed to the destructiveness of the other, resulting in civilian deaths alone of 14 million people in the so-called "bloodlands" between these two countries (Snyder, 2012). This staggering number was achieved through such means as state-manufactured famines inducing death from starvation, mobile execution squads, lethal slave labor conditions, and, of course, the infamous Nazi death camps in which the industrialization of murder utilized poisonous gases. Within Germany itself, as the inevitability of defeat became clear, even more civilian deaths occurred as Hitler staunchly refused to surrender. It was not until the dramatic murder-suicide of the occupants of his underground bunker that the war could finally end.

Extensive research into the phenomenon of murder-suicide has categorized it into four types, based on the manifest motivation of the killer. While these categories may be overlapping, they have been described as mercy killing followed by suicide, killing in the name of justice followed by suicide, killing another and then oneself out of a sense of duty, and, finally, committing murder and suicide in the name of glory. Such "virtuous" causes have been invoked by the murderers as the rationale for their behavior (Joiner, 2014) and, in Adolf Hitler's case, the glory of his Third Reich was a central tenet of his ideology (Koenigsberg, 1975). Writers have referred to this fixation, as an aspect of Nazi philosophy, as a "cult of death" (Friedländer, 2007). As a result, it might be considered that the German people themselves willingly or unwillingly participated in a societal murder-suicide guided by the delusional belief of being the master race entitled to world domination through enslavement and extermination of others deemed inferior. The notion of the Other (Lacan, 1982) is especially relevant here as it had life-and-death implications in Nazi-controlled lands.

Preamble

While it will require scholars many more years to get a fuller understanding of the historical, political, social, and psychological aspects of this period of time, much is already known about the importance of the psychology of the leaders of such regimes (Adorno, Frenkel-Brunswik, Levinson, & Sanford, 1950; Volkan, 2004). Nevertheless, there is a risk of jumping to reductionistic conclusions that oversimplify such enormously complex situations but may offer a false sense of comfort in the belief of our psycho-historical formulations. With this *caveat* in mind, I will endeavor to present the theory that Adolf Hitler's intolerable shame and humiliation, along with unresolved mourning, were major aspects of his development and that his characterological solution to these problems contributed to his unbridled destructiveness once he was in power.

I grew up with the absolute knowledge that Hitler was a very, very bad man who brought immeasurable sorrow to my family, my people, and to much of the world I knew. In the midst of so much uncertainty about the rest of my young life, there was something oddly reassuring about this unchanging fact—it was immutable and enduring. I could always set my moral compass by orienting it to Adolf Hitler, the most heinous, most despicable, most vile, and most destructive man in history. To assess one's character, I could always conjure up Adolf Hitler and gauge where everyone else stood in relation to him.

It was preached in religious and secular settings that it was both wrong and not possible to try to understand the man, not only because he embodied pure evil but also because of the remote possibility that such an attempt might result in humanizing him and having a speck of compassion for him. Rabbinical thought has even contended that Hitler was the reincarnation of Amalek, the archetypal enemy of the ancient Jews of the Hebrew Bible, that is, the Old Testament. Amalek would always be there, ready to attack, enslave, and kill. Throughout history, other malevolent figures bent on destroying the Jews have also been seen as reincarnations of Amalek. For example, the villain, Haman, described in *The Book of Esther*, whose downfall is celebrated during the holiday of Purim, has been considered such a manifestation of this perpetual threat to the children of Israel.

After many years of endeavoring to understand the psychological impact of survivors and their offspring of Hitler's genocidal policies, this is only the second time that I have put my thoughts down on paper about the "destructive prophet" (Redlich, 1998) himself. The indelible stain on humanity known as the Third Reich was masterminded by a very enigmatic and often underrated man whose "… recognition of cowardice and moral decay [in others] was uncanny" (Redlich, 1998, p. 166). Indeed, this capacity to exploit the vulnerability and corruptibility of others led to "… a war that took the lives of between 50 to 80 million soldiers and civilians" (Pressman, 2014, p. 251).

Adolf Hitler (1889–1945)

Our morbid fascination with him

There continues to be great fascination with Hitler's life. How could someone of his apparently unremarkable background be transformed into the dictator who catalyzed and unleashed such unprecedented murderous destruction? Hitler was extremely guarded and secret about himself and used the German propaganda machine, which not only manipulated words and created notorious euphemisms to hide its crimes, but also fabricated myths about his childhood and his "superman" image. He became a gifted orator who was described as hypnotic and irresistibly charismatic, able to ignite huge crowds into a frenzy. Yet, there is little known about his early years that could have presaged such meteoric success. It has been estimated that hundreds of thousands of publications have been written about this penniless, failed art student who became a decorated but very eccentric infantryman in World War I and then became transformed into *Der Führer* (Redlich, 1998, p. 1).[1]

Scholars most certainly try to understand his anti-Semitism and many have attributed great significance to his putative Jewish grandfather. A prevailing theory is that this man impregnated Hitler's grandmother who worked as a domestic. Significantly, one of the very specific provisions of the Nuremberg "Law to Protect German Blood and German Honor" was the prohibition against domestics under the age of forty-five working in Jewish households. It has been theorized that Hitler insisted on this detail perhaps because of a wish to prevent such a recurrence.

There is also some speculation that Hitler may have been born with two congenital defects—spina bifida occulta and hypospadias, a deformity of the penis. He was guarded about exposing his body. His sexual development is obscure, but he was very awkward with girls. A boyhood friend reported that as a prankish adolescent Hitler once urinated into the mouth of a goat, fueling rumors about a sexual perversion. Once in power, the mysterious death of his beautiful, beloved half-niece, Geli, who essentially became his prisoner, as well as the bizarre marriage to his longtime mistress, Eva Braun, on the day of their double suicide added to such formulations. Hitler refused X-rays presumably due to shame and paranoia over alleged deformities being discovered. Moreover, his personal physicians were not permitted to examine his genitalia or perform rectal examinations.

Hitler's father was a customs inspector, a mid-level Prussian bureaucrat. He was described as overly strict, punitive, and prone to violent outbursts at home. He evidently was a bastard in both the legal and the figurative sense. His early retirement from civil service may have been associated with an inheritance as well as alcoholism as he spent much of his time at the local pub. When he did come home, he brutally and regularly disciplined and humiliated his son and his wife. This, in concert with young Adolf's putative genital deformity, left the child feeling profoundly unloved, defective, and impotently enraged.

Although he did feel quite special and loved by his mother, her masochistic submissiveness to her husband left young Hitler feeling unprotected and unable to trust her.

Hitler's father died when Hitler was fourteen and this was followed four years later by his mother dying from breast cancer. Despite the competent ministrations of her Jewish doctor, whom Hitler quietly helped escape Europe years later, he was left on his own with no guidance. He quickly squandered his inheritance on the opera when he returned to

Vienna and had to live in a homeless shelter until the war broke out. He grew up in a house of death, having three older siblings who died in infancy before he was born as well as a younger brother who died when Hitler was eleven.

As a young man, Hitler lived in mortal dread of infections and diseases, especially syphilis, which he considered "the Jewish disease." He believed that it was inheritable and resulted in mental as well as physical degeneration. As he and his baby sister, Paula, were the only survivors of his parents' six children, he may have had an unconscious fantasy that his father was the source of this fatal infection. He may also have ascribed his congenital defects as well as his mother's cancer to his father.

Whatever the sense of inner shame and badness he may have felt would, therefore, have been externalized and blamed on others through displacement from the father and projected onto groups who he felt were degenerate and inferior, such as Jews, gypsies, homosexuals, the mentally ill, and the physically handicapped. In so doing, all of his doubts about his ancestry, his sexuality, and his physical and mental well-being would have been disowned and ascribed to others. In this vein, perhaps, a reason he had no children was because of a deep fear of transmitting his genetic defects and being "found out" as being far from perfect.

Hitler may have then grandiosely expanded his vision to include a contaminated, humiliated Germany, which then required radical measures to cleanse, purify, and free it from deadly parasites as well as excise its cancerous growth (Redlich, 1998).

Hitler's shame

Violent defenses against shame and humiliation can be traced throughout history, and likely our ancestral history (Thomson, personal communication, June 10, 2015), when those in power are so afflicted. Adolf Hitler's impact on the world exemplifies this phenomenon, which is still felt quite profoundly seventy years after his suicide. The accompanying mass murder of Goebbels's children and the suicide of the adults in his underground bunker was the grand finale of this tragic "hero" who refused to be captured and be at the mercy of his inferior enemies. Indeed, his overidentification with the mythical German heroes of Wagnerian operas would have left no other option in the face of imminent defeat. Moreover, his numerous military blunders and overreliance on developing super weapons, such as rockets and gigantic tanks, speak to a grandiose vision of victory that was unrealistic and not in keeping with the "facts" on the ground. His unpublished "second book" written in 1928 further documents his grandiose plan for global domination through a series of wars culminating in the conquest of the United States (Weinberg, 2006). He refused to listen to his military commanders and thereby sealed Germany's fate. It was as though he insisted on fighting a war that he knew he could not win, ensuring his inevitable, felt need for suicide just as he had brought unprecedented destruction upon his own people. And, certainly, to have diverted sorely needed manpower from the war effort in order to accelerate his annihilation of the dreaded Jews makes little sense strategically but might be somewhat comprehensible from a psychological perspective. They became the repository of every unwanted and disowned quality that had to be expunged from himself and the Aryan people (Volkan, Ast, & Greer, 2002).

As noted above, much has been said about his troubled childhood, being born to an older, disinterested, and brutal father and a much younger mother who died of breast cancer when he was a teenager. Even before this unmournable loss, Adolf and his younger sister were the only survivors of the six children his mother bore. He grew up surrounded by death and stayed by his mother's side during the excruciatingly painful last months of her short life. Furthermore, the possible congenital deformity of his penis would have affected his anatomy, urinary stream, and quite possibly his potency (Brenner, 2009).

A series of continuing, humiliating insults is known to have occurred throughout his young life from his rejection by his father, his failed attempt to gain entry to art school in Vienna, and failing his military induction physical for the Austro-Hungarian army after being caught while fleeing conscription by moving to Munich. Even his wartime record is clouded by controversy and shame. The temporary blindness that he sustained during the poison gas attack by the British toward the end of the war has been highly researched and considerable evidence suggests that his symptoms were in fact due to hysterical blindness. The nature of his treatment and the fate of his doctor are of great significance and will be addressed below. The fate of his mother's doctor is also of great significance and will be discussed as well.

The loss of World War I was the final blow for this now intensely preoccupied, odd little man who was, ironically, described by his superiors as having no leadership qualities. Interestingly, however, he seemed to have a sixth sense for avoiding the deadly explosions that killed many of his comrades in arms. His uncanny prescience has also been attributed to his having survived numerous assassination attempts. The corporal's seething rage and rambling rhetoric seemed to be the only salve (Akhtar, 2000) for his gaping, narcissistic wounds in which insult upon insult and humiliation upon humiliation only intensified the incurable shame of his childhood. But if, indeed, such developmental formulations have any validity, the role of his psychopathology and trauma in his transformation into the histrionically magnetic orator, political genius, and utterly ruthless dictator remains unclear. I will consider the role of affect intolerance regarding shame at three key nodal points in his life and will begin by presenting evidence of a grandiose defense against shame and humiliation in the orchestration of his suicide. I will then review the data on his putative hysterical blindness during the war and, finally, I will address the death of his mother and the evidence of its continued impact on his psyche in the "cult of death" that was a central part of Nazi ideology.

The musical accompaniment to his suicide

The impending death of the Third Reich was accompanied by the music and philosophy of Wagner, Schopenhauer, and Nietzsche (Demopoulos, 2014). Hitler's dramatic exit was echoed by thousands in a national mass suicide accompanied by a large-group fantasy of self-punishment and purification. One of his most prized possessions, which he kept in his bunker to his death, was an original manuscript of Wagner's *Rienzi* which in the final act declares:

> May this town be accursed and destroyed!
> Disintegrate and wither, Rome!
> Your degenerate people wish it so!
> (1840)

On April 12, 1945, as the Soviet army was fast approaching Berlin, the Berlin Philharmonic gave a concert. Albert Speer had intervened to save the orchestra's members from being drafted into the Volkssturm, the

German national militia created by the Nazi Party under the orders of Adolf Hitler during the last months of the war. He organized a concert in the Berlin Beethoven Salle, which was amazingly still standing amidst all the destroyed buildings. The hall was in darkness and the only illumination came from the lights on the music stands.

The program began with the finale of Wagner's *Götterdämmerung* (or "Twilight of the Gods"):

> Grane, my steed,
> Greetings!
> Do you also know, my friend,
> where I am leading you?
> In the glowing fire
> there lies your lord,
> Siegfried, my blessed hero.
> Are you neighing joyously,
> eager to follow him?
> (1874)

Here, Valhalla, the home of the Gods, was consumed by fire, and the people of Berlin also appeared to be "neighing joyously" as they followed their Führer into the flames.

The populace of Berlin suffered greatly in the last months of the war and may have found refuge in the music, especially in the face of imminent defeat and humiliation. Brunhilde's voice may have eased the fear of their inevitable destruction, as the remaining officers clung to the fantasy of military honor in not surrendering and thus guaranteeing the deaths of many thousands more civilians. There were two more concerts that the orchestra performed—the *Deutsches Requiem* by Brahms and *Tod und Verklärung* by Strauss. They were essentially a funeral march for the nation.

After Hitler committed suicide, his death was announced on German radio. Even the music played before the announcement was symbolically significant. At 9:43 p.m. on May 1, 1945, excerpts from Wagner's *Rheingold* were broadcast. Then at 9:57 p.m. the announcer added that the Adagio from Bruckner's *Seventh Symphony* would be heard. Significantly, Bruckner wrote the movement in memory of Wagner's death, and his *Seventh Symphony* was one of Hitler's favorite works. In so doing, the radio tried to mythologize the passing of the Führer through such music.

Incidentally, Hitler's teenage friend, August Kubizek, claimed (2011) that Hitler had predestined himself to be a leader of the German people and was inspired by Wagner's *Rienzi* as early as 1905. This account of an ecstatic, young Hitler imagining a future for his people after a night at the opera may have a basis in fact as he attended the opera almost every night in Vienna during this early time of his life. His immersion in this Wagnerian world became even more complete after the death of his mother.

In the last four months of the war, more than 1,500,000 Germans, including hundreds of thousands of civilians, had died unnecessarily as defeat was obvious and surrender was the most logical move. Music was exploited to exhort the German people to keep fighting and dying for the Führer. Ultimately, Hitler staged his own Götterdämmerung in his Berlin bunker as he refused to surrender. In so doing, he lived out his fantasy and favorite operatic scene, the final destruction of the gods and Valhalla.

Hitler's ideal was for his people to become an army of suicidal faithful, a glorious fate to fuel his malignant narcissism. The military oath of his time was as follows: "I swear by God this sacred oath that I shall render unconditional obedience to Adolf Hitler, the Führer of the German Reich, supreme commander of the armed forces, and that I shall at all times be prepared, as a brave soldier, to give my life for this oath" (Snyder, 1998, p. 257).

The cult of death

The myth of the Aryan superior race was a grandiose façade beneath which lies a very dark obsession with death and martyrdom. Hitler engineered a Germany built upon sacrifice, hero worship, fascist ideology, and a Nazi *Totenkult* or cult of death (Friedländer, 2007; O'Donnell, 2012). The future of Germany was to be based on world domination by the master race. The building of Nazi cultural monuments and art mirrored this quest in its efforts to change the image of Germany (and its leader) from one of shame and despair to one of great pride.

The roots of this Totenkult were based in *völkisch* thought of the late nineteenth century, which "showed a distinct tendency toward the irrational and emotional" (Mosse, 1964, p. 13), promoted the idea of "authentic German culture" (Levy, 2005, p. 743) and espoused the superiority of all things German. This new philosophy incorporated modern propaganda, technology, and warfare as well as darkness, destruction, and dramatic death.

The Nazi's appropriation of the work of Richard Wagner exemplifies the cult of death par excellence. As Hitler himself declared, "Whoever wants to understand National Socialist Germany must know Wagner" (Viereck, 2004, p. 126). Although Wagner was actually a product of nineteenth-century Romanticism, his art deeply influenced Hitler and became inextricably linked to the Nazi cause. Wagner's major operas, *Der Ring des Nibelungen* and *Tristan und Isolde*, exalted the superiority of the Teutonic race and glorified violent death. *Der Ring des Nibelungen* (The Ring of Nibelung) is comprised of four operas, the last one being *Götterdämmerung* (Twilight of the Gods). It was said that Hitler's favorite operatic scene was the finale of *Götterdämmerung* (Spotts, 2009, p. 114). Here, the hero Siegfried and his lover Brunhilde die heroes' deaths in an apocalyptic vision of the end of the world. During his brief imprisonment after his failed uprising in 1923, he wrote his manifesto, *Mein Kampf*, in which he declared, "A fire was kindled from whose flame one day the sword must come which would regain freedom for the German Siegfried and life for the German nation" (Michaud, 2004, p. 58). Thus, hero worship and memorializing the fallen soldier were essential elements of the Nazi ideology as it glorified death and kept such stories alive. As an example, during World War I, at Langemarck, Belgium, on October 26, 1914, hundreds of German soldiers knowingly marched to their certain deaths, allegedly singing *"Deutschland, Deutschland über alles"* ("Germany, Germany, above all things") (Mosse, 1990, p. 70). Thousands were ultimately slaughtered and the myths surrounding their deaths grew. In another example, Emil Alefeld, a soldier, wrote this letter to his family:

> We are Germans; we fight for our people and shed our blood and hope that the survivors are worthy of our sacrifice. For me this is a struggle for an idea, the Fata Morgana [mirage or illusion] of a pure, loyal, honorable Germany. And if we go to our deaths with this hope in our hearts, perhaps it is better than to have the victory.
> (Baird, 1990, p. 3)

An important martyr after Germany lost World War I was Albert Schlageter who, in 1923, bombed a railway bridge and was executed on the outer border of Düsseldorf by French occupation forces. The imposing of the Versailles Treaty was intended to bring Germany to its knees and prevent it from ever being able to wage another war. It was largely seen as a national humiliation spearheaded by France and its allies, which was taken almost personally by Hitler. Outraged at this punishment of one of its heroes, Germany erected a monument in his memory at the site of his execution (Baird, 1990, p. 33) and his story became a favorite source of inspiration for the Third Reich. An amalgam of such myths of dead heroes, Wagner, and *völkisch* neo-romanticism satisfied Hitler's grandiose vision, which quite likely served to eclipse his memory of an earlier dead heroine, his mother, and his failure to save her. To concretize this new vision, Hitler became obsessed with monument building, stating that "No Volk lives longer than the evidence of its culture!" (Romane, 2007, p. 486). Speaking at the cornerstone-laying ceremony of his new Congress Hall in September of 1935, he expressed his quest for immortality:

> On this day, we hereby lay for this new world of the German Volk the cornerstone of its first great monument. A hall shall rise that is to serve the purpose of annually housing within its walls a gathering of the elite of the National Socialist Reich for centuries to come .... Should the Movement ever be silent, even after millennia, this witness shall speak. In the midst of a hallowed grove of ancient oak trees will the people then marvel in reverent awe at this first colossus among the buildings of the German Reich. (Romane, 2007, p. 486)

As part of his plans for immortal monuments to the German Reich, he envisioned the building of many miles of mausoleums along the borders of Germany's newly expanded empire:

> "... to glorify war, honour its dead heroes and symbolize the impregnable power of the German race" as the massive stone structures would stretch "... from the Atlantic to the Urals, [and] from Norway to North Africa." (Spotts, 2009, pp. 116–117)

Hitler also reconstructed the mid-nineteenth-century Königsplatz tombs for the martyrs of the Beer Hall Putsch of 1923, Hitler's failed uprising, as a *Totenkult* monument (Spotts, 2009, p. 116). It became a sacred place where the Germans could celebrate their dead martyrs (Spotts, 2009, p. 116) every year on November 9th, the anniversary of their deaths. Incorporated into this dramatized, annual mourning ritual was the *Blutfahne*, or blood flag, the original swastika banner that had actually been carried in the 1923 Putsch, which Hitler marched with each November 9th. This bloodstained flag was considered to be the most sacred relic of the Third Reich, a national linking object (Volkan, 1981). However, this annual ceremony and its bloodstained banner may have also served to further shield and obscure the deeper, unmournable loss for the Führer.

The cult of death was a self-fulfilling prophecy that climaxed when Hitler and his followers committed murder-suicide in his Berlin bunker. On April 28, 1945, Josef Goebbels's wife Magda wrote to her eldest son stating: "The world that will come after the Führer and National Socialism will not be worth living in, and therefore I have taken my children away ... We have now only one aim: loyalty unto death to the Führer ..." (Goeschel, 2009, p. 163). She had taken her six children "away" by forcing them to swallow cyanide capsules. Shortly afterward, she and her husband committed suicide just as Hitler and his wife Eva Braun had done. United in death with his love object for eternity, this last act of his life may have also fulfilled a fantasy of reunion with his first love. Deluded into believing that this form of demise was glorious and exalted, it was Hitler's own "final solution" to his intractable, lifelong shame.

From temporary blindness to grandiose vision

Back to the pivotal time in his young adult life following his mother's death, Hitler returned to Vienna until he enlisted in the German army after war was declared. As with all aspects of Hitler's personal life, there is much uncertainty over both of these crucial periods in his "preFührer" life. This murkiness is especially evident regarding his wartime injury owing to the paucity of records and the propaganda machine both for and against him. However, there is a very strong suspicion that his temporary blindness after a poison gas attack was in fact psychogenic in nature, that is, a hysterical reaction (Lewis, 2005; Maranhão-Filho & Silva, 2010). Given the lack of understanding of post-traumatic disorders and the severe stigma of mental illness at the time, such a diagnosis would have been a humiliating disgrace of enormous proportion. It would have been the source of shame of such great magnitude that were it not very, very secret it might have undermined the Führer's credibility. It is, therefore, most intriguing that his treating psychiatrist, the eminent Dr. Edmund Robert Forster (1893–1933), was mysteriously found shot to death in 1933 in an apparent suicide with a handgun that his wife did not even know he possessed. It occurred after he attended a secret meeting. Shortly thereafter, he complained of being mercilessly harassed by the Gestapo and having his job threatened by a rambling, accusatory letter written by a virulent Nazi who did not even work at his facility.

The poison gas attack and its aftermath have been described as follows: On October 15, 1918, less than a month before the Armistice was signed on November 11, 1918, a small group of German soldiers in the Belgian mountains was surprised by the British army and attacked with either mustard gas or a chlorine-based poison gas. One of the minimally affected soldiers guided his comrades to a field hospital about three miles away from which they were transferred to a larger facility near Brussels the next day. Corporal Hitler, however, maintained that he was permanently blinded and was sent to a hospital in Oudenaarde, Belgium, for further evaluation. He was then transferred to Reserve Hospital IV in Pasewalk, a small town near the border with Poland, where he was treated on the psychiatric unit.

Hitler was evaluated by Dr. Karl Kroner (1878–1954), who was Jewish. Dr. Kroner had himself experienced a gas attack in the past and since he suspected that Hitler's blindness was of psychological origin he referred him to Dr. Edmund Robert Forster. Such a diagnosis at this time in history was typically seen as a simple failure of willpower in contrast to Freud's already developed ideas about unconscious processes and conflict. On October 25, 1918, Dr. Forster of the Charité Hospital in Berlin received the injured corporal's records. Dr. Forster had little time or patience for soldiers he felt were malingerers and many of his treatment methods, by today's standards, would be considered torture. He was known to employ not only hypnosis but also electric shocks, cold showers, nakedness, solitary confinement, and simulated asphyxiation. Dr. Forster's goal was to re-motivate the soldier to regain his courage. Reportedly, however, Hitler's case was unique in that he wanted to go back to the front. Dr. Forster reportedly modified his technique as he sensed the corporal's zeal and fervent nationalism:

> "I could show you the method by which you can see again, despite the fact your eyes have been damaged by mustard gas. With your symptoms an ordinary person would be blind for life. But for a person with exceptional strength of will-power and spiritual energy

there are no limits, scientific assumptions do not apply to that person, the spirit removes any such barrier ... You must have absolute faith in yourself, then you will stop being blind ... You know that Germany now needs people who have energy and faith in themselves." (Lewis, 2005, p. 239)

Dr. Forster reinforced Hitler's feeling of grandiosity by suggesting that a miracle might happen to restore his vision if he had in fact been truly chosen to do something great. This hypnotic suggestion apparently galvanized Hitler. His eyesight returned and his grandiose vision became crystallized. He then returned to his regiment in Munich on November 19, 1918, a week after the end of the war. He was infuriated that Germany had given up and vowed to do something about it. The rest is history.

Dr. Forster, however, was not a Nazi and later became very worried about Hitler's rise to power, fearful that he had created a monster. In an effort to stop this juggernaut, in the summer of 1933, he secretly met with a small group of like-minded German writers and journalists at the Café Royal in Paris in order to give them Hitler's medical file. This clandestine meeting was most likely known about by the Gestapo who already had these men under surveillance.

Dr. Forster reportedly gave his treatment notes to Ernst Weiss (1882–1940), a former surgeon and prominent novelist, in the hope that he would publicize Hitler's mental condition. Dr. Forster paid for his extraordinary act of bravery with his life. Dr. Kroner, who had confirmed the diagnosis of hysteria and referred the blinded corporal to Dr. Forster for treatment, was also persecuted. On the day after *Krystallnacht,* November 10, 1938, he was arrested and sent to the notorious Sachsenhausen concentration camp north of Berlin. It was located just a short train ride away on the S-Bahn in the picturesque little town of Oranienburg. He likely would have died were if not for high-level, political intervention by the Consul of Iceland in Berlin. When he finally escaped Europe and was debriefed by US intelligence officials in 1943, he re-confirmed Hitler's diagnosis of hysterical blindness.

Ernst Weiss incorporated the story of Hitler's condition into his novel, *The Eyewitness* (Weiss, 1977). The manuscript was originally written in 1938 and submitted to the American Guild for German Cultural Freedom in a literary competition. The thinly disguised story told of a patient (AH) who was treated in a military hospital identified as "P", and eventually became the dictator of Germany. Unfortunately, the manuscript lost the competition and it had no impact. Depressed and hopeless, Weiss committed suicide on June 14, 1940, just as the Nazis were marching into Paris. Curiously, the manuscript was filed away and forgotten about until 1963 when it was discovered and finally published.

The only survivor of that extraordinary meeting at the Café Royal was Leopold Schwarzchild and he kept silent until his death in the 1950s. Skeptics of this story question, among other things, why those privy to such explosive information did not go public with it immediately. However, for those who had lived in constant terror and knew of the long and lethal reach of the Gestapo, anyone with such information about the Führer would have justifiably feared for his life even long after the end of the war. Utterly merciless to his enemies and anyone who might reveal secrets that would humiliate and shame him, the Führer's heart hardened after his mother's death and his subsequent wartime experience.

Hitler's helplessly having to watch his mother die

It is this writer's opinion that the death of Hitler's mother was the central organizing trauma of his life from which he never recovered. All of his previous trauma and humiliation crystallized around her agonizingly painful death. Moreover, his subsequent experiences were interpreted by him through this lens of helplessness, loss, and a grandiose wish for her resurrection. The generally accepted story of her illness and early death is as follows:

Klara Hitler (1860–1907) essentially ignored the lump in her breast that she had actually discovered two years earlier at the age of forty-five. Already a widow and burdened with her many household chores, Klara typically put her needs last and neglected her health. By the time she was examined by her family physician, Eduard Bloch, MD (1872–1945), the malignancy had metastasized, and he accurately suspected that she was terminally ill. Dr. Bloch informed her children and it fell to Adolf to tell his mother the grave news, who, as Dr. Bloch reported, "… accepted the verdict as I was sure she would—with fortitude. Deeply religious, she assumed that her fate was God's will. It would never occur to her to complain" (cited in Olson, 2002, p. 94). Her only chance of survival, which was quite slim, was a radical mastectomy that was performed in Linz by a Dr. Karl Urban, a few days later.

Dr. Urban discovered that the tumor had spread to the pleural tissue and her condition was terminal. Again, Dr. Bloch delivered the bad news to her children, who moved back home to be with their dying mother. Adolf returned from Vienna where he had been rejected by the art institute but could not bear the shame of telling his mother in her condition. She had supported his effort at becoming an artist since he was a young boy. She had encouraged him to pursue his passion and not necessarily follow in his father's footsteps. Although very bright, he was not known to be enthusiastic about his studies—except that he did have a great interest in history.

Frau Hitler's health rapidly deteriorated by October of that year and her desperate son beseeched Dr. Bloch to do anything to try to save her. The only option at that time was the use of the antiseptic, iodoform. It is now known to have been of no help in treating cancer itself but it could be very useful in the cleansing of her extensive infected wounds. Every day for the last forty-six days of her life from early November until her death in December, 1907, Dr. Bloch dutifully applied iodoform-soaked gauze to her bloody, pus-filled mastectomy incisions in the vain hope of arresting the spread of the tumor. Her bedroom would have smelled like a hospital room as the pungent odor of iodoform would have filled the small space and might have irritated one's eye. Young Hitler would have also seen that the daily bandages were streaked with his mother's blood. Klara Hitler experienced enormous pain that was temporarily reduced by morphine injections. She allegedly developed iodoform toxicity resulting in an inability to swallow, which hastened her inevitable demise (Binion, 1973). Although frequently cited, this conclusion is controversial and, interestingly, the symptom of an inability to swallow is not mentioned in a review of the major signs and symptoms of iodoform toxicity (O'Connor, Freeland, Heal, & Rossouw, 1977). Regardless, she heroically fought to stay alive as long as possible for her beloved and dearest son, Adolf, whom she feared would be alone in the world without her. Her enormous suffering ended with her death on December 21, 1907, and she was buried near Linz, Austria, in Leonding. Dr. Bloch, many years later, was still so impressed with the intense mother/son relationship that he stated, "In all my career I have never seen anyone so prostrate with grief as Adolf Hitler" (Kershaw, 2008, p. 15; Zalampas, 1990, p. 17).

Another theory about the genesis of Hitler's unprecedented anti-Semitism, in addition to the Jewish grandfather theory, was that the

Führer blamed his mother's Jewish doctor for not curing her and subjecting her to extraordinary pain in her last days (Binion, 1991). However, this formulation for such an extremely complex and multiply determined phenomenon appears rather reductionistic and simplistic. In fact, Hitler personally intervened and quietly allowed the doctor and his wife to leave Austria. He was even heard to have said that if more Jews were like Dr. Bloch he would not have had such a problem with them. Dr. Bloch was a well-respected, local physician who treated the Hitler family with generosity, professionalism, and medical competence (Hamann, 2008; Kafka, 1995). Also, Hitler's malignant anti-Semitism was not evident in his Vienna years. However, being a pragmatic and extremely successful politician who could intuit the sentiment of the masses, Hitler's demonization and punishment of the Jews was an extremely successful campaign strategy (Hamann, 1999).

Upon his mother's death, the bereft eighteen-year-old Adolf took Dr. Bloch's hand and said, "I shall be grateful to you forever" (cited in Olson, 2002, p. 95). Following his return to Vienna, Hitler sent some of his own hand-painted, holiday postcards to Dr. Bloch. On one of them he wrote: "From Vienna I send you my greetings. Yours always faithfully, Adolf" (Bloch, 1994, p. 5). Parenthetically, when Hitler triumphantly entered Austria after the Anschluss, he briefly returned to his home town for the first time since he was a young man. The Gestapo confiscated the postcards from Dr. Bloch and gave him a receipt that was later donated to the US Holocaust Museum along with other important correspondence documenting the relationship that Hitler had with the Bloch family (Kafka, 1995).

Dr. Bloch's account of the treatment of Frau Hitler also includes important observations about young Adolf:

> "He slept in the tiny bedroom adjoining that of his mother so that he could be summoned at any time during the night. During the day he hovered about the large bed where she lay. In illness such as that suffered by Frau Hitler, there is usually a great amount of pain. She bore her burden well; unflinching and uncomplaining. But it seemed to torture her son. An anguished grimace would come over him when he saw pain contract her face. There was little that could be done. An injection of morphine from time to time would give temporary relief; but nothing lasting. Yet Adolf seemed enormously grateful even for these short periods of release." (Bloch, 1994, p. 4)

Dr. Bloch's awareness of the unusual mother/son closeness was revealed from the beginning:

> "Adolf Hitler's reaction to this news [that his mother was gravely ill] was touching. His long, sallow face was contorted. Tears flowed from his eyes. Did his mother, he asked, have no chance? Only then did I realize the magnitude of the attachment that existed between mother and son. I explained that she did have a chance; but a small one. Even this shred of hope gave him some comfort." (Bloch, 1994, p. 4)

After her death and modest funeral, young Hitler returned to Vienna and manifestly did not look back. He immersed himself in Viennese cultural life, living very modestly at best as a starving, young artist, attending the opera almost every night. It likely appeared to the outside as though he were not affected by his mother's death. However, with what we now know about unresolved grief and its associated powerful defenses, it is quite possible that he dissociated the emotional pain of her death and by employing a manic defense further retreated into the glorious fantasy life of the Wagnerian opera world. He slowly deteriorated until the outbreak of World War I at which he diverted his energies outward to the political situation consuming Europe. He felt a sense of purpose and soon joined the German army in search of his own glorious destiny.

Conclusion

When the idealistic young corporal was taken by surprise in the poison gas attack eleven years after the death of his mother, it is possible that the dissociated memories of her death were reactivated and threatened to overwhelm him. Analogous to the return of the repressed, the return of dissociated, traumatic memories during subsequent adverse life events can be quite destabilizing (Brenner, 2001, 2004, 2009, 2014). The gasses were known eye irritants, like iodoform, but they would actually cause blindness. In fact, the widespread fear of blindness had a demoralizing, contagion effect upon the troops and even the hint of exposure to these toxins could result in panic and psychogenic blindness for those vulnerable. Unlike those symptomatic individuals who could not wait to leave the battlefield, Hitler apparently thrived under wartime conditions but he, too, was apparently vulnerable to such a symptom. Perhaps his sense of helplessness in the presence of a pungent smell and the eye irritant due to the gas suddenly and unexpectedly brought him back to his dying mother's bedside, back to the worst sight of his life. Sensory memories associated with lost love objects and unresolved grief, that is, "multisensory bridges," were first described, ironically, in Holocaust survivors (Brenner, 1988) and may have been operative in Hitler's case. By becoming "blind," Hitler's conversion symptom would have represented his unconscious mind's desperate measure to protect him from the vision of his dying mother and all of its associated affects.

After his recovery and the restabilization of his defenses, five years later, almost to the day, on November 9, 1923, new martyrs and new mourning rituals were created. The iodoform and bloodstained gauze of his dying mother was replaced by the *Blutfahne*, or blood flag. Klara Hitler's modest cemetery plot in an obscure, small town in Austria got "replaced" by the Königsplatz in Munich, King Ludwig I Royal Square, which her son reconfigured to honor the fallen heroes of the Beer Hall Putsch. Annual parades and ceremonies marked this hallowed event. In so doing, the grief for his mother could be concealed and safely displaced onto his dead comrades. This became his chosen trauma (Volkan, 2001). In this way, like any good actor trained in the Stanislavski school of method acting, Hitler could draw on these affects and "use" them in the service of his performances. It could be said then that his fiery, impassioned rhetoric, which so magnificently resonated with the downtrodden, chain-laden masses, truly came from his heart. The extent to which he was conscious of a connection to his mother is unclear, however. But, certainly, the extremely personal nature of the origin of these affects had to be kept secret under the threat of death. Such is the nature of malignant humiliation and shame.

In keeping with Shakespeare's famous dictum that "brevity is the soul of wit" (1603, *Hamlet*, Act 2, scene 2, 90), Akhtar (2009) has written a concise and very useful definition of the affect of shame. He describes five components: deflation of self esteem, humiliation, self discontinuity, social isolation, and feeling scrutinized. In the foregoing chapter, I have tried to provide historical evidence about the centrality of shame in the life of Adolf Hitler. From his degradation by his father, whose own illegitimate heritage was "shameful," to his inability to save his mother from an excruciating death, and from his failed career as an artist to being a penniless drifter living in a homeless shelter in Vienna, young Hitler apparently fled a shame-laden existence to the refuge of an inner reality of Wagnerian glory and dark heroism. This psychologically defensive flight then found external resonance with the onset of the Great War, an unprecedented opportunity for glory, which ultimately only served to escalate his sense of humiliation to a national level. Along the way, he sustained psychogenic blindness, traumatic reactivation of his mother's death, and the fateful treatment by Dr. Edmund Forster, which helped transform him into a self-proclaimed messianic figure who promised to bring life back to the German nation. However, his murderous destructiveness and "cult of death" so greatly overshadowed any of his accomplishments that his legacy filled the postwar German people with the very same affect he so desperately tried to ward off.

In my own experience over the last fifteen years working with groups of young Germans who devote a year of their lives to social service projects, I hear about their wish to undo this legacy of shame and guilt, as they have a profound sense of responsibility and a wish to be ambassadors of goodwill abroad. Intergenerational transmission of trauma is observable in this group also (Brenner, 2014). These impressive young men and woman, many of whom are grandchildren and great grandchildren of Nazis, volunteer through ASRP (Action Reconciliation Service for Peace). It has grown into an international organization which sends about 180 volunteers to a number of countries, including the US and Israel, each year. Significantly, it was founded after the 1958 synod of the Evangelical Church of Germany which stated, "We Germans started the Second World War and for this reason alone, more than others, became guilty of causing immeasurable suffering to humankind. Germans have in sinful revolt against the will of God exterminated millions of Jews. Those of us who survived and did not want this to happen did not do enough to prevent it."

Note

1. Biographical details of Hitler's life throughout this chapter are derived from Redlich's text unless otherwise specified.

PART III

CLINICAL REALM

PART III

CLINICAL REALM

CHAPTER SIX

Shame and shamelessness

Salman Akhtar

Sixteen years ago, as I was writing a review of Joseph and Ann-Marie Sandler's (1998) book, *Internal Objects Revisited*, Joseph Sandler died and my essay took on the flavour of an obituary. I felt compelled to go beyond the confines of a book review and to survey the milestones of this distinguished psychoanalyst's career. I began this portion of my writing with the following sentence: "Joseph Sandler's contributions to psychoanalysis are wide-ranging and, with shameless brevity, can be summarized under four categories" (Akhtar, 1999, p. 533). Curiously, the phrase "shameless brevity" became a source of literary pride for me over time. But was I being really shameless? Or, was the ironic *mea culpa* a lexical veil to cover up the shame over what, of necessity, was a cursory treatment of someone's profound and vast oeuvre? In other words, was seeming shamelessness hiding shame? And, what is shamelessness anyway?

The fact is that we know little about it. While psychoanalytic literature on shame has grown in leaps and bounds over the years (Grinker, 1955; Kilborne, 2005; Lansky, 1991, 1994, 2003a, 3003b, 2007; Levin, 1967; Morrison, 1989; Spero, 1984; Wurmser, 1981), shamelessness finds little mention in this literature except in Wurmser's (1981) book on shame. There is no entry on "shamelessness" in the major dictionaries of psychoanalysis (Akhtar, 2009a; Auchincloss & Samberg, 2012; Eidelberg, 1968; Laplanche & Pontalis, 1973; Moore & Fine, 1968, 1990) or in the indices of the *Standard Edition* or monographs on shame (e.g., Morrison, 1989). And, PEP-Web—the electronic compilation of psychoanalytic journal articles spanning more than a century—contains just one paper with the word "shamelessness" in its title (Lowenfeld, 1976). This paper is essentially a culturally inclined lament about the "spread of general shamelessness" (p. 69) in modern society and deems such decline of shame to be a threat to civilized living. The paper does not deconstruct shamelessness along descriptive, developmental, or metapsychological lines and leaves us titillated but unfulfilled.

I intend to fill this lacuna in the psychoanalytic knowledge in this realm. I will delineate the phenomenon of shamelessness, and describe its various forms and the sociocultural slant that can be readily given to its perception and even its existence. I will also make a few comments about the technical implications of the concept of shamelessness and conclude with some summarizing reflections. Before undertaking this sojourn, though, it might seem advisable to reiterate briefly our psychoanalytic understanding of shame.

Shame

Freud's views

Sigmund Freud included shame among the "repressing forces" (1895, p. 221) acting against the sexual instinct. He proposed that hysterical conversion symptoms were attempts to avoid reexperiencing the shame associated with childhood sexual seduction. Shame, in such signal form, was a motivator of defense in neurosis. In perversion, however, the sexual instinct could go to "astonishing lengths" (1905d, p. 161) to override the barrier of shame. Besides this difference in the dynamic role of shame in these two pathologies, Freud (1897, 1905d) distinguished between the ontogenesis and severity of shame across genders. He asserted that the development of shame occurs in "little girls earlier and in the face of less resistance than in boys" (1905d, p. 219); as a result, the tendency toward repression of sexuality is greater in the former. This difference becomes more prominent during puberty when girls are seized by sexual repugnance and boys by sexual desire.

For at that period a further sexual zone is (wholly or in part) extinguished in females which persists in males. I am thinking of the male genital zone, the region of clitoris, in which during childhood sensitivity is shown to be concentrated in girls as well as in boys. Hence the flood of shame which overwhelms the female at that period, till the new, vaginal zone is awakened, whether spontaneously or by reflex action. (1897, p. 270)

Freud (1908b) also noted that shame functions as a powerful force to cause repression (and, later, reaction formation) of anal erotic impulses. Later, he observed that "It is very remarkable that the reaction of shame should be so intimately connected with involuntary emptying of the bladder (whether in the daytime or at night) and not equally so, as one would have expected, with incontinence of the bowels" (1918b, p. 92). Freud speculated that such reactions represent precipitates from the history of human civilization, an idea that he reiterated in *Civilization and Its Discontents* (1930a). There, he speculated that "Man's raising himself from the ground, of his assumption of an upright gait, made his genitals, which were previously concealed, visible and in need of protection, and so provoked a feeling of shame in him" (p. 99). In a later, full paper on the relationship between urination and shame, Freud (1932a) related man's domestication of fire to his controlling the desire to urinate on it and put it out; the loss of bladder control thus came to be looked down upon in man's history and became a source of shame.

Yet another realm in which Freud (1897, 1900a) talked of shame was that of dreams. He spoke of the common dream of being totally naked or inoptimally dressed in public with profound feelings of anxiety and shame. Curiously, the people around one in the dream do not seem to notice this state of undress. Freud attributed such dreams to the childhood experience of exhibiting oneself where the parental "horror" (actual or playful) is reversed by the process of wishful fulfilment.

Freud (1908e) also laid down the groundwork for distinguishing between shame and guilt when he wrote: "The adult is ashamed of his phantasies and hides them from other people. He cherishes his phantasies as his most intimate possessions, and as a rule he would rather confess his misdeeds than tell anyone his phantasies" (p. 145). Finally, Freud (1914c) noted that feelings of inferiority (from which shame arises) develop from the failure to live up to the narcissistic aspirations of the ego ideal.

Subsequent contributions

Fenichel (1945) discussed shame at length and concluded that it is deeply connected to urethral eroticism. Echoing Freud (1918b), he noted that while fecal incontinence in children receives direct punishment, deliberate and/or unintentional urinary incontinence (including somnolent bed-wetting) is often responded to by parental induction of shame. Internalization of this parental reaction causes vulnerability to shame, especially when urethral pleasure (and its derivatives) is in ascendance. Fenichel also noted that shame can serve as a defense against exhibitionism, and that the syndrome of "social anxiety," with its chronic dread of rejection and being shamed, exists midway between the child's fear of castration or loss of love and the adult's bad conscience.

Erikson (1950) included "shame and doubt" in the polarity faced by the child during his or her third year of life; the other end was constituted by a sense of "autonomy." Lack of self-control and over-control by parents lead to a lasting propensity for shame; this affect emerges from feeling exposed and conscious of being looked at. "Doubt is the brother of shame" declared Erikson (p. 253), adding that doubt has to do with continuing uncertainty about who (the parent or the child) is in charge of the child's sphincteric control and his sense of agency in general.

Piers and Singer (1953) located the origin of shame in the tension between ego and ego ideal. Shame, according to them, arises when a desired goal is not reached or one fails to live up to one's cherished self-image. Interestingly, Piers and Singer regard failing in one's own eyes as far more related to the feared and negative assessment by siblings and peers than by parents (and, of course, their respective introjects).

Kohut's views on shame were intricately related to his emphasis upon the self. Early on, when his concepts were ensconced in the structural model of the mind, Kohut (1966) proposed that shame results from the failure of the ego to "provide a proper discharge for the exhibitionistic demands of the narcissistic self" (p. 441). Ego ideal, in this formulation, attempts to keep exhibitionism to a minimum and thus becomes an ally of the superego. Later, Kohut (1971) changed his formulation and suggested that shame "is due to a flooding of the ego with un-neutralized exhibitionism[1] and not due to a relative ego-weakness vis-à-vis an overly strong system of ideals" (p. 181). Still later, Kohut (1972) traced the eruption of "narcissistic rage" to the experience of humiliation and shame. He also held that when, during middle age, an individual realizes that he (or she) has not lived up—or even come close—to his dreams, profound sadness and shame set in. Kohut (1977) spoke of a time:

> ... of utter hopelessness for some, of utter lethargy, of that depression without guilt and self-directed aggression, which overtake those who feel that they have failed and cannot remedy the failure in the time and with the energies still left at their disposal. The suicides of this period are not the expression of a punitive superego, but a remedial act—the wish to wipe out the unbearable sense of mortification and *nameless shame* imposed by the ultimate recognition of a failure of an all-encompassing magnitude. (p. 241, italics added)

Picking up the theoretical discourse where Piers and Singer (1953) had left off, Chasseguet-Smirgel (1985) delineated the following sequence:

> The wish to receive narcissistic confirmation from one's peers to diminish the margin between the ego and the ideal leads the subject to exhibit himself to them. If this exhibition fails to ensure such satisfaction (i.e. if a narcissistic injury or "social humiliation" results) ... the narcissistic injury [becomes] equivalent to a castration, and the exhibition to the exposure of the anus. This "about turn" (literally of a narcissistically cathected phallus) may be compared to the discovery of the fecal phallus beneath the guilt that seeks to mask it. (p. 161)

Chasseguet-Smirgel went on to add that the affect of shame can be disastrously painful and lead to suicide.

> This would then represent a realization of the phantasy that accompanies this affect: that of disappearing, of no longer having to meet the eyes of one's peers. The person who is ashamed is said to be unable to look others in the face, to be unable to face up to them, the hidden anus now being written on his face. One "dies of shame"; and to claim that ridicule cannot kill is but a denial. (p. 203)

Mention must also be made of the two important monographs on the topic of shame that appeared during the 1980s. These were *The Mask of Shame* by Leon Wurmser (1981), and *Shame: The Underside of Narcissism* by Andrew Morrison (1989). While it is not possible to summarize their entire contents here, it is important to list their major points of emphasis. Wurmser regarded shame to be a polymorphous constellation of emotions and termed them "shame affects." He noted that the content of shame clusters around six themes: (i) I am weak; (ii) I am dirty and am looked at with disgust; (iii) I am defective; (iv) I lack control over my mind and body; (v) I am sexually excited by suffering and degradation, and (vi) I fear that showing myself will result in mockery and punishment. Shame affects can be overt or covert and can serve as screens against deeper anxieties (e.g., castration, separation). On the other hand, shame itself can be defended against by reactive grandiosity, induction of shame into others, depersonalization, and masochistic flaunting of degradation. Wurmser distinguished shame and guilt on two grounds: (i) shame is felt in a split form: about the *function* of self-exposure and about the *content* of what is exposed, but guilt has no such inner division; (ii) shame is deeper and more self-oriented while guilt is the experience of a more coherent ego and is fundamentally object-related. He stated that "Teleologically, shame may be important as the protector of primary process thought—the language of the self. Guilt may fulfil the same purpose for secondary process thought—the language of object relations" (p. 67).

Morrison (1989) also regarded shame as essentially related to the self-experience, hence inadequately conceptualized in the language of the tripartite structural model. He felt that a consideration of identity and the self was central to shame; indeed, "Shame is a crucial dysphoric affect in narcissistic phenomena" (p. 8). Morrison noted that:

> There is an ongoing, tension-generating dialectic between narcissistic grandiosity and desire for perfection, and the archaic sense of self as flawed, inadequate and inferior following the realization of separateness from, and dependence upon, objects. Similarly, a metaphorical dialectic exists between the wish for absolute autonomy and uniqueness and the wish for perfect merger and reunion with the projected fantasy of the ideal. Thus, shame and narcissism inform each other, as the self is experienced first, alone, separate, and small, and, again, grandiosely, striving to be perfect and re-united with its ideal. (p. 66)

Citing Kohut's (1971, 1977) later views on shame but differing from them, Morrison asserted that shame reflects primarily a selfobject failure to meet the age-appropriate needs of the self, especially those of the self striving to achieve vigor through attainment of its ideals.

Finally, in a series of papers, Lansky (1991, 1994, 1999, 2000, 2003a, 2003b, 2004, 2005, 2007) highlighted a number of issues pertaining to shame. These included (i) shame resulting from the individual's sense of being incapable of sustaining meaningful relationships; (ii) the relationship between shame, narcissistic rage, and suicide; (iii) the central relationship of shame to core self-experience, not just the self's actions; (iv) the causation of inner shame by the awareness of increased neediness for human contact; (v) the role of covert shame in struggles over forgiveness; (vi) shame-related conflicts as instigators of dreams, and (vii) the paradox that acknowledgment of shame arouses more shame and the role of this paradox in driving shame underground.

Synthesis

Pooling the foregoing observations and deleting their antiquated and incorrect parts (especially those pertaining to gender and sexuality), one can safely conclude that shame refers to a dysphoric affect with the following components: (i) collapse of self-esteem, (ii) feeling of humiliation, (iii) rupture of self-continuity, (iv) sense of isolation and dysjunction from the surround, and (v) feeling of being watched by critical others, especially those from the peer group. Shame is similar to guilt insofar as both emotions cause distress and lower self-esteem. Both can act as guarantors of "appropriate" behaviors on the one hand, and both can drive one to self-laceration and suicide on the other. However, their differences are more marked than their similarities and include the following: (i) shame is visual, guilt auditory; (ii) shame is related to conflicts regarding exhibitionism, guilt to conflicts regarding transgression, (iii) shame is self-focused, guilt object-related; (iv) shame has physiological markers (e.g., blushing, palpitations), guilt does not; (v) shame results from failure to live up to a cherished self-image, guilt from disobeying actual or internalized authority; (vi) in structural terms, shame is a consequence of tension between ego and ego ideal while guilt is the result of tension between ego and superego; (vii) shame is developmentally earlier than guilt; (viii) shame pushes for hiding, guilt for confession, and (ix) defenses against shame include narcissistic self-inflation, social withdrawal, and shaming others; defenses against guilt include blaming others, fearing external punishment, and masochistic self-laceration. Having brought together the major psychoanalytic observations on shame in a harmonious gestalt, we are now prepared to address its absence.

Shamelessness

The dictionary definition of being "shameless" includes phrases like "having no shame" and "insensible to disgrace" (Merriam-Webster's Collegiate Dictionary, 1998, p. 1076). The first phrase is hardly informative. The second phrase tells us more. Implying that the individual who is shameless does not feel disgrace, it presents a portrait of social indifference. The shameless individual can express thoughts and opinions, use language, commit acts, and behave in ways that would send shivers of embarrassment over the spines of "civilized folk." He can belch, fart, and pick his nose with impunity. He can use foul language with a sailor's ease. He can ask favors upon favors without the slightest trepidation. He can give voice, with little hesitation, to his innermost fantasies including those of grandiosity and perverse sexuality. The shameless person seems to know no limits or, at least, not to care about any.

Drawn with such broad strokes, the nosological icon degrades into a caricature of ill-mannered psychopathy. In actuality, the phenomenon of shamelessness appears in myriad forms. These include, on the *normative pole* of the phenomenological spectrum: (i) development-based shamelessness, and (ii) dignity-based shamelessness, and on the *pathological pole*: (iii) defense-based shamelessness, (iv) discharge-based shamelessness, and (v) defect-based shamelessness. A brief comment on each form follows.

Development-based shamelessness

Although a modicum of "social referencing" (Emde, 1991) is evident in the infant from the earliest days, the experience of shame does not appear till the third year of life (Erikson, 1950). This is understandable in light of the foregoing consideration of shame which demonstrated that the capacity to experience shame is dependent upon a clear selfobject discrimination and the "forward projection of narcissism" (Chasseguet-Smirgel, 1984, p. 28) resulting in the formation of what Freud was the first to call the ego ideal (1914c). In other words, for shame to be experienced, there ought to be a "shamed" and a "shamer" present *and* there should be some sense that one has fallen in the eyes of idealized others and below the ideal view of oneself. These capacities arise over childhood development and so does the capacity to experience shame. Parental upholding of the ideals that the child must aspire to and parental vulnerability to shame over this or that specific matter also contribute to the child's acquisition of the content-based sector of shame (i.e., *what* to be ashamed of).

Not surprisingly, Freud attributed[2] the little child's polymorphous perverse sexuality to the fact that in him "mental dams against sexual excess—shame, disgust, and morality—have either not yet been constructed at all or are only in course of construction" (1905d, p. 191). However, even in the child, it is not an "either-or" issue; the capacity for shame can develop and yet certain areas might remain outside of its reign for quite some time.

Fart and awe

> A fellow psychoanalyst, Patricia O'Neil (a pseudonym, of course) relayed the following incident to me. She was playing, on the floor, with her beloved grandson, Tommy. Getting up to go to the bathroom, she emitted a loud and prolonged fart. The three year old stopped his play, looked up at Patricia, and said with earnest glee, "That was great, Grammy! How did you do it?!" He felt no trepidation in commenting upon my colleague's admirable "skill."

Such absence of shame can be termed "development-based shamelessness." Or, following precedence evident in terms like "un-pleasure" (Freud, 1915b), and "un-fear" (Akhtar, 2012a), it can be designated as "un-shame".[3]

Dignity-based shamelessness

It might, at first, seem preposterous to propose that shamelessness can occur in the setting of "dignity".[4] However, a contemplative pause might ease our way to seeing that this is not only possible but actually inevitable. Wurmser (1981) talked about "the 'shamelessness' of poets and scientists" (p. 52) and added that:

> The less vulnerable one feels about ordinarily threatened parts of the self, or in more technical terms, the more solid and conflict-free

the narcissistic investment, the self-valuation, becomes the less one will fear exposure, and hence shame. If we are confident of the value of our life as a whole, of its integrity and true wholeness, as we can assume Einstein and Freud were, we have less need to shield it against self-exposure. (p. 52)

The following incident, involving Gandhi, reported by Lapierre and Collins (1975) in their book on India's independence struggle, *Freedom at Midnight*, testifies to this type of healthy and glowing shamelessness.

The yogurt of reciprocity

While visiting Lord Mountbatten (then the Governor-General of India) upon his invitation to discuss some political matters, Gandhi was offered a cup of tea and some biscuits by the towering British figure. Gandhi accepted the offer and then produced a small container of yogurt that had been wrapped in his loin-cloth and forwarded it to Mountbatten, saying that the exchange of delicacies must be reciprocal.

Such proud and courageous forthrightness carries along with itself a certain sense of freedom from shame. Curiously, while the scientist and the leader feel *no need* to hide their conviction and hence are shameless, the writer and poet *render* the deeply private and conflicted into dignified forms and thus make the inner goings on shameless. Nietzsche (1886) said it most clearly: "The poets are shameless about their experiences; they exploit them" (p. 161). A more recent exposition of the same thought comes from Allen Wheelis (1975) that has the creative writer tell us the following:

My uniqueness must slip effortlessly into others' minds and there clone itself, my singularity then appear in the experience of everyone, spring up everywhere, like April flowers. What I lived alone in hideous idiosyncracy and pain will now be lived by all in acceptance and mutuality. I will have fathered the world; like God, will have created it in my own image. I create self, defiantly from the winds of contingency, then claim universality by extending that contingency to the furthermost limits of the known world. (pp. 82–83)

Thus the transformation of potentially shame-laden mental contents into a literary product yields aesthetic pleasure for all and confers dignity upon the creative writer (Freud, 1908e). He has nothing to hide anymore and through a circuitous route, joins the fraternity of healthy shamelessness of which the bold politician is already a proud member.

Defense-based shamelessness

Vulnerability to shame can, at times, be handled by counterphobic mechanisms. Fenichel (1945) mentioned a case where the attitude of shamelessness was a reaction to a preceding period strongly laden with shame. Wurmser (1981) also talked of the apparent shamelessness of sexual exhibitionists being a counterphobic operation against shame. He added that social exhibitionists and professional actors might utilize the same defense. Instead of being a regression to a psychic state before the establishment of the shame barrier, shamelessness, according to Wurmser, is the outcome of a complex layer of defenses.

> The shameless person is a variant of the "criminal from a sense of guilt" who commits a crime so he can feel guilty for and expiate some known and clearly defined misdeed rather than remaining saddled with a vague, shapeless inner guilt about unconscious wishes. It could be viewed as a "reaction formation against reaction formation"—a brazen violation of a taboo to defend against guilt, which in turn has been set upon a defense against the violation of a much deeper taboo. Similarly shamelessness is a reaction formation against shame, which in turn is a reaction formation against delophilic and theatophilic[5] wishes. Superficially, it simply appears as shame displaced. (p. 261)

Such shamelessness comes to serve as a transparent fig leaf against the dreaded experience of genuine shame. Individuals with the syndrome of "malignant narcissism" (Kernberg, 1984) display such defensive shamelessness. They seek to destroy whatever love is offered to them and declare that they are above the need for attachment and affection. Lurking underneath this cold superiority is "the shame of not having been loved" (Kjellqvist, 1993, p. 11) during childhood.[6]

Discharge-based shamelessness

Shamelessness can also serve the purpose of instinctual discharge. If a particular partial instinct (e.g., exhibitionism, sadism, masochism) is too strong, then it can override the customary barrier of shame; being shameless then facilitates the expression of the drive.[7] While this relationship was first noted by Freud (1905d) in the context of sexual perversion, it is also evident in the course of a "healthy" erotic encounter. Shedding one's shame over nakedness and gently overcoming the partner's shame are important constituents during foreplay (Kernberg, 1991). Anxieties regarding real and imaginary blemishes of one's body have to be put aside and this, in turn, requires genuine self-regard and trust in the partner's goodness. Another important aspect of foreplay is the emergence into consciousness of pre-genital drive directives (e.g., sucking, licking, biting, looking, showing, smelling) and their spontaneous expression needs to be shame-free in order to be pleasurable. Sexual intercourse too involves postures, acts, demands, and verbalizations that, outside of such context, could be regarded as shameful. In the context of erotic union, however, they are not; a robust and playful shamelessness prevails.

Discharge-based shamelessness can be witnessed in other realms as well. The drive to perform well (and therefore, win the love of real or imaginary others) in certain professions (e.g., striptease dancing, acting, salesmanship) can tip the balance of drive-defense in favour of the former and make shamelessness a psychic "wingman" of desire. At times, the environment can stir up longings that become too irresistible and lead to their shameless expression.

The director's plea

> During my college days, I used to act on stage. Once, as the play ended, one of my fellow actors walked out on the stage and announced that all the credit should go to the play's director, Mr. Mehra. Then, in the characteristically Anglicized manner of those days, he boomed, "Three cheers for Mr. Mehra! Hip hip hooray, hip hip hooray, hip hip hooray!" A year later, I was again in the college play but this time with a new director, Mr. Gupta, at the helm. Just as the play was ending and actors were lining up to walk onto the stage for a curtain call, I felt someone tap on my shoulder.

It was Mr. Gupta, who whispered to me, "Like last year's cheers for Mr. Mehra, can you say the same words for me today?" Drenched in the sweat of embarrassment at the old man's desperate hunger to be admired (and, his naked competitiveness), I was dumbfounded and could not utter those words once I was on the stage. He never forgave me for that!

Defect-based shamelessness

This type of shamelessness is found in the setting of severely narcissistic and antisocial personality organizations. According to Wurmser (1981), "Certain aspects of their self have become so dissociated and unimportant that they can be exposed without narcissistic pain" (p. 138).[8] Freud's (1914c) evocation of a truly hardened criminal for illustrating the smugness of primary narcissism is also a case in point here. And, it is true that the narcissistic person, especially the one with antisocial tendencies, can "shamelessly" make demands upon others' love, time, and material resources. The unconscious envy and hostility toward the benefactor is often striking under such circumstances.

The curious fate of a compliment

Catherine McCarthy, a thirty-seven-year-old attorney with a pronounced tendency to be flirtatious that arose from a powerful oedipal fixation, narrated the following incident during one of her analytic sessions with me. She said that the previous evening, she had given a compliment to her highly successful and narcissistic husband regarding his handling of the family dog. "You are far better with Jake [the dog] than I am," she had said. With disbelief and pain in her voice, she then told that he responded to her admiring comment by saying, "Darling, I am better than you in most things."

Whether one chooses to say anything about this remark or not, it seems clear that my patient's husband had difficulty accepting and enjoying his wife's "goodness" toward him. Her comment stirred up greed instead of gratitude in him; envy of her capacity for kindness perhaps also played a role in his devaluing remark. In addition to all this, there was a quality of shamelessness to her husband's self-centered boasting.

Sociocultural dimension

Since shame and shamelessness are essentially relational phenomena that arise from the era of early childhood, they inevitably become culture-bound in their prevalence, intensity, and the affected sectors of fantasy and behaviour. Indeed, the phrase "cultures of shame" has been around for quite some time and is intended to categorize some societies from others that are viewed as "cultures of guilt." Kitayama (2007) employs the term "shame culture," for instance, to designate the Japanese society which regards "life as a drama in which actors wear fragile masks" (p. 93). He goes on to state that:

> Anxieties about shame become stronger when their masks are stripped away and their real faces are exposed .... In the psychology of the awareness of shame, as Kenichero Okano (1998) states, it is easy to understand if we regard the self as carrying the duality of an "ideal self" and a "shameful self." It may be correct to differentiate the two by calling the former the adaptive self or the public self, and the latter the true self or the private self (Kitayama, 2004). This duality is repeatedly described in ordinary Japanese language, such as *omoto* to *ura* (front and back), *homae* to *tatemae* (what one says and what one means), and *giani* to *ninjo* (duty and sentiment). (p. 93, italics in the original)

With variations in nuance and focus, a similar proclivity of preserving one's public appearance at all costs prevails in many other cultures in Asia, especially, perhaps, the Islamic nations. Shame—or its dreaded anticipation—underlies "honor killings" prevalent in the less literate sections of these societies; the exposure of a transgression (especially by a female member of the family) is deemed worse than the transgression itself, and is to be strenuously avoided. Shamelessness in such settings can be fatal.

It is conventional to contrast such "cultures of shame" with the "cultures of guilt" which presumably inculcate greater respect for rules and give lesser weight to the fear of public exposure in the course of moral development. To be sure, such juxtaposition can have some heuristic yield but it carries the stale odor of Western colonialization which views its foundational structures to be superior. A more stark contrast might actually be between "cultures of shame" and "cultures of shamelessness." Talking specifically of the United States, Hoffer (1974) declared that "We have become a shameless society ... the loss of shame threatens our survival as a civilized society" (p. D-4). Christopher Lasch (1971) bemoaned such a "culture of narcissism" and Lowenfeld (1976) observed:

> Nowadays, even the bikini is often replaced by a thin string. Where formerly patients, even in analytic treatment, had severe inhibitions about speaking of their masturbatory practices and overcame their shame only against strong resistance, now lovers chat with each other about their masturbatory practices. Specially manufactured vibrators are displayed in the windows of reputable drug-stores. "Porno" literature and movies of polymorphous-perverse practices, once checked by shame, are now devoured by civilized people. The use of obscene language, mocking old fashioned feelings, has become quite general. (p. 67)

Shamelessness—whether era-bound or geographically located—can indeed raise a cross-cultural "confusion of tongues" (Ferenczi, 1933), so to speak.[9] What might appear normal and acceptable behavior in one culture can seem quite shameless to an observer who hails from a different culture. Look at the following examples.

- A tourist woman from Saudi Arabia (accompanied, of course, by her husband and/or other family members) happens to see a young American girl wearing a bikini on a beach and instinctively regards the latter as shameless. But is the American girl really shameless?
- A British couple invites a Pakistani friend to dinner. The latter asks if he can bring along his elderly father, who's visiting from their ancestral village. The hosts extend their hospitality to the older man who emits a loud and extended belch after the dinner. He regards that belch as an expression of his gustatory gratitude while the British couple blushes with shame on his behalf!
- An Iranian physician who is residing and practicing in New York returns to Shiraz for a visit. During one festive dinner, his deceased father's friend asks him—in sight and hearing of all present—how much money he makes every month. The Iranian doctor, who has become quite Westernized by now, finds the old man's inquiry to be intrusive but out of respect, decides to answer anyway.

Upon receiving this answer, the old man turns and loudly announces the figure to all present. This the young Iranian physician finds to be a shameless act.
- A female physician from the repressive and "proper" Tamil Brahmin community in Chennai feels horrified when, on her first day of internship in Chicago, she hears an American medical student say that he has done a "very good" write-up on his patient. She cannot fathom how one can praise oneself openly and finds the student to be utterly shameless.

These vignettes reveal that a considerable portion of the shame affect is context-bound, needs a shamed-shamer dyad, and is open to influence by the ethos of the two parties. All this, of course, has relevance to the conduct of psychotherapy and psychoanalysis.

Technical implications

By its nature, psychoanalytic treatment involves uncovering the prohibited, the transgressive, the infantile, and the profane, hidden in unlit corners of the mind. Patients might seek help for rational concerns (e.g., work-inhibition, sexual problems) and begin treatment with thorough elaborations of their complaints and by expressing sincere hopes for getting over them. Sooner or later, however, the cognitive sieve of free association permits the leakage of the seemingly irrational and the hitherto unknown material into the discourse. Secrets, long held deliberately, and fantasies that were repressed and "forgotten" now begin to surface. Shame enters the clinical chamber and self-revelation falters.

Clinical vignette: 1

Jules Levin, a fledgling businessman in his late forties, had had a painful childhood. Born with a visible deformity of his face, he was also short of stature. Throughout his childhood, he was mocked by his father and, over time, became acutely vulnerable to shame. He started keeping his thoughts and actions secret. One secret that came out early in his treatment was his sexually touching his younger sister while she was fast asleep; this began when Jules was eleven years old and lasted for a few months. In reporting his late night excursions to me, Jules felt shame but was unable to recall

> (or speculate about) his fantasies and expectations in doing this. He simply felt he had to do something odd, something bizarre, to have an alive psychic self since his normal self had been decimated by his cruel father (and ignored by his mother).
>
> During one session, while talking freely about how he sought vitality in lieu of his depressive existence, he suddenly stopped. Something had clearly come to his mind that was difficult to talk about. With gentle interpretation of his fears of my reaction, Jules became able to talk again. He revealed that he has the shameful habit of picking his nose and then eating his snot. I could sense a profound sense of sadness and solitude connected to Jules's behavior. I responded by saying that there seemed to be some connection between his touching his sister's genitals and his eating his snot; a certain audacity characterized both these behaviors. My voice was peaceful and conveyed my deep interest in his emotional life. Jules relaxed and began talking more fluently.

Since shame is invariably diminished by calm acceptance by the onlooker (or, the "on-listener"), the therapist's non-judgmental "holding" (Winnicott, 1960) goes a long way in strengthening the therapeutic alliance. This is true in instances where the patient is consciously experiencing the dread of being shamed but also applies to situations where he or she is not even cognizant that a particular behavior has the potential of becoming shameful.

Clinical vignette: 2

> At the end of a session in the second month of her analysis, Melanie Wright, an otherwise psychologically minded young woman, offered me a bag full of apples. She said that she had gone apple picking over the weekend and wanted me to have some. I was taken aback. Neither her characteristic way of being nor the material in the session had prepared me for this. I responded, "I appreciate your bringing me this gift but I cannot accept it. See, our task here is to understand, enlighten ourselves to your mental functioning and, thus, come to grips with your difficulties. We cannot, therefore, move into actions, especially ones whose meanings are unknown to us. Now, I regret if my stance hurts your feelings, but I do not apologise because my intent is not to

hurt you." She listened carefully and nodded in agreement. I then spontaneously added, "For instance, apples. What comes to mind about apples?" She answered, "Adam's apple! ... Adam and Eve ... forbidden fruit." She smiled, blushed, and left shaking her head, saying "I understand, I understand."

This vignette shows how the steadfast maintenance of a therapeutic frame and "invitation" for the patient to become more curious lays down the foundations of a good alliance. It also demonstrates that a sustained analytic attitude itself acts as a rescuer of the patient from the brink of shame.

This is not to say that the analyst himself is not vulnerable to shame. To be sure, healthy self-esteem, reasonably well-analysed personal conflicts, renunciation of omnipotent expectations from oneself, and availability of libidinal supplies protect the analyst from feeling shame in the course of his work. However, a patient in the throes of negative transference can readily demolish such resolve on the analyst's part, especially by attacking the latter's ethnicity, race, physical attributes, language proficiency, and technique. Feeling ashamed in response, the analyst can become defensive and, worse, retaliatory.

Besides such obvious triggers, analyst's shame can arise from associative recall of shameful experiences (old and new) outside his clinical life. And, at times, an inquiry from the patient that is in fact reflective of psychic growth can unexpectedly lead the analyst to encounter inner shame.

Clinical vignette: 3

A fifty-year-old Hindu Indian woman, Sunita Jha, had been raised by an instinctually repressed (and repressive) family in South Africa, and spoke mainly in English during her analysis. As early fears of criticism and rejection were interpretively softened, a devalued self-image emerged. While childhood experiences of prejudice due to skin color were emphasized at first, analysis gradually revealed profound rejection by her mother, a rejection centering upon her being female. Work along these lines relaxed her further and she occasionally began to speak in Hindi, her mother tongue. During one such session, Sunita very hesitantly revealed that she did not know the word for the female genital in Hindi and felt that it would

SHAME AND SHAMELESSNESS   111

help her to acquire this knowledge. Issues of maternal transference (i.e., can I label her body parts for her?; do I know and accept that she has female genitalia?; do I accept "my" female genitalia?, etc.) were clearly evident and I handled them in the customary analytic fashion.

However, in a later session, she quite earnestly asked me to tell her the word. Suddenly I found myself experiencing a dual dilemma. One was a purely technical dilemma, that of what would be the process-related pros and cons of telling her the word as against inquiring as to why she wanted to know it from me, and so on. The other dilemma which caught me by surprise involved my overall etiquette of life, as it were. Can I even utter the word in my mother tongue (spoken Hindi and Urdu have the same word for the female genital) in the presence of a woman? Or, would I feel ashamed while doing so? Experiencing the inhibition outlined nearly a century ago by Ferenczi (1911), for a moment, I became tongue-tied.[10] Then working through the inner block and in the spirit of "developmental work" (Pine, 1997) that includes occasionally providing patients with words for what is hard for them to express, I decided to tell her that it was called *choot*.

While this was a homoethnic clinical dyad, problems of the sort highlighted by it tend to occur with greater frequency in cross-cultural analyses (see Chapter Nine of this book). A culturally different patient's pointing out that the analyst has been mis-pronouncing his name, or the name of the city he came from, can cause embarrassment to the analyst. And, then there are narcissistic patients who are extremely prone to feeling ashamed and hardly need cultural pressure points to deposit their shame-laden self-representations (by projective identification) into the analyst. The latter's characterological resistance to shame, his capacity to contain such projections, and his ability to feel (and yet keep in abeyance) his sadistic desires to shame such patients, constitute important therapeutic tools in clinical work of this stripe.

Conclusion

In this contribution, I have provided a brief survey of the psychoanalytic literature on shame and, based upon that, delineated the affective and cognitive characteristics of this experience. I have, however, devoted greater attention to the absence (actual or seeming) of shame and have categorized such shamelessness into five types: (i) development-based, (ii) defense-based, (iii) discharge-based, (iv) defect-based, and (v) dignity-based. By carving out the first and last categories, I have rescued shamelessness from being regarded as necessarily pathological. Moving on, I have discussed the sociocultural dimensions of shamelessness and also addressed issues pertaining to it in the clinical situation. This has been a tedious but rewarding sojourn and has imparted an important lesson, namely that while Euripides (c. 413 BCE) called shamelessness "the worst of human diseases" (p. 37), it can also exist in the setting of a child's innocence and a great man's self-assurance. Thus not only shame but shamelessness, too, turns out to be a multi-determined, context-based, and complex phenomenon. In acknowledging that matters in this realm are not straightforward, one needs feel no shame at all.

Notes

1. Extending this observation to the malady of a "shy narcissist," I have noted (2000) that such a person feels "especially uncomfortable upon being photographed; the attention of a camera suddenly floods his ego with primitive exhibitionism and causes him much anxiety" (p. 115).
2. With characteristic misogyny, Freud (1905d) went on to compare such proclivity on the child's part with the disposition of "an average uncultured woman" (p. 191).
3. Such "unshame" can also be found in the setting of functional psychoses, advanced dementia, and traumatic injuries involving the frontal region of the brain.
4. For an elucidation of this elusive concept, see Akhtar, 2015.
5. Wurmser (1981), who coined the terms "theatophilia" and "delophilia," described them as follows. Theatophilia referred to "the desire to watch and observe, to admire and to be fascinated, to merge and master through attentive looking, operating as a basic inborn drive from earliest infancy" (p. 158). Delophilia stood for "the desire to express oneself and to fascinate others by one's self-exposure, to show and to impress, to merge with the other through communication. Again, it would originate in archaic times" (p. 158).
6. Though not naming it as such, I have elsewhere (Akhtar, 2011) described "the shame of the motherless child" in connection with the lifelong impact of early maternal loss.

7. "Such internal pressures are not exclusive in their capacity to override the shame barrier. Dire economic conditions and abject poverty can also drive one to behaviors that would otherwise be considered 'shameless'. An encounter with beggars in poor countries demonstrates this dynamic poignantly" (Priti Shukla, personal communication, May 28, 2015).
8. Shameless candor as a character trait was strikingly evident in the ex-marine officer, Jeffrey McDonald, who murdered his wife and children in cold blood (McGinniss, 1983).
9. The sporty practice of "skinny dipping" and the ever-so-slightly intimidating nude beaches and nudist colonies bring out the shame-shamelessness tension within one and the same culture.
10. A young Iranian psychoanalytic candidate once said to me: "I will die of shame if I have to say the words for sex and genitals in Persian to a patient" (personal communication, April 11, 2001; name withheld upon request). I smiled and encouraged her to explore this issue further on her own as well as in her analysis. I also reassured her that she was not alone in experiencing such anxieties, adding that even Freud lapsed into the Latin *matrem nudam* while describing, at age forty-one, the childhood memory of having seen his mother naked (Letter to Fliess, October 3, 1897, cited in Masson, 1985, p. 268).

CHAPTER SEVEN

Laziness and its links to shame

Jerome S. Blackman

The wish to be lazy is no doubt universal. You might argue with that proposition, but you will have to decide whether you want to work at it. Is it worth it, and how will you feel about yourself if you don't bother? When you stop to think about it (admittedly a form of work), the fact that any human beings do anything productive at any time is a remarkable phenomenon. Left to our own devices,[1] we would no doubt spend most of our time eating (Lewin, 1952), especially if someone is cooking for us; fornicating (Brenner, 1982), especially if the other person does the initiating; and sleeping (Lewin, 1946)—according to what Sigmund Freud dubbed the "pleasure principle" (1900a) and later the "Nirvana principle" (1920g). At least we might wish to (Schur, 1966).

But then again, if you are a history buff, you might wonder about the murder-suicide, in 1888, of Austrian Crown Prince Rudolph and his mistress, Maria Vetsera. The crown prince did not have to work. He ate well, had a wife and children who did not bother him much, and a mother, Empress Sisi, who loved him. He had not had to call for dates and get shot down by twenty women before he got lucky with Maria (she was selected for him by a female friend of the family). He even enjoyed, using a pseudonym, circulating, to underground newspapers, subversive missives against his father, Emperor

Franz Josef. But Rudolph was apparently not happy with a life of foxhunting, underground verbal aggression against his father, sleeping in, sex with his wife and a mistress, and eating extremely good food which he neither had to cook nor clean up after. He gave no reason for shooting Maria in the head in the royal cabin in the Vienna Woods and then himself (or if he left a note, it was destroyed). Moreover, the royal family covered up the truth, and the whole story was not learned until the 1930s (Morton, 1980).

We might ask: "What was this dude's problem, anyway? Why did he kill himself in the middle of all that (apparently) pleasurable activity?" One answer is that he probably felt *ashamed* that he wasn't doing anything useful for anyone (Erikson, 1950); another, often speculated on, is that his father prevented him from taking an active role in government, leading Rudolph to feel emasculated, or, as we analysts might say, to experience castration depressive affect (Brenner, 1982, 2006). In other words, it looks like damaged self-esteem played a part in his suicide, possibly some guilt (over cheating on his wife and sabotaging his father), and extreme shame over his unearned luxuriating—which apparently he equated with unmanliness. And just maybe he was psychotic, as well; hard to know.

Development and manifestations of laziness

Anyway, enough history for the moment. From a clinical standpoint, over the past ten or fifteen years, I have seen a spate of patients who have been successful financially; they had reached a point in their lives where they no longer needed to work to generate enough money to survive. They could retire or do anything else they want. And yet they developed panic attacks, depressions, and isolated themselves from pleasurable activities. There is a related group who have "come into" money, either through marriage or inheritance, who can't seem to stand the pleasure of not needing to work; they therefore work too hard. If we were texting, we might ask: WTF? And the answer might be similar—that they experience severe shame over the complete gratification of oral desires (to be taken care of like a baby). In such cases, exposure of infantile gratifications leads to severe inner conflict, the result of which is anxiety and defensive operations—all of which coalesce into symptoms and character traits, like depression, panic, and workaholism: compromise formations (Waelder, 2007).

How does all this occur? The answer is that development happens in myriad ways, and results in all adults living with some balance of laziness and work. Laziness inevitably becomes embroiled in mental conflicts, either between people or within a person; and the most common element of mental functioning that opposes laziness is shame. Perhaps I can shame you into working to read the rest of this chapter, or perhaps (as I have been trying to do) I can keep it enjoyable enough that it won't feel like work to read it—the latter an attitude Heinz Hartmann (1939) eschewed when he penned his masterpiece, *Ego Psychology and the Problem of Adaptation*.

And that brings us to another theoretical point: that is, in addition to there being a developmental line between play and work (Freud, 1956), I would like to add: *There is a developmental line between laziness and work*. Following this preliminary concept, we all start off lazy, and work is a human attitude almost entirely dependent on our experiences with the environment throughout life. We will expand on that idea in a bit.

There are many ways people can be lazy. Laziness is prominent during each stage of child and adolescent development, and persists in normal adults. I've made up a list of some of the most common presentations of laziness, but the number of types seemed so exhaustive that I didn't really want to bother knocking myself out to find them all—a case in point. If you put your mind to it, you will no doubt come up with more examples. Here's what I thought of:

- Not getting up on time
- Not meeting deadlines
- Carelessness
- Inattention
- Not doing homework
- Not doing housework (chores)
- Wasting time
- Procrastinating (putting things off)
- Not working productively
- Not earning an income
- Not being self-sufficient
- Gaming the system
- Failure to launch
- Not assisting others

- Sunning
- Eating at a restaurant where there is a wait staff
- Golf (the way I play it).

The first problem against which all these lazy activities bang their ugly heads is shame. Shame has several facets. It is at times conceptualized as the painful experience of having exposed to others some aspect of ourselves that is 1) deficient or 2) drive-related (oral, anal, sexual, and/or destructive). So being a student is always a mixed bag, since to learn anything, students must admit they do not know something, which is *prima facie* embarrassing, especially if you think you are smart. Et voilà—another facet of shame, 3) a negative comparison to what we expect ourselves to be, our ego ideal (Akhtar, 2014b, p. 20; Freud, 1923b).

Let's look at shame over exposure of a drive element[2] in our mental functioning. The conflict most commonly occurs over a tsunami of oral wishes: to be taken care of, to be fed, to be noticed, and to do nothing—this last being what we might refer to as pure culture laziness. Actually, laziness is not quite that simple; it is a compromise formation; but we'll have to work more to get our heads around that concept. It would be easier if I just explained what I mean right now, and spoon-fed it to you; but then if you were that lazy, you wouldn't even be reading this essay. So I'll presume (based on a projection that you're like me) that you have enough conflicts, yourself, about laziness, that you will follow along with me, and either learn something or make the effort to argue with me—either being an example of the obverse of laziness.

We should empathize with Freud (at least a little), who, between 1895 and 1923, struggled with his first theories that explained human symptomatology based heavily on the pleasure-unpleasure principle (that people move toward activities that are pleasurable and away from those that are unpleasurable). Must have been very depressing to him to realize, after twenty-eight years, that he had been barking up the wrong theory, and needed a better one.[3] So even though structural theory (id, ego, superego, but you already knew that) was riddled with internal contradictions (Brenner, 2006), we have to give Freud some credit for the amount of work he expended to come up with it. He could have just given up and gone back to taking cocaine, a lazier and potentially more gratifying solution, considering all the intellectual battles that ensued after 1923 with Jungians, Rankians, Adlerians, Kleinians, Bionians, sociologists, behaviorists, and the medical establishment in general.

To me, it would have been a great pleasure to get Freud in a room, trading ideas with Jacob Arlow, Harold Blum, John Bowlby, Eleanor Galenson, Heinz Kohut, Selma Kramer, Margaret Mahler, Henri Parens, Herman Roiphe, and Vamik Volkan, especially if I didn't have to prepare anything or, heaven forbid, moderate. Steve Allen (1977–1981) attempted something like this for history in his TV show, *Meeting of Minds*. Alas, the (sublimated) pleasures that show provided were less instinct-near than the recent *Bachelorette Show*, part of which involves young adult women, while cooing about who would be most fun in bed, choosing male dates based on physical appearance. No one has to compete for these men, nor, worse, has to assess them[4] for matching intellect, compatible social hunger, character traits, similar desires, and capacity for maintaining "optimal distance" (Akhtar, 1992), or common values (type of superego), all of which are requisite to actually sustaining a relationship. The women doing the choosing seem to have it easy, with the choices based heavily on acting on sexual fantasy (ahem, "romance").[5]

This brings up the next issue, although it is difficult to discuss due to the embarrassing (superego) pressures to suppress such discussion—namely masturbation and masturbation fantasies (Marcus & Francis, 1975). If we eventually get into what those fantasies are about, perhaps as in *Fifty Shades of Gray* (James, 2012), we will be led, as day to night, to formulate some kind of theory about fantasies of different kinds (including sex, violence, punishment, and laziness), as Freud tried to do in 1905, 1919 and 1920. In fact, some of the most exciting fantasies might include laziness and punishment.

One (but not the only) interesting thing about masturbation is that it is easy.[6] It doesn't take much effort. It could be thought of as lazy orgasms. A medical school friend of mine, who shall remain nameless to protect the possibly humiliated, once wrote to me (when I was also in medical school) in a letter, "I don't sleep at night; I swim." He was kidding, of course, but the joke involved the idea that he could get "laid" without bothering with a woman, and have orgasms whenever he wanted for relief without working at it too hard, so to speak; at the same time, he was making fun of himself, also a defense against shame.

OK, we've arrived at the part of this chapter where we will have to stop playing around and get to work on some theory to explain lazy, oral, and sadomasochistic fantasies that so frequently enter masturbatory thoughts. And it will probably be theory that is not based fundamentally on attachment. One might wonder if attachment theorists ever get a good grip on themselves. Oh well. They make some good points

(Bretherton, 1992)—for example, that secure-organized attachments foster affect regulation—but their theory doesn't help too much with understanding laziness and the conflicts human beings get into about it. On the other hand, aspects of separation-individuation, identity, and conflict theories may come in handy.

Clinical vignette: 1

A middle-aged male patient of mine once dreamed that after being tried in some fantasy tribunal, he was alone, sitting on top of a mountain, sucking his own penis, which was three feet long. He joked that he was not from, nor planning on visiting Nantucket any time soon; nevertheless, we had both associated to the ribald limerick as soon as he told me the dream.[7] The dream indicated, in part, that he was tired of trying, and wanted to be lazy in getting sexual gratification by himself. To use Volkan's (2012) theory of the "look upward," we figured out he was sexualizing his wish to suck on a woman's breast, in turn symbolizing oral dependency wishes that caused him extreme *shame*. He felt relieved that his penis was three feet long, but the sucking was still embarrassing.

In addition, he was creating distance from his fiancée, in reality, by avoiding spending as much time with her as she wanted. He opined that depending on her interfered with him feeling "like a man." Distancing also protected him from a more primitive anxiety he called "being controlled," meaning she would also take over his thinking and make him into her "marionette, with her pulling the strings." My observation that he still defended himself against identity diffusion as he might have done during adolescence: a partial reconstruction (Blum, 2005), led him to think of how he had hated going to "Cotillion," an antiquated formal social event his mother pushed him into as a teen.

In addition, when he told his mother he wanted to go to medical school, she was critical, opining that it was a "chauvinistic" occupation run by a "good-old-boy network." She suggested he continue writing poetry, as she did, and as he had during college; but he considered poetry-writing "mental masturbation." Becoming a good-old-boy doctor, as he did, gave him control over his own thinking (individuation) and a sense of masculinity. Meanwhile, he had transferred from his mother onto his fiancée—a woman who had expressed a desire to marry him—a fear of being controlled and emasculated (marriage=Cotillion equation); he then was protecting himself by limiting his contact with his fiancée.

By using "pseudoindependence" (Blackman, 2003), he defended himself from *shame* over his symbiotic dependency wishes, from fear of mind-control ("self-object fusion": Mahler, Pine, & Bergman, 1975), from fear of castration, and from *shame* over his wish to be like his mother, who symbolized, to him, laziness=femininity=castration.

Compromise formations underlying laziness

I like the idea of compromise formation better than the concept of dialectic. Every time I see dialectic, I look it up again, and it makes sense briefly, until I forget it. Maybe that's because dialectic reminds me of communism, a philosophy that abrogates human autonomy.

Compromise formation, on the other hand, helps explain symptoms and character pathology so that, as people know more about their compromise formations, they can become more autonomous—that is, freer from constrictions of their own making. Freud (1926d) first explained that if people are inhibited (not getting enough sexual or aggressive pleasure), it's probably because they are assuaging some shame or guilt (superego). At the same time they regress as a defense, they obtain pleasure on an oral or anal level. To follow Freud's formulations, a woman with a phobia of going over bridges might be, simultaneously 1) limiting herself (defense), 2) expressing a(n oral) wish to be taken care of (someone must make special arrangements for her to take a ferry or something), 3) expressing anal control (saying no and making everyone do things her way), 4) punishing herself (staying in a kind of prison by not going places), 5) avoiding the reality of getting caught in traffic or getting killed if the bridge collapsed, 6) expressing hostility to foster autonomy (getting everyone who has to deal with her irritated with her self-centeredness), 7) castrating her husband by making him take care of her (like a mother), 8) becoming the center of attention, a distorted version of an exhibitionistic/sexual wish, 9) avoiding shame over wishes for sexual intercourse (where the bridge is symbolic of such a connection), 10) bringing shame on herself for being infantile, and, actually, an infinite number of other possible combinations based on the specifics of her history.

A skeletal way of looking at these matters (Waelder, 2007) is that five essential elements of a compromise formation make up painful symptoms (like phobias) and character traits (such as passivity or obnoxiousness): wishes, superego activity (guilt/shame), reality perceptions, affects, and constellations of defensive operations. As a matter of fact, if you really get into this, you can describe any thought or action not only as a combination of the five factors in one compromise formation, but as consisting of multiple compromise formations layered over each other from every developmental phase (Blackman, 2013). Now we're thinking like a three-dimensional chess player, except with an infinite number of planes. That's what I call pleasurable work, but some would disagree.

Now, let's apply this notion of compromise formation to laziness, which turns out not to be as simple as oral gratification (although I would argue that's still a big piece of it—the spa, the massage, breakfast in bed, your money—not you—making money through compound interest). First, consider the common-day phenomenon of people, after finishing college, returning home to live with their parents without looking for a job; sometimes, the returners just smoke pot all day, and have sex with other failure-to-launch types all night. Their parents criticize them, but they maintain their putative torpor. What compromise formations are at work?

The failure to launch person

1) *achieves high levels of oral gratification*: fed by parents (like newborn infants); not working (no effort); smoking pot (oceanic feeling, like an infant).
2) *is humiliated as a defense against shame*: snubbed by others who are working; nagged by parents.
3) *asserts autonomy*: does not do what parents want—so feels "independent"; does not do what the culture values—so feels "different".
4) *receives genital gratification*: has sex promiscuously; feels "superior" to peers who try too hard.
5) *obtains gratification of competitive wishes*: outwits parents and authorities; has sexual relations without commitment—goes against the "norm."
6) *uses rationalizations about not finding work*: makes excuses to relieve guilt and shame; bases excuses on generally agreed-upon realities such as poor economy and shortage of jobs.

7) *obtains anal gratifications*: does not clean room; does not help in house; says "no" to what parents want; leads a messy life.

The workaholic

This is the person who works too hard at everything, all the time. The workaholic cannot relax, and either stays at work too long, is too perfectionistic, or comes home only to work on something else. The workaholic is restless and cannot stand being lazy. Why?

Clinical vignette: 2

A successful woman attorney, on turning sixty-five, presented for evaluation because of anxiety attacks and insomnia. Although she had saved over $20 million, she bitterly complained about many of her clients, who were demanding of her time and complained about her fees. She had to work an average of twelve hours per day to get her work done on time, and "went in" on weekends to clear up paperwork, finish time sheets, and answer emails she had not answered during the week. Her husband suggested she retire, as he had a few years earlier. But she felt she did not have enough money to do that yet. As I got to know her, I learned that her husband disagreed with her about work, and that part of her anxiety, which she had denied, was based on a reality perception that her husband was becoming more distant from her; he played golf with men she knew to be alcoholics and philanderers. He protested that being friends with them did not mean he was the same.

The patient had had a mother who was a homemaker and doted on the patient; however, the mother was stupefyingly narcissistic, often taking it on herself to advise her daughter about legal matters. The mother felt the patient's father had died due to the patient's neglect of him, and often brought this up in phone calls to complain that the patient did not call her mother enough.

Over a course of analytic treatment, we figured out the following: (i) working relieved a fear the patient harbored that she would have to listen to her mother; (ii) working represented a disidentification from her "lazy" mother who just complained all the time about not being attended to; (iii) working made the patient feel autonomous (she did not need to depend on her husband and did not want to give up her identity as an expert; (iv) by working, she alleviated shame over a conscious wish to be "lazy" as she had been in college, when she had drunk alcohol too much; (v) working relieved her depressive affect over her father's death (kept her from thinking about it); (vi) working was an identification with her father, who had worked hard as a chemical engineer for a large corporation; (vii) working helped her earn money which represented mother's milk (the patient wanted more, but was ashamed; she was ashamed of the money she had saved, which she described as "obscene"; she continued to suffer and be ridiculed by her clients for having high fees, relieving her guilt and shame over her enjoyment of making money), and (viii) working involved certain other dynamics pertaining to control, gender, avoidance of sexuality, and self-punishment.

For the purposes of our theoretical understanding of laziness, the factors that this person considered "lazy" caused her so much shame that she developed reaction-formations (the opposite of wished-for laziness: perfectionism, punctuality, and cleanliness). She also used reality rationalizations about why she could not yet stop working. She was a prototypical workaholic.

As analytic therapy uncovered these and many more meanings, she cut back to half-time work, hired other attorneys to work for her (which she had previously been bad about), and spent more time with her husband. He became less distant and much happier. Their sex life picked up. There was an "alteration of defenses" (Brenner, 1975) that led to different compromise formations.

Two compromise formations that work

My grandfather, Theodore A. Blackman, was a refugee from czarist Russia. He was glad to be alive. His advice to me was, "Find something lucrative, and learn to like it." As much as I loved my grandfather (I was much like he was), I did not take his advice. I chose psychoanalysis, which I enjoyed, and tried to learn to be good at it.

My grandfather's idea is a common solution to the balance problem. As much as people philosophize that you should "love your work," I believe this is a rare solution to the problem of laziness *vs.* working. Most people do not love their jobs. If they are fortunate, they get good at their jobs, and are able to survive (in Western civilization, that usually means making money). Like the French, many would like to have a thirty-two-hour working week and long vacations in the summer—to get away from work and to enjoy themselves.

My own personal solution—to find something I enjoyed studying and doing, and then try to make a living doing it—is a much more difficult proposition. This solution involves considerable sublimation: symbolic displacement of drive wishes welded to developing ego functions (Blackman, 2010). Of all the high school football players who love channeling competitive hostility into the game, only a tiny fraction of a percent ever get to make money playing in the NFL. Of all the people who love (curiosity plus reading) Shakespeare, only a relative few succeed in making a living as an actor or an English professor. Of those students who loved math and science (curiosity and aggression coupled with a certain type of intellectual aptitude), only a relative few succeed in tech startups (Messrs Gates and Zuckerberg notwithstanding). There is, I believe, a need for talent, training, and luck to succeed financially in pleasurable, sublimated endeavors. Either solution avoids the shame of not working, and either should afford sufficient gratification to make life worth living.

A controversial area: to homemake or not to homemake

You already know about this issue: women who decide to be "stay-at-home moms." And women with children who have decided to reenter the workplace (and perhaps share childrearing evenly with their husbands). Without repeating what has become so common that it is almost a cliché, the problem for such a woman starts with her ego ideal. From what activity does she obtain self-esteem? Does she consider herself lazy for not making money? Or does she criticize herself, while making money, for not being an attentive-enough mother? Does she criticize herself so much that she becomes depressed (Blatt, 1992)? Especially— are things in the house going to pot while she is working?

The solution for any woman must somehow balance pleasure, duty to children and home, and identity and reality issues surrounding work. If the ego ideal is too ideal, perhaps based on an identification with a fantasy, an identification with her mother or father, or a disidentification from either of her parents, she will become anxious and depressed no matter which choice she makes—to work outside the home (even part-time) or to homemake. There isn't any very good advice about this. The best an analyst (or anyone) can do is to help any particular woman understand the bases for her ego ideal, the shame that emanates from the ego ideal when adequacy is not felt in either activity, and any compensatory (compulsive) defensive operations. In other words, it comes down to deconstructing whatever compromise formations are present, so that the woman can make decisions that are self- and reality-syntonic.

Some parting thoughts

If, like me, you usually take the lazy way out and read summaries of book chapters first, so you don't waste your time working to read something you won't find worthwhile, here's a précis of what I have tried to contribute.

Laziness is primarily a perpetuation of orally-based wishes which can be normal, but can also disturb the development of reasonable work habits. In addition, laziness itself is a compromise formation with multiple meanings deriving from solutions to conflicts at various levels of psychosexual development. Some of the multiple meanings of laziness involve object relations compromise formations—gratifying symbiotic and separation wishes simultaneously (Blum, 2015). Other meanings derive from conflicts about aggression and sexuality. Those conflicts involve shame over unproductiveness and failure of identity formation. Normal laziness could be considered a phenomenon where respite and relaxation have been earned, survival has been assured by sufficient work, and individuation is not threatened by indulgence of drive wishes.

Shame, in lazy adults, is managed by constellations of defenses, especially reality rationalizations and subtle defiance, which relieve the shame that would, during normal development, incur too much self-esteem damage to be acted on for long. The reality rigors of survival usually push even the lazy individual to do some work, although that person may fail and wind up a ward of the state, deriving self-esteem from gaming the system, and thereby relieving whatever shame had been generated. Workaholics are, at base, lazy people who can't stand themselves. They have similar compromise formations to those of lazy people, but add reaction-formations and some other compulsive defenses to relieve their shame over various lazy wishes.

Thanks for reading. I hope the pleasure in the theories expounded herein have outweighed the labor it took to read through this—a philosophy I try to apply to myself as well as to those I care about and treat.

Notes

1. That is, without laziness conflicting with survival (reality), other pleasures, and, in particular, *shame*.
2. For a more complete dissertation on drive elements, see Blackman (2010).
3. For a neat review of how Freud changed his theory in 1923, see Arlow and Brenner (1964).
4. Using the ego functions of perception, integration, abstraction, reality testing, and executive functioning.
5. According to I. Marcus (2013), men began to appeal to women's romantic fantasies sometime during the Renaissance, as a way of competing for desirable women.
6. Although a comic once quipped that he did not masturbate because he wasn't good at it.
7. For those readers unfamiliar with that vulgar, hermaphroditic limerick, you may find it at http://motd.ambians.com/quotes.php/name/freebsd_limericks/toc_id/1-0-9/s/670.

CHAPTER EIGHT

Shame and the aversion to apologizing

Melvin R. Lansky

In this contribution, I shall explore the difficulties posed by aversion to apologizing and the relation of this difficulty to the anticipation of shame at the self-indictment that inevitably accompanies acts of apology. This is a widespread problem and, more often than not, the shame dynamics do not manifest themselves as the overt affect of shame or the conscious apprehension of having been shamed. More often, we see reactions to the failure of apology in what later may become understood to be the wake of the anticipation of a shame experience—a paling or diminution of intensity in a relationship or an outright severance of a bond without any official declaration of the rupture of the relationship. In this regard, the reader may recall that the great twentieth-century philosopher, Martin Heidegger, never apologized for his membership in the Nazi party. This omission was not an episode, but continued throughout his life. Whether or not this failure to apologize was part and parcel of Heidegger's philosophical concern for authenticity is impossible to determine with certainty. I am presuming that all relationships, close ones especially, need repairs, whether very brief ones acknowledged in our code of manners, or formal apologies in which the offender presents himself to the offended and apologizes. Without some ceremony of apology—in person or by phone or letter or card—bonds are more likely to be damaged irreparably or relationships lose any quality of intimacy or nourishment.

Preamble

As a prelude, I turn to George Bernard Shaw's *Arms and the Man* (1894). In this play, the young Bulgarian officer, Sergius, engaged to the heroine, Raina Petkoff, is put up as a model of pompous and shallow standards of honor. He is pompous with an overarching preoccupation with his public image as valorous. Sergius led his cavalry brigade into an almost certainly suicidal frontal attack on enemy cannons. However, Captain Bluntschli, the Swiss officer in charge of the enemy forces, was given the wrong size ammunition on the battlefield, so the foolish Sergius was acclaimed a hero when his regiment overcame the opposition. Bluntschli fled and found his way (unintentionally) to the home where Raina resided. He scaled the wall and entered her bedroom, pointing a gun at her. We learn later that the gun was not loaded since the avowedly unidealistic Bluntschli kept chocolates in his ammunition belt instead of bullets. With his pistol without bullets, Bluntschli forces her to hide him. Soon, he falls in love with her. The situation provides the opportunity for Shaw to lampoon the canons of military honor:

> Sergius: "You see the young lady's concern, Captain Bluntschli. Denial is useless. You have enjoyed the privilege of being received in her own room late at night."
> Bluntschli: (interrupting him pepperily) "Yes, you blockhead! She received me with a pistol at her head. Your cavalry were at my heels. I'd have blown out her brains if she'd uttered a cry."
> Sergius: (taken aback) "Bluntschli! Raina: is this true?"
> Raina: (rising in wrathful majesty) "Oh, how dare you, how dare you?"
> Bluntschli: "Apologize, man; apologize." (He resumes his seat at the table.)
> Sergius: (with the old measured emphasis, folding his arms) "I never apologize!"
>
> (Act IV)

I use this brief excerpt as an illustration using a comically explicit example of the need for social repair and the blocking of that repair by failure to apologize. Shaw's genius provides the opportunity to lampoon the military ethic, but also its mores in respect to which apologizing was in and of itself disgraceful. Sergius's trust of his (entirely innocent) fiancée has been damaged by the news that a man—an enemy soldier—had climbed up into her bedroom and hid out, keeping Raina from seeking help with a pistol that she had presumed was loaded with bullets. Shaw's portrayal of the pomposity and rigidity illustrated in Sergius's reply farcically illustrates the inability to deal with repair of any disruption of the relationship, great or small, by apologizing. Viewed psychoanalytically—as though he were an actual person seen through a psychoanalytic lens, the pompous Sergius would seem possessed of an ego ideal, that part of the conscience dealing with ideals and aspirations, that is rigid and uncompromising and will accept no departure from the ideal of military honor and valor with which he was acculturated. The title of the play, borrowed from the opening line of Vergil's *Aeneid*, draws from a Roman standard of honor in battle—the very standard that Shaw sought to lampoon throughout the play. We can draw from the dramaturgic preposterousness of Sergius's refusal to apologize without presuming that we are engaging in the dubious activity of psychoanalyzing a literary character. Shaw is lampooning the idealizations of his age that are used to justify an absurd ethic.

My intent is not to view this brief excerpt from the point of view of literary criticism, but rather, of psychoanalytic exploration of the predicament, specifically in relation to anticipated shame over the self-indictment that is inevitably part and parcel of the act of apology. Some of this predicament is sociological and is an aspect of what we call manners (P. Post, A. Post, L. Post, & Post-Senning, 2011). For example, a simple "sorry" when one jostles another hurrying along a crowded street is a case in point of what we may call the apologizing of everyday life. Later, I give some clinical examples of the failure to apologize, fairly brief sketches that illustrate the dynamics and the cost of difficulties in apologizing. Then, I turn to the analytic situation itself and consider the impact of failure to apologize on the part of either the patient or the analyst to apologize when apology is indicated in the clinical situation. I move on into the dynamics of the moral emotions, shame and guilt, insofar as they concern the problem of apology.

Apology is a social event, one between two or more parties, so it is not surprising that sociologists and psychologists have paid serious attention to it. Helen Block Lewis (1971), using refined techniques in her groundbreaking research on the natural history of disruption of relationships, found that shame played a key role in the disruption of relationships if that shame was bypassed and unacknowledged by the person experiencing the shame. Lewis demonstrated with elegant empirical evidence that unacknowledged shame had a wide-ranging impact and gave rise to disruptions in treatment and to varying manifestations of anger and disruption in relationships. Lewis's influence extended to Thomas Scheff (1987) and Suzanne Retzinger (1991a, 1991b), sociologists at the University of California, Santa Barbara. Scheff, studying international conflict, pointed out that the Treaty of Versailles, by forcing the disarmament of Germany, humiliated her in such a way as to promote the rise of the Third Reich and the leadership of Hitler. Retzinger, within a clinical context, studied videotapes of her sessions with marital couples and developed an important theory of shame in relation to the escalation of marital conflict in which one partner, upset, shames the other, who in turn reciprocates by shaming the first, who then responds in kind by further shaming.

Apology refers to an attempt to repair a rift in the social bond and is part of a larger picture of disruption and repair that often, though not always, includes forgiveness (Akhtar, 2002). In an early work on apology, A. Goldberg (1987) does not take cognizance of the dynamics of shame, further asserting that: "Apologizing *per se* is not treated as a normal part of psychoanalytic technique" (p. 408). I shall take issue with that assertion in the next two sections, pointing to the necessity of apology in the analytic situation.

Clinical examples

Clinical vignette: 1

> Carolyn, a woman in her forties, for many years had a close relationship with her neighbor, Sue, a woman five years her senior, who played a motherly role in Carolyn's life. The relationship was satisfying to both of them. This was particularly important since Carolyn's relationship with her own mother had been quite strained, and she felt the need of a motherly presence in her life. Over time, Carolyn appreciated the closeness to Sue, but Sue repeatedly called at times when Carolyn was sleeping (she was

afflicted with a chronic fatigue disorder and needed her rest). Sue kept calling, despite Carolyn's telling her not to, and never apologized. She simply wouldn't do so. Repeated continuations of the offense and Sue's serious failure to apologize led to a rupture of the heretofore close and satisfying relationship. This rupture lasted for many years. This rupture eventually subsided, but still, Sue could not apologize for a character trait that others noticed as well. The relationship became much less robust and satisfying for Carolyn, and Sue remained dismayed that Carolyn kept her at a considerable emotional distance.

Clinical vignette: 2

Carl, an old friend of Tim, visited Tim and Donna, his wife, coming from a long way away. Carl and Tim had been school fellows forty years previously and the friendship had continued albeit with very infrequent reunions, since they now lived a great distance apart. On one visit, Carl said to Donna that the first time he met her, he disliked her immediately. This is just when Carl and his wife Joan were leaving. Tim and Donna were too shocked to address the matter immediately; there wasn't time to bring this matter up for discussion and insist on an apology. The couples parted and did not communicate for some time. A serious, but unacknowledged rift occurred. The situation would in all likelihood have been reparable had Carl made amends at the time or subsequently, perhaps said, "I disliked you at first, but ours has developed into a warm friendship." But Carl said nothing. Tim and Donna remained shocked. They did nothing to continue the friendship, and the holiday cards sent by Carl and Joan were sparse and businesslike. Tim and Donna sent equally pale cards for a few years. The friendship trailed off entirely and seemed to expire after a few years without the basic shaming act by Carl ever having been addressed by anyone; Carl and Joan said nothing, nor did Tim and Donna feel that it was their place to bring the matter up. Christmas card exchanges soon ceased. The relationship extinguished because of sheer lack of contact, since it was not resuscitated by an act of apology; essentially, it was extinguished without any attempt at repair on either side. The failure of an act of apology had obviated the resuscitation of the relationship entirely.

Clinical vignette: 3

Shannon, a forty-five-year-old woman, successful in her business pursuits, broke off relations with her mother, a volatile woman, who repeatedly exploded with rage at whoever frustrated her, but never acknowledged her impact or apologized for her temper and its impact. Her mother regarded herself as piously religious, and a dedicated and loving mother who, somehow, had to face disrespect from every quarter in her immediate family. The family was replete with dissension. Shannon moved across country and kept contact with her mother to a minimum. Her father had presumed himself her ally, but in her treatment, Shannon realized that he had placated her for his own interests and never actually stood up for her. He might be seen as co-dependent in this abusive relationship—not participating in the verbal brutality, but enabling it at the expense of his daughter. In the course of her long and productive therapy, Shannon finally confronted her father specifically about his cowardice in this matter. But the mother could never apologize for the verbal and physical abuse that continued, and the father eluded any unpleasant confrontation with the mother. Some similar scenarios had occurred with two of Shannon's siblings. Shannon's relationship with her parents was restored somewhat, albeit to a superficial level, and never came close to providing the emotional nourishment that she wanted. These difficulties in repair in her family of origin also affected her ability to see clearly and either repair or leave relationships with men or hold them accountable for abusive or exploitative behavior. In her professional life, she remained competent and successful, albeit personally unhappy.

Clinical vignette: 4

Gene and Bob became friends as sophomore pre-professional students in a large Southern university. They were both strong students, though Bob was a bit stronger. When Gene decided to move to a more highly-rated Northern university, he convinced Bob to join him the next semester. Gene was a child of divorce. Both parents, quite brilliant and well educated intellectuals, placed him in the middle of marital quarrels. Gene became quite angry and this anger spread to his social circle, where he resorted to bullying when he felt threatened.

Bob had always felt that he was overprotected. He valued Gene's friendship in part because it helped him separate from his parents, with whom he was not at war. He decided to get an apartment with Gene. The two had a convenient symbiosis: Gene liked to lead, though he was often bluffing about his capacities; Bob, ashamed of his inexperience in the world, liked to be led. The friendship worked well for a time, but tensions arose. Gene attempted to bully Bob into resuming the *status quo*, but Bob would have none of this. He felt that he had outgrown the friendship and resented Gene lording it over him. He took a stand and the relationship ruptured. Bob was admitted the first time he applied to law school in the same town, but Gene was not. Gene reapplied and was admitted the next year. Though both wanted the relationship restored, neither could take the step of approaching the other for a reconciliation. The two met in the course of their studies and the friendship resumed, but never with its former intensity.

Clinical vignette: 5

A young physician in analysis with me for four years came to his session and declared that he had been up most of the night thinking about something wonderful I had said during the previous session. He declared that it was an astonishing experience for him, and he couldn't get it out of his mind. Since I do not utilize grandstanding interpretations, I was lost in dismay over what he was referring to. After a few minutes, I said, "You talk as though I know what you're referring to, but I don't." He fell silent for a few minutes, then said, "Wait a minute, wait a minute, you lost me." I was even more dismayed, but soon he burst out, "That son of a bitch would never care to find me." This man had idealized his family, parents, siblings, and grandparents, all of whom had lived close by in the Midwestern town in which he grew up. His outcry was the beginning of his giving up his idealization of the family and considering some features of the relationship that he felt had damaged him, especially his academically aspirant parents' constant preoccupation with academic matters to the point that they virtually ignored both of their sons. The matter further came to a head when the patient's brother committed suicide after a rejection by his wife and a divorce. We were later able to return to the cost of his idealization of his parents in terms of his failure to separate emotionally from them and to deal successfully with relationships with women, which he usually limited to short sexual encounters. What emerged as the analysis continued was his shame about himself for his failure to have relationships in which he fully participated and his anger at his parents that he could not hitherto acknowledge. He remained close to his family, but was able to achieve enough of an emotional separation so that he could have a richer intimate life.

Clinical vignette: 6

Ralph was an internist. He was well trained and well respected in the medical community and his manner was pleasant. His standing in the professional community rose. He was something of a perfectionist, though, and could not easily face admitting errors that he made. Typical of his difficulties was a case in which he told a patient with a serious leg injury that had become infected and who had allergies to many antibiotics that she didn't need hospitalization. The woman did not receive timely treatment and was hospitalized, clearly because of Ralph's error in not taking the infection seriously enough. To make matters worse, when confronted, Ralph dismissed the issue with a brief, "Well, I'm sorry," and rushed off to see other patients. The patient in question left his practice as did many others and his reputation suffered significantly. Ralph's "I'm sorry" was not, in fact, a serious apology so much as a quick attempt to disarm the person who confronted him.

Apology and failure to apologize in the analytic situation

Although the necessity of apology and situations in which apology should be forthcoming are widespread, the topic does not make significant appearance in either oral or written psychoanalytic discourse. The fact is that hidden or overt resentments when apology is not made are ubiquitous in psychoanalytic practice. "Mini offenses" may pass unnoticed by either patient or analyst, but the failure to deal with them, even by just acknowledging them, has potentially erosive consequences for the analytic relationship and for the treatment itself.

Failure to apologize on the part of the patient

On the patient's part, such breaches as the frequent missing of sessions, or lateness to, or interruptions of sessions, have significant impact on the process and must be considered. So is any offhandedness about frequency of absences or lateness. Also important to acknowledge are snide overt or indirect comparisons of the analyst to previous analysts or therapists or analysts of others that the patient knows, lateness of payments, and missing of sessions without notice or explanation.

Clinical vignette: 7

> Drew, a successful attorney, came in accompanying his wife with whom he had a loving relationship. She had complained that Drew, instead of dealing directly with her complaints, acted seductively with her and won her back. In his treatment, which became an intensive individual treatment, he often didn't show up or didn't call. He was charged for the sessions, but the analyst still kept the absences in focus. Eventually, the work got to his struggle against identification with his enraged and abusive father and his brutal humiliation of his own son. The analyst was more active in intervening with his degrading his son, and that behavior subsided substantially when Drew began to appreciate that with his son he was giving what he'd gotten. This humiliation of his son subsided after some years of analytic work. A significant part of the work was the analyst's keeping in mind the sense of being insulted and disrespected by Drew's persistent unannounced absences. The analyst's consulting of his own feelings enabled him to sense something of the emotional world that Drew experienced in his growing up. When this insight into the shame dynamics in Drew's family of origin projected onto Drew's son and onto the analyst was brought into the treatment, things began to change for the better; absences stopped, and the patient was able to experience some remorse for what he had done to his son over the years.

Clinical vignette: 8

> Lina, a young physician, was the daughter of a well-known psychiatrist. She came for treatment after the father came into a brief psychotherapy with the analyst to check the analyst out before

referring his daughter for treatment. The analyst noted this bizarre method of embarking on treatment and later was able to use it in Lina's treatment. Lina was very bright and successful, but gravitated toward abusive relationships with men who invariably treated her shabbily and left her. She had requested early morning therapy hours, but would often miss them. This missing of hours was explored with the analyst opining that she was inflicting on the analyst what she had suffered from her parents—frequent desertions—when she wanted a kind of predictability and safety that she could never get from her family of origin. After many years of treatment with a focus on her projective identifications, she finally began a relationship with an attentive and loving man whom she dated for several years before marrying. With the combination of interpretive work and steady support for her needs from the analyst and her husband, she became able to understand the basis for her masochistic excitement which had its own gratifications but of which she was greatly ashamed. Once she could acknowledge the underlying shame that prompted her self-sabotage, Lina could enjoy her marriage and distance herself from her quite toxic family of origin. She was not able to hold them accountable, though, or to insist on apology and a change of behavior.

Apology on the part of the analyst

The analyst, too, must apologize more often than is commonly realized. Consider how frequently one must say, "I'm sorry I'm a few minutes late, can you stay so we have the full time?"; "I'm sorry to have to interrupt when you're so upset, but we do have to stop"; "I'm so sorry my time away coincides with this very difficult time for you"; "I'm sorry to have to be out of the office on such short notice"; "I'm sorry, but I'm expecting an urgent call, and I'll have to answer the phone in this session"; "I'm sorry, you told me this, but I can't recall and have to ask you again"; "I'm sorry, I can't remember your sister-in-law's name"; "I'm sorry about the noise, [or the room temperature, or the lighting]—it isn't as it should be today"; or, "I'm sorry the construction going on in the building next door is intruding on our session today."

I have deliberately included fairly trivial situations for which the analyst should apologize. Such apologies are not simply trivial social niceties, they convey an understanding of the patient's predicament and empathy for what the patient is going through and the putting aside of self-protection of the analyst by "stonewalling" it in the face of these disruptions of the patient's experience. I presume that patients note a failure to issue an apology that is in order and accommodate to the realization that the analyst needs to save face even if it is at the patient's expense. My experience has rather consistently been that patients take in at a very deep level any apology on the part of the analyst. Such comportment summates to generate an atmosphere of true compassion and empathy for what the patient is experiencing about the relation to the analyst. I apologize quite often in the treatment, sometimes directly with a clear-cut apology, but at other times with an observation, for example, "You've said nothing about the fact that I've had a number of absences recently that have interrupted our work." My acknowledgment of such events that may upset and humiliate the patient—prior to my apologizing—often have a very strong impact.

Shame dynamics driving the aversion to apology

Apology is an inevitable part of the process of repair that is absolutely vital to the attention to the health of the interpersonal bond and the vicissitudes of the injuries to that bond that are central and primary to the work of psychoanalysis and psychotherapy. The clinician will very often find that when interruptions, large or small, occur in the analytic setting, some form of shame experience—one of which the patient is too ashamed to admit to consciousness or to bring up with the analyst—is operative. This applies both to the patient and to the analyst. I am emphasizing that the need for explicit apology and the experience of shame for both patient and analyst is ubiquitous for both—much more so than either finds convenient to acknowledge. This is profitably borne in mind by the analyst even if the event in question seems trivial.

In psychoanalytic discourse and in writing, it is usually the case that we are able to talk about guilt and guilt dynamics more easily than we can talk about shame and shame dynamics. When we acknowledge guilt for transgressions or omissions that harm the other, we are presenting ourselves as strong in some way: we have *done* something that is harmful. With issues involving shame, one or the other or both of the parties are seen in the light of being weak, vulnerable, or otherwise "less than" what their standards hold them to. It is important to note that people tend to be ashamed of being ashamed and will often generate some line of thought or action that generates guilt as a defense against their acknowledging shame at weakness or incohesion of their personalities (Kohut, 1971; Lansky, 2004, 2005) that engenders shame. When we apologize, we acknowledge ourselves as carrying a burden of shame: we have failed in terms of our own ideals and aspirations for social conduct in ways that have harmed the other. It is not just wordplay to assert that we are ashamed of being ashamed—being "less than," "clueless," "clumsy," "inconsiderate," "self-centered," and the like.

Just as there is unconscious, there is also unconscious guilt (Freud, 1916d), so there is unconscious shame (Lansky, 2004, 2005). That concept is what H. B. Lewis (1971) was getting at when she wrote of unacknowledged or bypassed shame—the shame that is not experienced as the emotion itself, but as omission or defect or poor comportment that harms the other. We require the notion of "signal shame," the anticipation of shame to more fully understand the psychology and sociology of human interchange.

Conclusion

The line of thinking I have developed in this chapter highlights the role, not simply of the overt affect of shame, but also "signal shame," the anticipation of shame and the deployment of unconscious defensive activity to avoid the experience of unbearable shame in our relationships with ourselves and with others. The shame arises not necessarily with consciousness of the overt affect, but as an unconscious or preconscious trigger, in the present discussion, to the inhibition of apology with the anticipation of shame at the self-indictment that is inherent in the process of apology and may pose insuperable difficulties in the process of apologizing, and, hence, in the necessary repair of damage to the bonding with others. We tend to be ashamed of being ashamed, and that is why there is to some extent a "shame gradient" inevitable in the process of apology. We must give up the notion of our perfection and face shortcomings to be able to apologize and repair damage to relationships or we will remain, like Shaw's Sergius, unable to make repairs because we cannot tolerate putting forward to others and to ourselves our imperfections so that damage to relationships can be addressed and ameliorated.

CHAPTER NINE

The dialectic of shame in cross-cultural therapeutic encounters

Christie Platt

It is easy to regard racism as an issue that affects people of color more directly than it does white people. To grow up as part of the majority culture is like growing up in a world of affirming selfobjects. It is as if the culture is looking into your eyes and saying, "Yes, you belong." While one's individual family may not be able to provide the same kind of affirmation, the cultural matrix is secure and can be taken for granted. There is no need to look beyond this world. By contrast, members of racial and ethnic minority groups are forced to confront the implications of their racial identity every morning the minute they walk out the door, regarding the world with vigilance because their safety and well-being depends on it.

We grow up in an infinite variety of Americas, many or perhaps most of which are unknown to one group or another. As Scott (2014) observed in his recent review of *Dear White People*, a movie that explores sensitive racial and cultural issues, "We are all stereotypes in one another's eyes and complicated, unique individuals in our own minds" (p. 1).

A bit of personal background

Like most white people in the United States, I took my white privilege for granted. I didn't even know I had it. It just was. When I learned to read, I read about brown-haired Dick, blonde-haired Jane, and their dog, Spot. I watched white cowboys such as Maverick or the Lone Ranger defeat bad guys and Indians. During commercial breaks, I saw white mothers and daughters wash their hands in detergents that left them with creamy smooth hands. Cereal commercials featured white families getting their kids off to school with a healthy bowl of sugared cereal. Barbie dolls were white, as were action figures, as were the children who played with them in the commercials that presented the world to us. "Colored Francie" was the first African-American Barbie doll and was introduced in 1967 but because her features were made from the molds for white Barbies, she didn't look very African-American. It wasn't until 2009 that Mattel manufactured an African-American Barbie who looks like an African-American. A study conducted by the City of New York Department of Consumer Affairs (Green, 1991) revealed that out of 127 general interest magazines, African-Americans represented less than 5 percent of the people in the advertisements. When they did appear, it was generally in situations that replicated white suburbia. In 2013, Cheerios depicted an interracial couple with their daughter having breakfast. "The commercial generated such a racist backlash on YouTube that the comments section had to be closed" (Huffington Post, May 31, 2013).

I grew up with all of the above as my context for learning about the world, but learning about the world in white suburban Middle America provided a narrow sense of what the world was like. Without the internet, the rest of the world stayed far away. It never occurred to me that I *wasn't* the norm.

By the time I first considered training to become a psychotherapist, I was worried that I had nothing to offer to people of color because I *am* white. By then I had been to college and had friends who challenged any white person to comprehend someone from another culture. Could the patients I would see look beyond my color and want to talk to me? Could I understand what I had not lived? Becoming a psychologist opened up many possibilities, among them working with people from backgrounds unlike mine. After my sheltered upbringing, I longed to meet people who were different from me. Graduate school externships brought those opportunities in abundance.

During my training in the 1980s, we were encouraged to ask our patients to tell us if they had any feelings about working with a white therapist, but there was little discussion about how *we* felt as white therapists working with black patients and what challenges we faced working with patients from different backgrounds. Today, there are many more diversity awareness trainings built into graduate schools and continuing education requirements. Back then, these were "training cases" for us; we knew that we would inevitably move on, leaving clinics and patients behind for the next group of interns. We hoped to help them, but there was an unspoken, implicit sense that they were lucky to have treatment of any kind, even if we were green.

One year I got a glimpse of what it feels like to be a majority of one. I was assigned to work on a ward at a state hospital where I was the only white person. Other staff and all patients were, in this case, black, and I felt exposed and alone in a way that I hadn't experienced before and have not since. The first day I walked into the staff room, people greeted me perfunctorily, with what I perceived as little interest. I was assigned a spot off in a little corner for the time that I was there. I watched the interactions between psychiatrists, psychologists, and nurses, and it seemed that everyone instinctively understood the milieu in a way that I didn't. I wondered if they were watching me. When they laughed, I wondered if there were inside jokes about me that I couldn't understand. Much of the time, I felt invisible and of little consequence. As a result, I moved cautiously and tentatively through my days there and felt gratified when I felt included or shared a laugh with people. Was that an accurate sense of what was happening? Did my presence disturb a certain equilibrium or feeling of ease that existed during the shifts when I wasn't there? There was no one to ask, no one like me.

On one of my first days, my supervisor suggested I "mingle with the patients to see what it's like on the floor." There was an elevated nurse's station that overlooked the lounge where the patients were lying around, in the various states of sedation induced by antipsychotic drugs. As the staff watched, I self-consciously walked out on the floor. I felt ashamed of my naïveté and mortified as I tried to wake several of the patients to invite them to talk with me. Not surprisingly, none of them wanted to talk with me but I felt my inability to break through the patients' states of isolation on display. One patient was finally willing to talk to me. He was wearing fingerless gloves so I asked about them in an effort to strike up a conversation. He told me that they covered up the burns that covered his body from an awful accident that had occurred when he was trying to acquire some crack. I murmured something back to him and gratefully slunk off the floor when my supervisor decided to stop the experiment. I felt paranoid: Was this to help me or to provide entertainment for the staff? I never asked but there was a feeling of shame in being so exposed. I felt like I didn't have an ally, that day, but also in the subsequent months I worked there. It got better, but I never felt I belonged. This very brief year of my life gave me a visceral appreciation of what it might be like to *not* be part of the cultural majority.

Years passed. Barack Obama was elected as our first black, biracial president. Now, the phrase "post-racial America" got bandied about a lot. Yet it seemed that cultural biases and prejudices had become more nuanced, taking the form of "microaggressions" (Sue, 2010) in the interpersonal context. There was a popular consensus that the election signified that "things were getting better in America," but recently, we witnessed the high profile deaths of several young black men, and the conversation about race reemerged explosively. Never has there been so much conversation about race and culture as there is today. Because sensitivity has been heightened, there is also awareness that it is also more likely that one may unwittingly reveal one's unconsciousness about these matters. White therapists such as myself may wish to be particularly careful not to say anything that could be experienced as racist or culturally insensitive. Paradoxically, such sensitivity can inhibit the psychotherapeutic dyad from talking about important elements in a patient's family history, cultural experience, intrapsychic dynamics, and transference-countertransference issues that would enliven and enlighten the work.

In the following pages, I hope to elucidate some of the issues that may arise when the therapist is white and the patient is a person of color. In particular, in what ways might shame operate in both, inhibiting each in the attempt to uncover delicate, painful feelings that are generally not shared, especially with someone of another culture? I will refer briefly to the specific challenges ethnic and racial minorities face in regards to developing a healthy self-esteem and the consequent vulnerability to shame that may accompany that.

Some general remarks on shame

If we are lucky, we have grown up in what Winnicott (1960) called a "facilitating environment" for healthy development, by which he meant both reasonably nurturing caregivers as well as a safe environment. Such a facilitating environment suggests that a child can grow up with the expectation that both physical and emotional needs will be gratified in a reasonably predictable fashion. It is the consistency with which this cycle is repeated that instills a child with confidence that one's needs can be successfully expressed and that people in the immediate environment are able and willing to respond to them. If, on the other hand, the child wants for something, and wants for something and it does not come, confusion and self-doubt will likely ensue. As the child struggles to make sense of this lack of responsiveness, it is easy to wonder whether one is inadequate, defective, or unlovable? Or are those around the child unreliable, untrustworthy, or hostile in some way? Is the world a hostile place? Failure to obtain what one needs can occur on the most basic levels, food and safety, but also warmth and holding. Early childhood studies demonstrate that even very young infants try to engage their caregivers, making attempts to fascinate them into the pleasurable experiences of mutual gazing and play. It has also been shown that when mothers turn away from these intimate interactions, even for seemingly benign reasons such as answering the telephone, the baby becomes confused, subdued, and researchers speculate, ashamed (Ayers, 2003).

When a child experiences a pattern of rejections and ruptures, feelings of self-doubt as well as mistrust of the holding environment can develop. The environmental factors that contribute to a susceptibility to feeling shame are in place. Feelings of shame can be excruciating. "Shame is fundamentally a feeling of loathing against ourselves, a hateful vision of ourselves through our own eyes, although this vision may be determined by how we expect other people are experiencing us" (Morrison, 1994). Kaufman (1989, p. 29) writes of the internalization of shame. A significant person ruptures the mutual pleasurable experience of engagement and this leads to ambivalence about the object, who becomes both desired but also hated. The "defective self" is dealt with by splitting and turning on the perceived negative aspects of the self, creating an internal feeling of shame that is ongoing.

While all people experience feelings of shame, for some it is a more pervasive experience. Living in a culturally inhospitable milieu exposes one to shame experiences from an early age, so having a "good enough" experience is complicated, if not almost impossible, for persons of color growing up as part of a minority culture. Immigrants from other countries frequently write that they didn't "know" they were black or Asian until they came to the United States and discovered that they were now classified according to their minority status (Adichie, 2013; Akhtar, 2014b). Children of color in the United States witness the ways that their families are treated and the consequent challenge to a sense of dignity. Fleeting instances of disrespect can exist at the end of a spectrum that begins with so-called "microaggressions" (Sue, 2010). At the other end of the spectrum is the ongoing threat of more aggressive assaults that can result in death to the victim. Vigilance is necessary for survival.

Parents cannot seem omnipotent if children witness their fear, compliance, or second-rate status in society. Years after his father told him the story, Freud (1900a, p. 197) recounted the disappointment he felt when his father told him about the time an anti-Semitic youth knocked his hat off and shouted, "Jew, get off the pavement." To Freud's shame, his father simply retrieved his hat in order to avoid an altercation. "This struck me as unheroic conduct on the part of the big, strong man who was holding the little boy by the hand." It is more difficult to continue to see one's parents as invincible gods to idealize when one observes them in situations such as these or worse. Developing a healthy ego ideal is complicated when one's grandiose childhood wishes are dashed early and one's parents cannot seem omnipotent in the face of these cultural assaults (Freud, 1914c; Sandler & Holder, 1963).

Clinical illustrations

The following cases are intended to illustrate some of the ways that the complexities of racial and ethnic differences played a role in two patients. These brief examples bear as much resemblance to actual patients as I felt I could share without compromising their privacy. At times, the issues that are inherent in being part of a racial minority seemed to serve as a defense against psychological issues arising from family circumstances, internal conflicts and so forth. At other times, race or ethnicity was a very real issue that needed to be acknowledged as a reality.

Vulnerability to feelings of shame in a biracial man

In the following case, I wish to highlight the ways that the experience of growing up as a minority person can compromise one's ability to trust others and to consolidate a positive sense of identity. Despite the fact that these issues do get raised in treatment, both patient and analyst tend to tread softly around them. The analyst might hesitate and want to avoid provoking feelings of shame in the patient, given the injuries the latter has already suffered. It is the patient who then regulates the pace of unmasking such issues, in order to preserve his sense of dignity.

Clinical vignette: 1

> It was not easy for Mr. B. to seek a consultation because to do so stimulated the same feelings of neediness and vulnerability that he was experiencing in the relationship with his girlfriend. These were feelings that he hated. Over the course of his four-year relationship with S., there had been frequent and tempestuous arguments followed by periods of frozen silence. Her cruel iciness could render him helpless. When she was angry with him, she adopted a sullen, contemptuous stance toward Mr. B. that made him feel pitiful and impotent.
>
> The issue of Mr. B.'s ethnic origins permeated our work together from the beginning. He warned me about the mistrust he felt for many people and linked it to the experiences of being discriminated against in his town. It was clear that he would feel safe to talk about things only if he felt that his strengths would also be recognized. And because strength was very much associated with virility and physical prowess, he was afraid that these strengths would be overlooked if he became too emotional or felt too dependent on women, be it his mother, his girlfriends, or his female therapist.
>
> He was a handsome man in his late twenties who worked out regularly. While he was proud of his physique and dressed with an edgy panache, he was extremely sensitive about his short stature and ethnicity. His father was South Asian while his mother was a blonde Russian beauty. During elementary school, he was

not particularly aware of his ethnicity despite having grown up in an affluent white suburb. When he was twelve, a boy in his class called him a "dirty Indian." He was surprised and hurt. Perhaps that was the first time he truly became aware of his ethnicity, only vaguely realized before. He never mentioned the event to his parents. Instead, he suffered alone, blaming himself in some inchoate way for eliciting the slur. Because he still maintained vestiges of his childhood fantasies of his father's omnipotence, he had the notion that his father handled his minority status more successfully. In his efforts to metabolize this episode, he blamed himself for being defective, thus activating a split between a wish to be loved by the rejecting others as well as a burgeoning mistrust and dislike of his white counterparts at school.

In fact, his father sounded like something of a bantam cock who was trying to protect his boy by toughening him up to meet the challenges of this new country where the father was also an outsider. Father frequently praised another boy in his class for being a math wizard, apparently to whip Mr. B. into a competitive frenzy that would spur him to excel in all areas. The (unintended?) consequence of this strategy was that whatever Mr. B.'s accomplishments, he felt inferior and disappointed in himself, feeling that he could neither measure up to this rival nor succeed in pleasing his father. As if this were not enough, the father seemed to boost his own narcissistic needs by drawing comparisons to himself and his son, for example, "When I was your age, I had already left my family and was putting myself through college. I married your mother and I didn't ask anyone's permission." Sometimes he hated his father but more often he hated himself. He especially hated that he could be so wounded because then he felt weak, like "damaged goods." These feelings surfaced in dreams in which he was trying to drive to an important event, but found that someone had tampered with his car and he was powerless to drive it.

There was one way that Mr. B. felt he bested his father and that was in his relationship with his mother. Initially, he described her as a wonderfully nurturing presence whom he adored. He told me that he had spent many happy hours talking to her after school while she prepared dinner. She was always there, always supportive. However, over the course of his treatment, Mr. B.'s representation of his mother took many forms, not all of which were so benign. Her efforts to shape his character were subtler than his father's but were equally coercive. She tried to get him to do her bidding by shaming him into complying. When he was still very young, she could make him feel miserable for failing to take out the trash by telling him that she had thought he was a responsible boy, but apparently he was not. He would feel banished from the warmth of her affection and would retreat to his room, feeling ashamed of himself and guilty. There, he would spend hours obsessively putting together intricate ship models by himself. Like the baby who feels he is successfully fascinating his mother, but whose mother then turns away from his gaze, Mr. B. felt humiliated when his mother seemed to turn on him.

Mr. B.'s oedipal strivings were stimulated by his need to also serve as his mother's protector on more than one occasion. Occasionally, Mr. B.'s father would have a very stressful day at work and then become verbally abusive and physically menacing at home. As a child, Mr. B. would overhear the increasingly heated conflicts between his parents and worry about how far things might escalate. When Mr. B. was twelve years old, on the cusp of becoming an adolescent male, he heard his father shouting at his mother and threatening her. After listening for an endless couple of minutes, Mr. B. successfully intervened, shouting at his father to stop, thus enabling his mother to extricate herself from the situation.

Mr. B. was sensitive about being sensitive, and this triggered feelings of emasculation. The cumulative effects of his father's challenges, racial epithets at school, being at one moment his mother's knight in shining armor and in the next, her unreliable little man, left him with precarious feelings of self-esteem that he struggled to regulate. For the first few months of our work together, if he exhibited sadness or hurt in a session, he would leave the session and become angry at me and particularly at himself for revealing such softness. Occasionally, he felt that he had been manipulated into exposing these vulnerabilities and he would show up at his next session and take his distance by expressing his wish to not be there. In spite of this, he almost always arrived on time and never missed an appointment because of these feelings.

Although Mr. B. had excelled in school, graduated from excellent undergraduate and graduate programs, he frequently felt inadequate. He was drawn to the arts, visual and literary, but these did not comport with what he knew his father wanted for him. Mr. B. complained about his father's insistence that he do something practical, but he complied. His father had come to America with almost nothing and was a self-made man and Mr. B. admired him for it, albeit begrudgingly at times. He wanted to make his father proud of him and he certainly did not want to depend on his father financially. While Mr. B. could be defiant and blame his father for preventing him from following a passionate goal, it proved difficult for him to choose a more unconventional occupation or even to know what that might be.

Instead, he chose a profession that would garner financial rewards and respect, but was constantly ambivalent about it. Although he chose opportunities in cities and universities where he felt diversity was valued, he felt marginalized and opted out of many social and extracurricular activities where he felt self-conscious. His default defense was to say he didn't care or he didn't really like the people in his program (in graduate school) or at the investing firm where he worked. He always had a plausible excuse for his diffident attitude and failure to actively engage with his cohorts. I was always cautious about prematurely raising subjects that had the potential to make Mr. B. feel exposed, knowing that it would be injurious. While we often talked about his critical observations of others, it took time before he could fully acknowledge the extent to which these negative assessments protected him from feeling like an outsider who also longed to be an insider. He spoke often of how he never gave 100 percent of himself and couldn't understand why. It was too risky for him to try to become part of things and fail than to hold himself apart, superior in his observations of the inauthentic behaviors of others. At work, he felt excluded from the inner circle of colleagues and attributed this either to his ethnicity or the fact that "this just isn't what I want to do and I don't care." He was confused about how to be assertive or aggressively competitive as a minority male at work and likened his dilemma to Obama's problem campaigning against McCain. "He can't decimate him in a debate because if he does, he'll look like a savage. You can be a savage or a slave." Mr. B. wanted so badly to be perceived as an alpha male, but as the last statement shows, he also feared the consequences. This conflict was manifested in his extreme weight lifting regimen. He was highly competitive with the other men at his gym and frequently injured himself so that he was in a great deal of pain and had to interrupt his training for long periods of time.

> In fact, part of Mr. B.'s attachment to his brooding and erratic girlfriend had been her mixed ethnicity. Although he never articulated exactly what her ethnic roots were, I sensed that they differed from his. Why I didn't ask him directly pertains in part to my being uncertain of how to ask the question. How complicated would it have been for me to simply ask directly? I stumbled on what language to use and may have asked so euphemistically where her family was from that I learned the name of her hometown but not the answer I wanted, which was her precise ethnicity. Was her culture quite different from his or complementary, or comforting simply because she knew what it was like to grow up as a person who didn't quite belong anywhere? Undoubtedly, it would have been an avenue worth pursuing. I say undoubtedly it would have been useful, but as we never discussed it I don't know that for a fact. Nonetheless, the fact of her being what he called "happa" (a term that originated in Asia and is defined loosely as someone who is part Asian and part European) allowed him to feel that he was not alone because "she knew the dark places, too."

Unlike this case, there are others where racial issues are not discussed for a long time after the beginning of treatment. Often this happens because the analyst admires the patient and believes him (or her) to be capable of considerable social success. This can contribute to the analyst's failing to understand that the variable of race might still be precluding the patient from reaching his full potential.

The shame of being exposed for trying

Finding a patient smart and engaging, and noticing that he makes many references to restaurants, plays, and books that the analyst is familiar with might lead the latter to assume a greater similarity between their situations than actually exists. The clinical vignette that follows consists of such an occurrence.

Clinical vignette: 2

> On a sunny fall morning, Ms. P. arrived for her first session. She reported that she had been feeling depressed for over a year following the death of a much-loved aunt. Her friends had been urging

her to seek treatment. She was a very pretty woman with fine features and an intelligent look, neatly dressed, and well spoken, with an excellent ability to express herself and a sense of humor about herself that seemed to forecast a good prognosis. Ms. P. was a single African-American woman in her late thirties. She told me that she was ashamed to find herself still single, working at a job that had proved increasingly disappointing over the past several years, and apparently going nowhere.

I had the naïve sense that all she needed was support with her bereavement process and to have her obvious strengths mirrored to her. With a positive holding environment, she would be on her way. Because Ms. P. seemed so extremely competent and insightful, I underestimated the intractability of her increasingly negative view of herself. She had admired her aunt's independence and ability to live life on her own terms. They had shared similar intellectual interests in the theater and the arts, "NPR-type stuff" more often embraced by white people than her black friends. Her aunt's shared interests dignified her own and created less conflict when she recognized her preference for hearing an opera than seeing the Grammy Award shows the rest of her family preferred. She never wanted to be perceived as "uppity" so she was perpetually at odds with herself because in truth, she was an intellectually curious person with sophisticated taste. If she followed her internal directives, she found herself at odds with most of the black people she knew. And, more specifically, she despaired of finding a mate.

More recently she had felt resigned about it. The *New York Post* reported on November 2, 2014: "Indeed, of all US demographic groups, African-American women are least likely to date or marry across ethnic lines. Fewer than 10 percent of black women have non-black spouses—less than half the number of black men." Part of this is external: troubling 2013 and 2009 reports from dating network, OK Cupid, revealed that black women are the site's least-desired demographic—even by black men.

Ms. P. was keenly aware that her chances of finding a mate diminished with each passing year. Losing her aunt eroded whatever dignity she had felt in being single. In her entire extended family, almost everyone had found a mate, even her troubled sister. So what made her so undesirable? This had become the question that permeated her life, not only in regards to finding a partner, but also at work where she failed to achieve promotions and pay increases time after time. Since her aunt's passing, she had felt the absence of a partner acutely. She did not want to call on her many friends who would have been more than willing and eager to support her because she felt that to do so only emphasized her unmarried status. She dreaded the thought that her friends would feel sorry for her so she suffered alone, quietly, suddenly unmoored by the lack of a person who "got" her.

It was easy for me to admire Ms. P. and to imagine that with a little time she would be able to get herself out of this rut. I resisted her efforts to persuade me that she felt as badly as she actually felt. This was due in part to her excellent sense of humor. She seemed to have a sense of perspective about everything that she told me. She was so likeable and astute in her observations that I didn't appreciate the extent to which her sense of humor kept me from seeing the depth of her pain. I made far too many interpretations about why she might be failing to take into account her capabilities. In my own defense, I knew that she had been a star throughout her childhood, excelling academically as well as athletically. She had been awarded a scholarship to an excellent college where she had graduated with honors. It did become evident that her expectations for herself were unrealistically high. When she did not meet them exactly, she felt that she had failed.

Over time, I learned from her how this uncompromising ego ideal had been formed. Ms. P. had grown up in a part of the South where segregation persisted long past legislative rights for African-Americans. She had lived in a white neighborhood that sought to keep it that way. As one of the few black families, they were unwelcome. The family's home was vandalized on more than one occasion. Every day at school, kids jeered at her and called her the "N word" (i.e., "nigger"), even when she was a very young child. On one occasion, she made a friend, who invited to play at her house. She and her friend played outside until Ms. P. said that she needed to use the bathroom. Her friend explained to her unapologetically that she wouldn't be allowed in the house. She slunk home, never telling anyone of her pain and disappointment, the failed friendship a secret humiliation.

As she grew up, she walked an almost impossible tightrope. On the one hand, her family was sacrificing to make it possible for her to go to school in a good school district. She was expected to take advantage of these efforts by being an excellent student and participating in extracurricular activities of all kinds, which she genuinely wanted to do. At the same time, she did not want to draw attention to herself, inviting envy or worse from her white fellow students. So she tried her best to be outstanding without being noticed. For her, being superior at everything she attempted was necessary for survival and self-respect but it also felt like a dangerous enterprise that could result in any number of consequences.

Throughout the course of her career, she always sought challenging situations that allowed her to contribute in meaningful ways to those in need. When she spoke of her work, she was thoughtful and well informed. As she told me more about her workplace, I had the sense that she covered for her superiors who were often, according to her stories, inept. I thought about the political climate of the country where many organizations find it advantageous to hire women for high-level jobs as well as people of color. So why was she stuck in this modest position when she was outperforming her managers? It became evident that no matter how good her performance, she never received credit. She had learned her lessons well and was faithfully reproducing her high school experience. Her immediate manager appeared to like her, but did nothing to champion her cause. Colleagues in other parts of the organization gave her glowing reviews. This only highlighted the discrepancy between these evaluations and the one she received every year at headquarters: "Meets expectations." She told me that the only people who seemed to get ahead were the bubbly, blonde girls. She could tick off the names of women who had completely bungled assignments but were rewarded with new prestigious positions that required less work. I found myself being more and more supportive and less and less exploratory as I encouraged her to let people in positions of authority know all of what she really did. She would accept these suggestions politely but it was clear that she would never follow them up.

Session after session, we discussed her feelings of denigration at work. I was puzzled and frustrated by her resignation and halfhearted attempts to find a new job. Her refusal to use connections impeded her efforts, but she was embarrassed to tell her friends that she still had not found a job and was reluctant to ask them to put her in touch with their connections. If they tried to help her and she failed to get a job again, she would be mortified. In a similar vein, she made disparaging remarks about her appearance despite being an attractive woman. That too, was hidden beneath baggy brown sweaters and pants that camouflaged her beauty. Here again was the compromise formation that made her invisible to people around her, whether it be colleagues, managers, or potential suitors. She dreaded the idea that people would think she was trying to look attractive because if she failed she would "just look stupid and pathetic." When a friend at work gave her a colorful top for her birthday, she insisted on interpreting this as a criticism of her frumpy way of dressing rather than a vote of confidence. She returned the blouse without even trying it on.

After many iterations of this dynamic, we talked about why I seemed to be carrying the hope for her future and the confidence in her abilities while she was becoming more and more despondent. She slumped back in her chair and said that I was becoming just like her friends, believing in her, and that her inability to produce the results that we all thought she was capable of just made her feel pitiful and ashamed. To believe in her was to cause undue pressure, not to believe in her was to collude with her self-doubt. She was correct. Rather than joining others whose confidence emphasized her underperformance, I needed to simply remain empathic with her conflict.

Perhaps it was at this point that we began to talk more openly about racism in her workplace. I realized that I had been resisting her efforts to tell me that she was experiencing discrimination. Because I saw her in a positive way, and because I hadn't experienced discrimination in any consistent way, I hadn't been able to hear her. One hot humid day, she came in and decried the frizziness of her hair. I had been reading *Americanah* (Adichie, 2013), in which every other chapter described a scene at a braiding salon. Up until I read this book, I had felt as if I "should" know about braiding, weaves, hair straightening, and all of the politics involved therein. I had protected myself from saying something stupid, or even worse, inadvertently racist about hair by skirting the subject. This time I said, "Hair's really a big thing, isn't it?" She agreed, "One of the top five problems for African-American women." I told her that I had been reading this book that talked about braiding salons and she immediately identified the book. She was clearly pleased that I had read it. We went on to discuss the author and she told me that she was going to tell one of her best friends who hadn't read it yet that even her therapist had read it. This opened the door to more frank discussions of what she faced at work. We talked about the hierarchy of discrimination she perceived, with African-Americans at the bottom, then Hispanic, Asians, with whites on the top. She told me how often powerful women of color were described as "crazy." The more powerful they became, the angrier and crazier their descriptors. This elaborated earlier themes regarding her fear of being noticed for her strengths. She told me that she worried about how her fellow black colleagues at work would feel if she found a "better" job and left them behind. Would the unintended consequence be to make them feel betrayed or demeaned by her departure? This fear can apply in any job situation of course, but in this case the complications of race added layers of complexity to the quest for bettering oneself.

In this psychotherapy, my belief in her capabilities proved to be an impediment to her expression of deep shame regarding both her professional and personal life. It was important that I give up my white perspective about what she told me so that I could truly hear that her experiences in the world were different from mine and that my interpretation of them could be based on hers rather than mine.

Shame as a source of the analyst's inhibitions

There is a great fear of exposing oneself in a negative way that is endemic to the experience of shame. With regard to issues of cultural difference, there is a fear of exposing one's ignorance about the patient's background and especially that one will stumble upon unexamined prejudice in oneself in the midst of a therapeutic encounter. In addition, the analyst does not want to injure the patient by expressing some inadvertent microaggression. Terminology changes and the question of whether it is appropriate to say black, Black, or African-American can interrupt the free flow of the analyst's communications. The race conversation is once again part of the zeitgeist and it is more evident than ever before that any point of view can be construed as racist. In an effort to be racially sensitive, some well-intentioned analysts have questioned whether Euro-centrically derived psychoanalysis is the treatment of choice for African-American patients (Leary, 1995). But some have reacted to that effort to be sensitive to cultural difference as condescending in its own way. In addition, Leary (1995) points out that the therapeutic community has focused on race as an issue for minorities but not for whites, ignoring the fact that whites are an ethnic group as well. The US Census Bureau states that the US is projected to become a majority-minority nation for the first time in 2043. While the non-Hispanic white population will remain the largest single group, no group will make up a majority (www.census.gov/newsroom/releases/archives/population).

In therapy sessions with white patients, I have found that issues of race come up infrequently, as Holmes (2006) suggests, but when it does, there is shame associated with it. Recently, a prosperous white male patient told me about an incident on the subway where he moved to make way for a black man. At first, he did not tell me that the man was African-American but when he did, he expressed his shame that he felt proud of the fact that he moved for this particular man. He had wanted to tell me about it precisely because he felt proud. At the same time, he felt that his pride also exposed a streak of "noblesse oblige" that embarrassed him. He was afraid of appearing as if he felt superior for putting a black man's needs on the same level as his own. This highlights the degree of self-consciousness that accompanies many of our interactions with people who are from a different culture as well as our internal dialogue. Most of the time, we just don't discuss these feelings with anyone. After we discussed this incident, he was more able to plunge into a conversation about him being Jewish and perceiving me to be a WASP.

In the case of the Indian patient, there were a number of factors in myself that I didn't want to get "caught" having with him. I had been intrigued by India for many years and had recently realized a lifelong dream of traveling there for several weeks, so I was aware of trying to restrict my curiosity about the entire country to matters pertinent to his situation. At the same time, I felt that my knowledge was also superficial, based on novels, some history, some travel but not enough to even know the questions that might invite deeper exploration of his own ambivalent relationship to his Indian roots.

He had emerged from his early experiences of being denigrated as a "dirty Indian" with a deep vulnerability to feeling humiliated. His father's efforts to shame him into both academic and physical excellence that would ultimately protect him from the slings and arrows of a culture with much to offer but with the potential to exclude had made shame an intimate part of family life as well. Our sessions left him much more exposed and at times distraught than I realized, threatening his masculinity each time he revealed something he perceived as weak or soft. Handling such material required much tact; this involved an intuitive evaluation of the patient's problems, choosing the "right" one among many possible interventions, and retaining a fundamentally affectionate relatedness to the patient (Loewenstein, 1951; Poland, 1975).

While I was endeavoring to do this, Mr. B. needed his virility to be recognized and I was conflicted about his efforts. He was a very attractive man, smart and engaging, and I shied away from interactions that would expose my own feelings of attraction. Growing up in a family that seemed blandly without ethnicity, I have always gravitated toward people whose family histories and origins differ from mine and seem to have flavor that my own "white bread" background has lacked. Thus, in my efforts not reveal my fascination with what I saw as his more interesting background and his more exotic appearance, I subtly deflected any discussion of the sexual energy that existed between us. Toward the end of the psychotherapy, he admitted, with embarrassment, but also with the newfound confidence to tell me about it, that he'd had a crush on me. Had I been less worried about my own countertransference and being exposed myself, we might have worked through some of this together. His mother had been such a key figure in his life, depressed, demanding, and alluring, and he had felt both dependent and protected by her. Had we been able to explore more of this together, I believe it would have been helpful to him.

In the case of Ms. P. who didn't want to get caught trying too hard, I presumed that I understood her worth in the marketplace and as a person and that underneath her protestations, she felt about herself as I did but was too conflicted to reveal this. Much of this could be attributed to my personal lack of exposure to the kinds of prejudice, subtle and frightening, that she had experienced since she was a small girl. Holmes (2006) suggests that there is a "culture-wide defensive barrier" that allows us "to keep hidden what threatens us" (p. 221). I had taken innumerable diversity training classes and lived on the African continent for a year. The difference was, I had taken these classes and lived in Africa as a white person. As we say of the proverbial fish, it doesn't know it lives in water because it has always lived there.

Concluding remarks

I have tried to demonstrate some of the ways cultural differences interfere in the psychotherapeutic work of a white therapist working with people of color. We no longer think of the psychoanalyst as an omniscient "tabula rasa." Relational and intersubjective perspectives may contribute to better ways of working together as an analytic dyad to address cultural issues more openly. When the analyst recognizes that there are certain inevitable lacunae regarding cultural and socioeconomic factors affecting a psychotherapy, she is freer to explore them, rather than feeling ashamed of her ignorance. These factors are essential to keeping the treatment alive for the analytic couple. Avoiding them perpetuates the cultural barriers we seek to dissolve. Whenever we are successful in speaking authentically about these issues, both patient and analyst are enriched by the encounter.

CHAPTER TEN

The role of shame in treating maniacal triumph and paranoia

Patricia L. Gibbs

Both higher functioning neurotic patients and those experiencing regressed psychotic levels of functioning will be included in my illustrations of the psychoanalytic treatment of what I call *maniacal triumph and paranoia*. Because the negative therapeutic reaction occurs and is worked through in the transference and countertransference, Riviere's (1991) work has indicated that it was actually the strong loving attachment to the analyst—however masochistically or psychotically organized—that often contributes to the patient's refusal to recover. If the patient recovers, so the unconscious fear often goes, the patient will lose the therapist or analyst. There is often shame regarding the patient's awareness of what they feel to be their dependence upon the treatment and the analyst. Clinical vignettes will illustrate these dynamics shortly.

The work of Erving Goffman (1963) refers to the "spoiled identity" that often results in people who believe that they have suffered from stigmatization because of mental illness, physical deformities, blindness, and other psychosocial, racial, or ethic prejudices. Goffman says that the stigmatized person tends to have the same beliefs about his identity that non-stigmatized persons do, such that: "His deepest feelings about what he is may be his sense of being a 'normal person,' a human being like anyone else, a person who deserves a fair chance" (p. 7). Yet, "He may perceive, usually quite correctly, that whatever others profess, they do not really accept him and are not ready to make contact with him on equal grounds" (p. 7). Goffman concluded that the central feature of the stigmatized person's identity is acceptance, and focused his work on the lack of acceptance others accord to stigmatized individuals.

The main premise of this chapter is that self-acceptance is often a challenge for our patients, and contributes to negative therapeutic reactions and treatment impasses. Most importantly, I argue that for those in our profession, the stigma associated with both providing and receiving psychotherapy and analysis can have dangerous consequences. There is an unfortunate weakness in the common public understanding of psychoanalytic treatment and theory. Psychoanalytic theories of personality development can be easily misunderstood and used to assign blame to someone for the patients' symptoms or personality organization. How many times have we all heard patients being afraid that they will be blamed for loved ones' mental difficulties and suffering? It can become too easy to formulate a psychodynamic explanation of our patients' conditions that essentially amounts to blaming the parents—or the greedy and perverse uncle, the absent father, or the depressed mother—leaving a patient feeling even more stigmatized and ashamed. Goffman's work illustrates the crucial therapeutic task of helping our patients bear intense feelings of rage, shame, depression, and self-destructiveness during therapy. This chapter will focus on using analysis to work through the destabilizing regression accompanying the analytic treatment of shame and paranoia, thus avoiding analytic impasse.

Our culture's current focus is to demand empirical evidence to prove the efficacy of all psychotherapies, educational practices, and medical treatment. The pressure to produce empirical measurable evidence and predictable psychotherapeutic outcomes could easily leave many patients, candidates, and analysts quite consciously searching for certainty and normalcy in an effort to guarantee our claim to professional supremacy. I argue that the pressure to perfect not only the human condition, but also our psychoanalytic methods, would seem to only increase the likelihood of stigmatization against those seeking a type of mental health treatment that will not claim such certainty and perfection. I also assert that psychoanalytic methods often align with the aims and benefits accrued from the arts and humanities.

The widespread use of psychoanalytic and dynamic treatments in community clinics and the public sector will both reduce stigma and facilitate the widespread use of psychoanalytic and dynamic treatments. After witnessing the pervasive hopelessness, shame, and guilt expressed by patients whether in community clinics, hospitals, or my private practice, I have concluded that taking steps to bring psychoanalytically oriented treatments into widely available community and outpatient clinics will help to reduce the destructive effects of stigma preventing people from getting quality interventions. Psychoanalysts were once routinely included on the staffs of local private and public hospitals, and were also supervising in outpatient clinics. Psychoanalytically informed treatment was done with most, if not all, patients at one time. Furthermore, the line between patient and doctor could involve no sense of "the superiority of the doctor," as psychoanalysis rests on the premise that all aspiring to become psychoanalysts must be in their own analyses.

I have two objectives in this chapter. The first objective is my usual goal to demonstrate the power of the psychoanalytic approach using detailed clinical vignettes, largely to the "faithful"—or other psychoanalytic clinicians. The second objective is one of advocacy for both our patients and *the professions of psychoanalytic and psychotherapeutic practice*. I am advocating that we, as a profession, marshal our efforts to make analytic and dynamic psychotherapies available to the "widening scope of patients" we now routinely see in our private practices. The clinical vignettes I present will provide a basis for discussing the power of our psychoanalytic method, with the hope that we will come to widely apply our craft not only in private practice, but also in community mental health clinics and hospitals. It is here, in the public and community centers, that I believe we stand the greatest chance of fighting the stigma seen against those seeking mental health treatment.

The role of shame in treating maniacal triumph and paranoia

Understanding the role of shame in patients has been central for me in helping patients who are working through paranoia and maniacal triumph in psychoanalytic treatment. Grandiosity combined with vengeance, hate, and rage, or what I refer to as *maniacal triumph*, was observed frequently in the analytic patients that are considered here. Some of these patients had significant paranoid personality features, and paranoid associations during their treatments.

Paranoid patients have a tentative and impaired capacity to trust others, judge others' intentions, and maintain interpersonal relations without disruptive projections and introjections of hostility and terror, which Klein (1946), Freud (1911c), and Kernberg (1994) have all addressed. I have also found a strong sense of justice and an impassioned "pursuit for the truth," in the paranoid patient as "the search for truth" is repeated in the transference-countertransference. It is often important to these people that they are *believed*. I have concluded that the difficulties paranoid patients have in tolerating feelings of shame, as well as the analyst's collusion to avoid working with shame in both the transference and countertransference, perpetuates paranoia and repeated responses of maniacal triumph. This results in analytic impasse.

Shame proneness

Klein's (1940) connection of superego development to the process of mourning identified by Freud (1917e) is especially germane here. She states that the inner world is destroyed when actual loss occurs. Reality, then, is seen as impinging too harshly to allow the continued denial of loss without retreat to the primitive defenses associated with the paranoid-schizoid position. For paranoid patients, we can see that repeated childhood trauma and loss can be sufficient to largely confine adult functioning to that characterized by the paranoid-schizoid position (Davoine & Gaudillière, 2004; Lansky, 1992). Such conscious memories of violation would be expected to be extremely painful to bear affectively. Paranoid patients will initially struggle to face the awful truth—especially emotionally—of bearing the murderous feelings associated with the awareness of their abuse, as well as their own hateful negative introjections. Paranoia and the related feelings of vengeance, murderous rage, and hate are understood as being related to a profound sense of betrayal associated with unconscious violent persecutory anxieties. These anxieties over the course of development are then infused into the patient's basic object relations capacities, and compromise the ability to establish basic trust (Bion, 1959; Erikson, 1950).

A number of researchers, family therapists, and analysts have identified personality vulnerabilities that predispose individuals to shame

(Lansky, 1992; Schneider, 1977). Lansky has specifically identified a background of childhood trauma and violent abuse as such predisposing factors. Unconscious identification with a family member, commonly the same-sex parent who is held in contempt, is also a factor that predisposes individuals to disorganization and shame. Lansky concludes that this personality fragility is associated with an excessive need for a person or persons to stabilize personality cohesiveness. Riviere (1936) and Kohut (1972) have both discussed this excessive need for selfobjects, or a narcissistically organized dependency on others, which often contributes to analytic impasse.

The understanding of impulsive and violent acts within an understanding of shame-proneness offers compelling insights into clinical work with adults having backgrounds of childhood abuse, and those caught in the paranoid-maniacal triumph impasse. Many analysts conclude that the source of shame in impulsive acts such as self-mutilation, impulsive sexual encounters, violent acts, and binging, is preexisting. Shame, then, is evoked when a narcissistic wound is experienced by exposing the patient's desperate dependency on self/objects (Lansky, 1995; Retzinger, 1991a, 1991b).

Boundaries, analytic progression, and regression

Shame-prone paranoid patients must find effective ways to protect themselves and their fragile sense of boundaries, while slowly coming to trust the analyst within the deepening paranoid transference. I have found that the patient's unconscious experiences of boundaries will then take center stage in the clinical moment. For this reason, technical adherence to analytic technique can be important in keeping boundaries predictable and safe in the treatment. Once the patient begins to experience boundary violations in the transference, depression would be expected. The continued persecutory anxiety of intense paranoia, however, can eventually lead to the reliance on primitive defenses associated with psychosis. Both Helene Deutsch (1933), Melanie Klein (1935, 1952), and Joan Riviere (1936) have all described the manic character's inappropriate, omnipotent, and distorted sense of external reality. Joan Riviere, in speaking of such omnipotent denial, states that it "relates especially to the ego's object relations and its *dependence on its objects*, as a result of which *contempt* and depreciation of the value of its objects is a marked feature, together with attempts at inordinate and tyrannical *control and mastery of its objects"* (p. 139, italics in the original). This type of omnipotent denial is especially seen in a more thorough discussion of the paranoid patient's remarkable ability to both progress and regress in analytic treatment. The clinical vignette that will be presented shortly is typical of a high-functioning paranoid patient in analysis or psychodynamic psychotherapy. After periods of analytic progression, where intermittent psychotic functioning was repeatedly avoided, I would observe these patients defensively return to fantasies and behaviors based on maniacal triumph.

Subjectively—to the patient—there may seem to be a great deal of initial benefit derived from the active and aggressive emotional expression of hate, vengeance, and grandiose retaliation. I concluded, however, that ongoing maniacal triumph was associated with analytic impasse. This kind of impasse manifested when patients repeatedly returned to unmodulated expressions of rage, hate, profound mistrust, and depressive withdrawal and isolation. The patient's relinquishing of omnipotent attempts to "suffer no loss" would have to be done slowly. Only this painful work could allow mutative analytic mourning in the transference-countertransference (Gibbs, 2007a, 2007b).

Clinical vignettes

The first clinical vignette of analytic work will illustrate the role of shame in working through paranoia and maniacal triumph. We will observe the features of a deepening working alliance with an analytic patient, as well as the eventual return to expressions of maniacal triumph and impasse. The patient was in a four days per week reduced fee analysis for eight years. He mostly used the couch, though he would occasionally sit up.

Clinical vignette: 1

> Mr. T., a successful young businessman, began his session by asking if I was familiar with a particular movie series. He went on to recall how he would view these movies as a young boy, with his siblings and cousins. Mr. T. was the eldest boy, thirteen at that time, and was left in charge of his older sister, and younger sisters and brothers. He came from an upper middle class and socially prominent family, and explained it was yet another weekend that they

were all left alone. Mr. T. recalled a particular movie in which a man working in a doll factory puts an evil soul into a doll. He described in detail how frightened they all were—though the boys, he said, "were trying to act brave and 'macho.'" *His mood suddenly changed*, and he went on: "It was so funny! My little brother would take a big cushion and put it over his head. I would laugh at him and call him 'a little chicken!' He would say—'Ah, I'm not afraid—just bored.'"

He continued describing his confusion: "I knew it was just a movie—but I don't know—it seemed pretty real. And so I would tell myself, it isn't real, it's only a movie. I'd say it all through the movie." *His mood again changed, as he seemed to delight sadistically in his own terror and confusion, as well as that of his siblings*: "I mean it was really funny! My sisters would scream—*but they wouldn't leave.*" After some brief silence, he said he believed he was only four years old when he began watching the horror films alone with an older teenage cousin.

He went on: "I don't know why I'm thinking of this, but when we traveled overseas, my mother, sisters, and me ended up going together to a festival while my father went somewhere else with my little brothers and uncles. I was about nine, and I didn't speak French, of course. My Dad would always go off with his brothers, and leave me to take care of my Mom and sisters. So my Mom gives me some money to buy tickets. I come back with the change and tickets, and my Mom and oldest sister start yelling at me: "Are you stupid?! You were *cheated*; he took your money, and didn't give you the correct change!" They all started laughing at me. I really hate my Mom when I think of it. It was awful!"

I said: "The terror and shaming was real, you knew that, and you tried to tell yourself, 'It's funny, it's not scary, it's no big deal.'" Later in the session he said: "I think I was about four years old when my father ..." and Mr. T. trailed off. He shortly said, in a calm and articulate manner: "No one ever knew what would happen—it could be really bad." He went on to recall how his father and mother and extended family would argue all the time. "The yelling, the damn yelling—all the time. Then, just cover it up. No one talked about it. Everyone would keep everything quiet, of course .... The whole time I was watching those movies I remember thinking: '*Did the people know that Jason was going to kill them? Did they know what kind of person he was?*'"

Mr. T. missed the next session and did not call until well into the hour to say "an unavoidable meeting had come up!" He walked into the following session looking irritated, and before lying on the couch, *looked at me and sharply said*: "I'm sure you understand about the missed session." Mr. T. then repeated that a meeting had required much more time than anticipated, though he also soon revealed that he had known about this extended meeting for some time. After stating my decision to bill Mr. T., and my refusal to simply reschedule the missed appointment, Mr. T. sighed angrily, and said nothing. I said: "You seem quite angry that I won't reschedule, though you knew of this meeting and didn't bring it up months ago, when we could have talked about it." Mr. T. then graciously replied that he completely understood, denied any anger, and said he would of course pay for the missed session. The remainder of the session seemed superficial, with Mr. T. discussing business and financial plans in minute obsessive detail.

About a month later, Mr. T. came in saying, as he lay down on the couch: "I curse the day I met my stupid wife! The bitch, I hate her! I have more important things to think about than her! Her—her!" There was a brief silence. Saying no more about his wife, he said: "I know the managers at [a competing firm] have been fraudulently billing. They've gotten the contract retainers based on this crap, while they're trying to cozy up with our guys! I know who they're getting their leads from—my guys know it. Everyone knows it! They're *cheating* us! So I walked right in—I filed a complaint with the Commission, and handed a copy of it to Ralph [the competing firm's CEO]. The bastard! I put it in his hands! There—fucker—there is the bomb, it's right in your hands! You feel it ticking!"

There was silence, and after a few minutes, I said: "Could we imagine that you feeling cheated by the competing firm is related to you feeling cheated here—feeling that I've cheated you out of a session by billing you, instead of rescheduling?" Mr. T. quickly said: "That has nothing to do with this! *They're crooks, I'm telling you! Bastards! They won't get away with it!*"

The remainder of the session was filled with Mr. T.'s intense emotional expressions of hate, rage, and vengeance. Much later, after several months, Mr. T. expressed amazement that he had been so nasty, eventually saying: "I can't believe that I blew up at the guy like that. I was shaking; I could feel my face turning red as he walked in. I knew I had to say something—my mind just went blank—then I exploded."

It was difficult for Mr. T. to see that he was not-so-unconsciously speaking to me in the session *as if* I was his wife—"Her! Her!" A deeply religious man, he could not entertain the notion that he could even remotely view someone other than his actual wife as his spouse. I came to understand that this may have helped Mr. T. express his extreme contempt and hate in the sessions to me. He reported avoiding talking with such emotion and rage to his wife. Only after years of analytic work did Mr. T. begin to report the arguments he was having with his wife.

Mr. T. frequently returned to expressing rage, hate, and vengeance in the treatment. This portion of clinical material reveals Mr. T.'s paranoia, and his childhood experiences involving humiliation, and verbal and physical abuse. He ends the last session of this clinical vignette repeating in the transference the same rage, hate, and vengeance toward his business associates, wife, and me, that he had described in his home growing up. While Mr. T. was repeatedly exclaiming: "It is so funny," about his siblings' terrified responses, I knew it was important to speak to the reality of the terror that he was describing. Mr. T.'s insistence that horrified reactions were "so funny!" are evidence of his confusion regarding *affective realities*, as we then see Mr. T. marshal his manic defenses against the denial of the reality he recalled in his sessions (Gibbs, 2004; Lewis, 1971).

In the following vignette, we will also see Mr. S. working through paranoia and maniacal triumph; however, Mr. S. presented himself differently than Mr. T., especially in terms of temperament and affect expression. Mr. S. was mild-mannered and calm. His rage and vengeance was directed inward masochistically. Such was not the case with Mr. T.

Clinical vignette: 2

Mr. S. was a middle-aged professional in health care technology. Prior to going into this field, he had served as a federal police officer for several years. He was raised in a middle class family whose members prided themselves on being hard-working. Both of his parents were first-generation college graduates. They were "'intellectuals'—but not snobs," Mr. S. explained. Early in Mr. S.'s initial two days per week psychotherapy he reported he had been severely bullied as a school-age child. As his psychotherapy progressed I recommended increasing the frequency of his sessions, which was done slowly over a two year period until he was on the couch four days per week. He reported seeing another therapist years prior to consulting me for "depression, low self-esteem, and a constant sense of hopelessness and dread," which years later continued to be pervasive in his daily life. He said medication had been intermittently tried, to no avail. He did report being happily married, with three children. Throughout his analysis he reported his greatest satisfaction coming from being with his children and wife. His dread, depression, and dissatisfaction were understood by Mr. S. as being the result of feeling no satisfaction at any point in his adult work life.

Mr. S. begins his session saying he is "disgusted" with a number of internet posts which colleagues had made in his field of health care technology. Some of the posts are authored by peers or friends outside of work, though most were made by those completely unknown to him. He states angrily: "It really infuriates me! They are *so* certain that their viewpoint is the only right one! The conceit, the judgment—condemning the other guys—so *sure* that they are right. It reminded me of being in the Reserves. In a way I can see what some of them were saying. The military had—at least in my opinion as I saw it—a very dark view of human nature. Essentially they believe that people will rob, cheat, steal, kill—that people are inherently self-centered. 'Kill or be killed,' you'd hear it all the time. So their bottom-line argument was since this is the way people are, it's best to make sure—no matter what you have to do—that you are on the winning side," he said. "No matter what you have to do," I said. "Exactly!" he continued, "no matter if you have to lie, cheat, steal, kill—sell-out your principles or your buddies—exactly right!" "Sounds similar to your experience playing football in high school," I said. "Yes, it was funny—I remember I could never feel good about winning. I always felt—I don't know, I didn't really enjoy it," he said. "It was obvious that most of them loved it—smashing someone. In the locker room they would say the meanest things. The worst thing you could say was: 'You are weak—a loser! Just like a girl!'" He continued: "It was disgusting to me.

My brother told me he would feel the same way—guilty: he would feel ashamed if he won academically—which he always did."

"They did it because they could get away with it," I said. "That's exactly right," he said calmly and with conviction. "It's hard to see—this dark side of humanity," I said. "It's hard for me," he continued. "But it's also hard to be so cynical. One of my friends posted something I have very strong feelings about. We have very different opinions about things—opinions about the way a company or government should distribute resources and motivate people. I said what I had to say—I wouldn't say I rained on his parade—well, maybe I did. He was feeling very good about his viewpoint, which I disagreed with vehemently, and so I—right there where everyone could see it on the website—did a pretty good job of backing my opinions up. I was very civil and articulate. I actually prefer this kind of debate. Really, if I hadn't cooled down, I would have torn him apart. I wanted to call him an ignorant selfish bastard!"

"We might ask—why do you always have to be the nice guy, the civil reasoned one?" I said. "Yeah, that makes me think of my father," Mr. S. said. At his funeral, some of his coworkers said that he was known to be outspoken. He would argue and debate a point, and never back down. I know he could be that way. I remember thinking growing up that I didn't want to be like him—it was embarrassing to me. He'd get going on something: I just wanted to disappear." "He called attention to himself," I said. "Yes," Mr. S. replied, "and I hated that. I didn't want to be the center of attention." There was silence for a few moments, and then Mr. S. said, "Everyone knew us in town. And especially my father. Everyone knew my brother and me."

As I was listening to Mr. S. I noticed that he had not connected his previous experiences of being bullied to his awareness that he had to be "the nice guy," and to his inability to enjoy success, victory, and pleasure. We had already observed these connections by that time in his four days per week analysis. His unconscious resistance to experiencing pleasure and victory had been well cemented by his identification with the bullied and defeated. Mr. S. would simply feel shame, disgust, and deep unworthiness were he to identify with those who had prevailed over him as a bullied child. This type of self-defeating masochism I have found to be especially common in men. Mr. S. reacted in the transference with experiences of shame, feelings of dread, and expectations of inevitable failure. John Steiner's work, *Seeing and Being Seen* (2011) was particularly helpful in describing shame-infused experiences of masochism and guilt. Being seen with the critical gaze of the Other, Mr. S. unconsciously concluded he could not construct a Self he could protect and take pride in—which became a primary analytic goal of the remainder of his eight year analysis.

The bullying that Mr. S. experienced was found to be central to understanding him, and what appeared to be his self-sabotaging masochism. This masochism was directly related to his experiences of shame, providing an affectively intense underpinning for his repeated experiences of maniacal triumph. The repetition of these masochistically organized expressions of maniacal triumph was pervasive in the course of his treatment. His masochism contributed significantly to analytic impasse and negative therapeutic reactions in working through maniacal triumph.

The following clinical vignette illustrates the difficulty that the negative therapeutic reaction can present for some patients in their efforts to be less masochist, suicidal, anxious, and depressed.

Clinical vignette: 3

Ms. C. came from a working class background. Both of Ms. C.'s parents were children themselves of parents who lived through the Depression. This sociocultural factor seemed to repeatedly impress its shadow on Ms. C.'s temperament and ability to trust, even precipitating events which led her into my practice. She had enjoyed a successful career in finance and manufacturing until her early forties. She frequently reported liking her work and many responsibilities, and said she was on friendly social terms with most of her colleagues. After over two decades of such stability and satisfaction, a long-brewing political change at her employment resulted in colleagues she once trusted "setting her up" to cover their own mismanagement of funds.

I have seen this a few times in my practice, and imagine many of us have: I immediately had the sense that Ms. C. was *too good*—too keenly trying to please; too ready to give the benefit of the doubt when it seemed clear no such benefit was warranted. In the ensuing years, she felt less fulfilled in her marriage, and was generally unhappy and overwhelmed. Yet she said she seldom expressed anger at her husband, boss, colleagues, or children. When I would suggest Ms. C. was angry with someone currently, or had been angry at her mother and father, she would calmly say: "Getting angry never solves anything."

Perhaps because I did work in inpatient facilities and community mental health clinics, I saw many people with a history of inpatient hospitalizations. After four years of psychoanalysis with me, starting at three times weekly, and eventually moving to four times per week, Ms. C. told me she had been hospitalized for a "nervous breakdown." She had never revealed this until well into her analysis. She also reported that her previous therapist told her that she would no longer see her after her hospitalization. After four years in Ms. C.'s analysis with me she had long ago returned to work. We carried on as we had—now with this new revelation of her prior hospitalization.

Ms. C. reported that she was functioning well in her high-stress home and career duties—or so she would say in the analysis. Curiously, though, in the analysis she became more dependent, calling me frequently and urgently pleading that I call her between sessions. Fortunately, I had reason to go back to studying the work of Joan Riviere and other Kleinians. This was not the first time I had read this work, though upon reading Riviere, I was able to see both my patient and my own countertransference much more clearly. I'll discuss how Riviere's work was helpful in my work with Ms. C. toward the end of this chapter.

Now into a four days a week analysis, Ms. C. came to her session after work, and reported exhaustion. She began: "I don't know if I am depressed—like I was before ... and does it really matter? Who cares? The budget is still due. The kids still have homework. My husband still can't drive them to soccer ..." Her resigned soft voice tailed off. "I really hate this time of year. The days are getting darker, shorter. My brother is going out of town ... So we won't see them for quite a while ... That was one thing about my Mom—she did the whole show—all the relatives came over a lot, food galore. She was so busy ... of course, she worked, she had to—but she did it all. I was the oldest, so I was expected to take care of all my brothers and sisters. I resented them—maybe I still do [there was several minutes of silence] .... So, I'm sorry I kept calling you. I can't explain it … just hearing your voice makes me feel better." I said: "You said you didn't know if you could make it if I didn't call you back." She pleaded: "*I told you* I just needed to hear your voice. Are you to get rid of me too?!"

Such an encounter was frequent with Ms. C., and also with other patients from time to time in my practice. Ms. C. would describe years of crushing depression during which she would wish she would die in her sleep, and wish she had never been born. Although she never made a suicide attempt, she did put herself in relationships and work situations where she was deceived, manipulated, cheated, and abused. She consciously knew she was in a good marriage and now, a good career, yet she constantly expected the worst, and felt disappointed and hopeless. This pattern only seemed to harden the further we went along in the analysis.

Several themes began to emerge in my mind in an attempt to understand what appeared to be masochism, dependency, self-hate, and depression. Extreme anxiety regarding any change, and Ms. C.'s absence of the expression of anger in sessions, as well as her *insistence* that she felt no anger, were all fairly constant. Changes, such as the seasons changing, or seeing her children graduating and moving away, would bring months and sometimes years of her attempts to suppress her feelings of anger and bitterness, as well as her intense experiences of anxiety and depression. Ms. C. would isolate herself from relatives and colleagues, though, being a gracious lady, she would be careful to put the blame on *herself*, never others. She was raised in a conservative and religious family where "women were to be pleasing and supportive." Though this seemed to be a rather typical presentation of "anger turned inward depression" I frankly marveled at her ability to *never* express anger.

Always impeccably dressed, with a purse, dress, and high heels, Ms. C. entered her session: "So, you never called me back," she softly said. "What comes to mind?" I asked. There was considerably more silence, and then she said: "So, you are giving up on me?" I knew I had to choose my words carefully, and remain calm and compassionate. Ms. C. was all too ready to blame herself for everything, and turn her feelings of vengeance and hate on herself. I eventually said: "Your call indicated that *you* were giving up—giving up on the analysis, on me, on yourself. You did everything but state that you would kill yourself if I didn't call you back.

We have talked about how you now believe these very kind of calls were what resulted in your previous therapist committing you to the hospital." It was not an unusual confrontation, and we had talked of this very topic repeatedly by this time in her analysis.

Ms. C. slowly sat up from the couch and then looked at me. She then immediately *screamed*: "Oh—so—I can't need you! You can just ignore me! You'll never see me again—don't worry about me!!" She ran from the couch, picked up her purse, and made haste to the exit door.

I stood up and said: "Please come back and lie down on the couch." I knew I had to remain calm and sincere. She turned around and looked at me—and we looked at each other for several seconds. I knew I had to try to prevent her from leaving, and make it as safe as possible for her to stay. Beyond my initial plea that she *not leave*, I cannot remember what I said. I suspect whatever I said could not be learned from a book or technique seminar—only from my own analysis. Upon writing this chapter, I did think about two supervisors who would essentially say: "Go with your gut—the words will come."

She slowly came back and sat on the side of the couch. "I just feel so *scared every time* I think of another shrink giving up on me. But I think it's more than that. It's like my boss—I never thought he would betray me like that—I lost my career. I think he became too successful—had too much power. I was nothing to him—*nothing*. He got rid of me .... *I feel so embarrassed that I yelled—I'm sorry—I didn't mean to do it*." "Hard to trust that anyone would want to hear it from you—that anyone—even here you tell us, could or would hear of your anger," I replied. "Yeah," she said. A few minutes later the session ended with Ms. C. quietly and calmly walking out the door.

The next session, which was the next day, Ms. C. came in and began talking about her father. She was animated, seemed excited, and talked quickly: "I think I am a lot like my father. You know he had a nervous breakdown too, and couldn't work for a while. We were all still pretty little, and so my Mom went to work. She worked, and Dad was home with us for a few years. But he was always in his own little world. He would just do his puzzles, and read the paper—all day. So last night I was thinking—maybe it is just hopeless—maybe it is all in the genes." She paused for a bit, and then seemed more reflective. She eventually said: "I remember when he found out that I was really having trouble with depression when I was working before I got married. He said: 'Don't worry, things will get better when you just stop giving a damn.'" Then angrily, and with anguish she said: "I wish I could stop *caring* about losing my old job—and about all those people there. I wish *I could hate them!*"

The next several years until Ms. C.'s successful termination she talked about the enormous shame she felt about being hospitalized, her old therapist no longer being willing to see her, and her colleagues betraying her. This shame was woven around the shame she felt about being fired—"cast out" as she would say, by "everyone."

Discretionary shame, boundaries, and masochism

The Kleinian view of narcissism provided me with a conceptual link that helped redirect my technique to include working through affectively charged experiences of shame. This proved to be key in resolving the repetitive paranoid-maniacal triumph cycle. As has been pointed out by many contemporary analysts, Freud focused on feelings of anger and guilt, to the relative exclusion of shame. The Oedipus complex and the role of the repetition compulsion were both central in Freud's construction of narcissism, and can help to illuminate analytic impasse and treatment failures: "… a force that is defending itself by every possible means against recovery which is absolutely resolved to hold onto illness and suffering" (Freud, 1937c, p. 242). I believe that it can be argued that Freud identified the consequences of unresolved shame, without specifically using the word "shame" to explain the mechanisms of analytic impasse. Today we know that many analysts have equated the omission of shame work with analytic impasse (Bion, 1959; Lansky, 1992; Lewis, 1971; Retzinger, 1991b; Schneider, 1977; Steiner, 2011, 2013).

Freud's neglect of shame may be significant, though I believe it is Freud's early view of narcissism that is most problematic here (1914c). Klein came to see narcissism as a symbiotically organized object relations capacity centered on possessing, merging with, and controlling the object. This view of narcissism illuminates the paranoid mechanisms of projection into—and control of—the Self and the Object. Klein's view of narcissism is compatible with the use of Self/Objects to stabilize the fragile personalities I often saw in my paranoid patients. This Kleinian understanding of narcissism makes is readily apparent that paranoid patients—even when psychotic—are object related.

Klein's understanding of narcissism, then, differs from Freud's view that narcissistically organized individuals are self-absorbed, often to the point of not having the capacity for object relatedness. The problem in paranoia, as I came to see it, is with the patient's difficulty establishing *stable and safe* Self and Other boundaries. The affect modulation necessary to have a more whole object relations capacity is not easily possible for the paranoid patient. Thus, we see possessing, merging with, projecting into, and controlling—the Self/Object in paranoid patients (Bion, 1959; Freud, 1911c; Klein, 1940).

Carl Schneider's work (1977) proposes two types of shame: disgrace-shame and discretionary shame. The essential nature of shame, Schneider explains, is ambivalence: "If one stands judged and inadequate before one's better self, one still possesses that better self ... while shame may separate the self from the other, it also points to a deeper connection. In shame, the object one is alienated from, one also still loves" (p. 28).

Of course, one can also be alienated from one's self. In discretionary shame one exercises an appropriate restraint for a valued relationship, as well as often exercising this restraint in the relationship one has with oneself. This type of shame does not involve exposing discrediting qualities, as in disgrace-shame, but rather arouses shame simply by the act of exposure.

Schneider's clear illustrations of discretionary shame helping to protect oneself, and one's relationships, helped me to direct my technique toward integrating shame by focusing some treatment interventions on establishing boundaries. The initial subjective sting of shame is often experienced as self-negation, for example: shame and self-negation were experienced by Mr. T. when his face turned red, his mind went blank, and he could not confront his associate while appropriately protecting himself. We can also see this sting of shame in Ms. C.'s experience of dependency on me and her previous therapist. Helping patients to identify and use experiences of discretionary shame—in the clinical moment in the transference-countertransference—can be a powerful affective tool to help patients establish appropriate and protective Self boundaries, and regulate affect.

In considering the shame that Mr. S. felt, it was clear that it was associated with his self-destructiveness especially in terms of his self-worth. I concluded that it was related unconsciously to his dependency needs, his fear of losing important people, and his fear of losing the respect and love of other people if absolute obedience and perfection was not accomplished in the eyes of the Other (Riviere, 1936). Here, Freud's (1924d) guilt-based understanding of oedipal rivalry combined with masochistic attempts to atone for one's aggression, was also theoretically helpful to me. Unlike Mr. T., with Mr. S. his competitive edge only seems to inflame his feelings of shame and humiliation rather than help him to resolve his oedipal fixation or his masochistic stance. Interpretations based on Riviere's negative therapeutic reaction—his need, dependency upon, and fear of losing his primary objects—were initially necessary for me to consider technically in both Mr. S.'s and Ms. C.'s narcissistic vulnerability and masochistic stance. With Mr. T. I found direct interpretations of his competition could be handled when combined with Kleinian object-related interpretations of Mr. T.'s envy and manic-omnipotent tendencies early in his analysis.

Working through paranoia and maniacal triumph

The literatures on the effects of trauma and the expression of violent emotions are directly relevant to working through paranoia and maniacal triumph. Lansky (1995) and Retzinger (1991) have found that victims of physical, verbal, and sexual abuse are known to be highly sensitive to shame. The affective experience of shame is associated with both the violent boundary violations occurring during *actual* abuse, and the overwhelming feelings of dependency and helplessness on a shaming object during the abuse, *and in the transference.*

We can refer back to Mr. T.'s violent outburst following my charge for his missed analytic session. The expression of rage toward his wife, business associates, and me are understood as Mr. T. feeling small, embarrassed, or *shamed in the transference.* Such expression of Mr. T.'s rage, of course, is also associated with me charging him for his missed session. Helpless dependency in the transference can be seen in Mr. T. reporting his feelings of terror watching movies with his siblings—and his denial of this terror: "It's so funny!" These feelings of impotence and shame, however, were to remain too affectively overwhelming for Mr. T. to be contained by my verbal interpretation, without frequently resorting to maniacal triumph. Thus, Mr. T.'s experience of shame and impotence could not be contained by *his verbal expression of his feelings*, but instead were *acted out* in his verbal explosions. Bion's (1962) work on the precursors to thought—namely action, perceptual hallucinations, and psychosomatic symptomatology—provide a conceptual understanding of Mr. T.'s frequent return to explosive *action*, prior to his ability to contain his rage with appropriate, self-protective verbal expression.

When working with psychotic patients who are actively hallucinating and delusional in the analytic hour, the analyst must find a way to connect with the patient's reality without the patient being too overwhelmed with shame to contain the analytic work in the transference (Gibbs, 2009a). My encounter with Ms. C., and her desperate plea: "Oh! I'm not allowed to need you! Are giving up on me?!" illustrates the affective intensity, as well as the object-relatedness needed between the patient and analyst for productive analytic work to occur with shame.

Retzinger (1991b) a family and marital therapist and researcher, found that videotapes of marital and family treatment with patients involved in highly conflictual verbal interchanges have shown that the most explosive verbal expressions are associated with a person feeling unconsciously helpless and shamed. Thus, the recollections of verbal and physical abuse by Mr. T. were associated with him feeling helplessly dependent on the Self/Object in the transference. In Kleinian terms, his narcissistically organized symbiotic object relations capacity was centered on possessing, merging with, and controlling his wife, business competitor, and me. My comments, such as: "It was hard to keep your cool and think clearly when you saw him. Only later were you able to think clearly—of what you wished you had said," were used, and seemed to slowly facilitate Mr. T.'s establishment of protective Self boundaries.

After two more years of analysis, Mr. T. reported being able to confront the same colleague assertively, and without verbal abuse. I believe that his older male colleague had unconscious transference associations with some of Mr. T.'s most painful childhood experiences of shame, helplessness, and rage. Though a highly educated and articulate man, Mr. T. struggled for years with such verbal assaults when his feelings of hate, vengeance, and rage were triggered by unconscious shame.

Mr. S. was a large man and presented himself with a commanding and self-assured manner, initially putting others at ease. He was known for playing aggressive sports into middle age, being well-spoken, and usually calm. I came to see his initial presentation as an effective disguise for both himself and me in the transference-countertransference. Initially, my own countertransference made it difficult for me to identify his masochism and self-defeating dependency that impeded his analytic progression. I had used Mr. S.'s calm and commanding manner to block my awareness of his masochism. Mr. S.'s dependency was initially associated with my anger linked with the necessity to recognize the limits of my own omnipotence. Once I was both consciously and unconsciously able to return the responsibility of the analysand's role to him, I could contain my own frustration and anger, rather than continue to enact with the patient a sadomasochistically organized impasse (Boesky, 1982; Joseph, 1988). Mr. S. became increasingly able to relinquish his negative therapeutic reaction, with the analytic work becoming again productive. Though he could be mistrustful, I eventually came to see the shame Mr. S. felt as being significantly related to his masochism, and much less to paranoia. My comments, "So we might ask, why do you always have to be the nice guy, the civil reasoned one?" helped to facilitate Mr. T.'s working through his masochistic resistances.

Mr. T., Mr. S., and Ms. C. were all able to accept transference work and interpretations very gradually after years of slowly working through the painful affects associated with paranoia, shame, and masochism. These initial years of analysis involved periods of analytic progression, followed with a return to maniacal triumph impasse. The clinical material of Mr. T. and Ms. C. are examples of patients slowly working through the paranoid-maniacal triumph impasse.

I cannot deny that it was not easy to sit with Mr. T.'s maniacal and explosive rage. I could certainly feel the pull of my own anger toward him, as well as my own feelings of full-blown maniacal triumph and vengeance for *all crimes ever committed towards me*. It was neither pleasant, nor anything to be proud of. I did understand how Mr. S. was avoiding his feelings of loss by refusing to sit with his painful feelings of grief, sadness, shame, and regret. Moral outrage, vengeance, and retaliation were all more active than sitting helplessly with feelings of loss and grief (Gibbs, 2009a, 2009b, 2011).

Knowing of Ms. C.'s numerous threats of "wishing she was dead" and her hospitalization, and having other similar patients in my practice, made me more than once not only question my own judgment, but incur the expense of costly consultations and further personal analysis. Mr. T.'s well buried masochism could only be addressed when I was able to face my own masochism, omnipotent denial of human limitation, and depressive feelings of defeat and hopelessness. I mention these countertransference challenges as a reminder of the fallacy of finding a "guaranteed" type of psychological, psychosocial, or psychoanalytic intervention that will always work with every analyst/patient dyad.

Concluding remarks

The role of shame in creating self-inhibition, self-blame, paranoia, hate, and vengeance, in what I have called maniacal triumph, across the functional axis, has been the focus of this chapter. It is my position that the role of shame contributes to analytic impasse, and the ongoing expression of self-destructive self-blame, hate, vengeance, and paranoia. I have argued that the power of working in the transference-countertransference is that such work allows strong affective realities to be reworked to a fuller maturity and capacity. Only this can eliminate empty intellectualization and validate operationally our developmental object-related understanding of the conscious and unconscious mind. It is here, I believe, that we will have to be content to rest our case in terms of psychoanalytic clinical evidence.

I have further argued that psychoanalysts are uniquely trained to provide effective psychoanalytic treatment to individuals across the neurotic-psychotic functional axis, within a variety of community, inpatient, and private clinics. This brings me to my final question: *Could shame also be playing a role in our profession's retreat from the widespread treatment of psychological disorders and everyday life stresses outside of private practice?*

I believe that psychoanalysts have a unique opportunity to hone their craft with all who need and want psychological intervention—thereby keeping the role of *stigma* from preventing those who could benefit from our approach from ever receiving it. I would like to conclude by briefly returning to the role of stigma associated with receiving treatment for any mental health condition. An appreciation for the humanities within our psychoanalytic profession, I believe, is one of the most powerful means of reviving interest and confidence in psychoanalytic treatment, especially for patients experiencing paranoia, maniacal triumph, and shame proneness.

Recently, psychoanalysts, psychotherapists, journalists, philosophers, and a host of other social scientists have made a broad call to justify the legitimacy of their methods to advance the human condition based on more than empirical evidence, economic profit, or other quantifiable measures. I would like to add my voice to this chorus. Azzone (2013) considers that depression is best seen as a psychoanalytic problem, stating: "Moral and subsequently psychological causes of depression have always played a secondary or marginal role in the history of psychiatry" (p. 9). Calling depression "socially shared representations of pain" (p. 49), Azzone takes a historical view of humanity's understanding of depression, quoting the Ancient Greeks, and the philosophy of the Hellenistic and Roman periods. He concludes, "Most symptoms included in the DSM-IV list of diagnostic criteria for a major depressive disorder had already been mentioned in the *Aphorisms* of the *Corpus Hippocraticum*" (p. 7). Azzone concludes, "The role of empathy is acknowledged in all therapeutic approaches. However, in psychoanalytically oriented treatments, the therapist's emotional processes and reactions to the patient's statements play a role in both the establishment of the therapeutic alliance and the processing of the countertransference. They are the engine that fuels the treatment" (p. 61).

Fusella (2014) states, "Psychoanalysis has situated itself as a hybrid science, not quite a pure hermeneutic one on the one hand, and not quite a pure science on the other" (p. 871). He argues that three features essentially comprise all psychoanalytic work: presence, engagement, and framing. Fusella concludes that in limiting his investigation to a phenomenological exploration of what occurs within psychoanalysts' consulting rooms, he has "offered an overarching view of the psychoanalytic process … helpful in efforts toward reunifying *an unfortunately fragmented profession*" (p. 920, italics added).

Leon Wieseltier (2015) in a brilliant review of Mark Greif's (2015) book *The Age of the Crisis of Man* concludes with a strong defense of the value of Greif's call for a return to an appreciation to the humanities. Wieseltier states that "The view that the strongest defense of the humanities lies not in the appeal to their utility—that literature majors may find good jobs … but rather in the appeal to their defiantly non-utilitarian character, so that individuals can know more than how things work, and develop their powers of discernment and judgment, their competence in matters of truth and goodness and beauty, to equip themselves adequately for the choices and crucibles of private and public life" (p. 14). In our efforts as psychoanalysts, I could think of no better aim for our patients and ourselves.

Note

In the interest of confidentiality, identifying patient material has been changed, omitted, or compiled.

CHAPTER ELEVEN

The analyst's sense of shame

Anne J. Adelman

In St. Exupery's (1943) *The Little Prince*, a young boy, a naïf from another world, encounters a range of damaged yet sympathetic characters who open his eyes to the complexity, loneliness, and isolated nature of mankind. One such character, The Tippler, is a sad drunkard who spends his days lost in the bottles, both empty and full, which surround him. His futility and hopelessness confuse the Little Prince and arouse his curiosity. "Why are you drinking?" demanded the Little Prince. "So that I may forget," replied The Tippler. "Forget what?" inquired the Little Prince, who was already sorry for him. "Forget that I am ashamed," The Tippler confessed, hanging his head. "Ashamed of what?" insisted the Little Prince, who wanted to help him. "Ashamed of drinking!" (p. 35).

The Tippler's story speaks directly to the entangled nature of shame. It shows how shame can wrap around itself like a spiral staircase, keeping us entrenched and compelling us to repeat the very behaviors that generate shame. Like The Tippler in St. Exupery's *The Little Prince*, shame itself is what drives us to engage in ways that only serve to compound it. As he reveals to the Little Prince, shame is what we most try to escape and what hounds us most unrelentingly.

Shame is a potent affect state that binds us up in knots, with the power to obscure our thoughts and interfere with our actions. While guilt is an internal acknowledgement of a "bad deed," shame is a perception of a "bad self." Shame occurs when a taboo has been breached unwittingly, in spite of one's good intentions and clear conscience. It has to do with being surprised or mortified by a violation of one's internal standards, or one's failure to fulfil external demands. Shame is a response to the discovery of such an unintended breach—one that is motivated by unconscious forces.

Shame is a physical, biologically driven sensation as well as an emotional one. You feel shame in your bones, in the pit of your belly, where it burns, in your inflamed cheeks, in the tears that sting your eyes, in your racing, sinking heart, in the heat that courses throughout your body. Consumed with shame, we bow our heads and seek relief. When shame overtakes us, it is a moment of total exposure, raw and naked, whether it is on display for others to view or kept tightly under wraps, known only in the most private alleyways of our minds.

While shame is a profoundly internal experience, it differs from other emotions we may feel toward others in that it is uniquely transparent and easily observed by others. Shame is there for all to witness: We blush, we avert our eyes, we shift in our chair, we move our hands unwittingly to cover our mouths. We cannot control or conceal the reddening that creeps over our features, or the wavering in our voice, or the way that our eyes shift slightly to the left and down. With shame we are in the spotlight: All eyes are on us. Our mortification is evident; we feel alienated, disgraced, humiliated. Like a scarlet letter, we cannot hide—shame leaves its mark. Then we must work to regain our footing, to find a pathway to make use of our shame in the service of self-understanding.

In her memoir, *Autobiography of a Face*, Lucy Grealy (1994) offers a moving and poignant account of how shame unfolds out of a complex and painful string of circumstances: illness, physical deformity, bullying, shaming, and self-denigration. She depicts her shame as a bodily experience of hyper-exposure that then takes root in the psyche. As a child, Grealy was diagnosed and treated for bone cancer. After a complicated surgery to remove a Ewing's sarcoma from her right jaw, her face was left deeply scarred and malformed. The young Lucy avoided gazing at herself in the mirror for a long time after the surgery. In her memoir, she takes the reader through the complex narrative of a child's pragmatic realism mingled with magical thinking and avoidance. For a long time, she allowed herself to believe that people were staring at her because of her hair loss due to the chemotherapy, and she defiantly rejects her mother's offer of a wig. Little by little, however, it dawned on her that there must be something else that causes others to stare at her. Finally examining her scar in the mirror for the first time, she writes:

> … my chin seemed so small. How had it gotten that way? … with a bit of angling, [I] looked for the first time at my right profile. I knew to expect a scar, but how had my face sunk in like that? I didn't understand. Was it possible I'd looked this way for a while and was only just noticing it, or was this change very recent? More than the ugliness I felt, I was suddenly appalled at the notion that I'd been walking around unaware of something that was apparent to everyone else. A profound sense of shame consumed me. (pp. 111–112)

Grealy's shame arises when she sees for the first time what others have been seeing without her awareness. It contains elements of exposure, violation, and intrusion—a puncture of one's sense of boundaries and privacy. I believe that is the essence of the shame experience—to be taken by surprise, to be suddenly denuded and laid bare for all the world to see.

Shame and the analytic situation

In many ways, shame lies at the heart of the analytic process, in that psychoanalysis is, in a sense, a quest to uncover what is hidden, to reveal what is concealed. As analysts, our quest is to search for the truth—not a factual truth, but the deeper, psychological truth that our patients unknowingly seek—who are they really, what are they made of, how did they come to be so, and what do their actions reveal or conceal? We come to the analytic situation with good intentions—we have a clear conscience, we believe we can be helpful, we think we understand something about the nature of the mind and our patients' struggles. Yet, lo and behold, with each new patient we are surprised again, never knowing at the outset what will be in store for us.

Every analytic treatment must deal with shame in one form or another. The very notion of having a private, confidential, one-on-one relationship shields our patients from the humiliation that would bear out if their shame were made public. As Sandra Buechler writes, "It is a priority for patients to be able to trust that, generally, I wish them well and I am trying to preserve their self-esteem as much as I can without sacrificing the treatment's effectiveness" (2008, p. 69). Held securely within a serene and benevolent analytic surround, the intimate and delicate exchange between patient and analyst makes shame bearable. Only if it can be borne together can the deepest truths—those that also are most painful and conflict-ridden—become fully known. In the course of the treatment, the analyst, too, must contend with her own shame. We cannot hope to help our patients with their shame unless we can sort out our own.

In the analytic relationship, we strive for openness, yet at the same time we inevitably strive to conceal those aspects of ourselves that cause us shame. In fact, in the analytic situation it can be said that we literally hide—we sit behind our patients, with the intent to free them and ourselves to enter into reverie, but by being out of their sight it protects us from the shame of being witnessed by our patients. They cannot see our cringing, mocking, musing, or pain.

Likewise, our theoretical constructs guide and inform us, but they also provide us with a safe hiding space, one where we can conceal what we do not yet know. Somehow, our theories fall short in one way or another in each and every analytic treatment. The analytic process demands that we struggle with our shame and bring it into the treatment either in our own private musings or our own reflections, in order to shed light on those aspects of the patient's and our own experience that may be just outside our view.

As therapists and analysts, we are no more invulnerable to shame than we are to rage, fear, or joy. The problem is in sorting out what are we to do with it. It is not a place where we want to dwell, but rather a feeling we want to escape. Often, we turn to colleagues and others for help, for forgiveness, for absolution. Indeed, sometimes patients come to treatment seemingly in order to confess, as if entering the confessional looking to unburden their soul and finally put their feelings of shame to rest. When that isn't possible, shame can take up residence in the unconscious layers of the mind, where it becomes a distorting lens through which we view our entire self-worth. As it is with our patients, so it is with ourselves: In the face of our shame, we seek to be exonerated, yet hold tight to the notion that we are too inadequate to be forgiven.

Shame is best understood as an interpersonal experience. Many investigators (Bromberg, 1998; Buechler, 2008; Kohut, 1971) have pointed out that shame likely occurs in relation or in reaction to another—whether we feel too exposed, inadequate, helpless, or dependent. Shame may also couple with other powerful emotional states, such as rage, anxiety, or despair, that render it even more tenacious and, at the same time, more nuanced. Thus, shame requires a minimum of two players—one to feel ashamed, one to hold the mirror. The mirror-holder is, at times, another person, and at other times, an internal voice, the never-ending loop of self-attack that can be easily set off in each of us.

For the analyst, shame serves as an alert, a wake-up call of sorts: Why am I feeling so uncomfortable? What is needed in order to rid myself of this feeling and return to my former state of well-being? If we think about the state of well-being as having to do with the regulation of our healthy narcissism, then we can understand shame as, in effect, a result of a significant narcissistic injury. Our basic sense of self-esteem is disrupted. We cannot go back to feeling good until we have done something about it. Furthermore, as Goldberg (1989) points out, shame serves a constructive and necessary function. He postulates,

> The willingness and ability to pursue self-knowledge is generally a more arduous task than simply meeting the expectations of those who have established the basis for our feelings of culpability. In short, because of its central role in the pursuit of self-knowledge, the awareness of shame is crucial to a morality based on autonomy and responsibility. It is the fine edge of shame as a function interfaced with creative and defensive aims that has interested me … (p. 598)

Shame is, then, a powerful attention-getter. It beckons to us, forcing us to reckon with it. While shame serves as a signal function, it can intrude on our ability to think clearly, recognize transference-countertransference dilemmas, and make clear clinical choices. When we feel shame, we doubt our minds and our sound judgment. We hesitate, naturally wanting to hide our mistakes—or what we think of as mistakes. Our ability to function effectively as a therapist, or even simply as an individual out in the world, is impaired. The task of the therapist, then, is to recognize shame as a signal affect and to try our best to make use of it to guide our understanding, the decisions we make, the recommendations we give, the interpretations we craft. As Silverman (2006) writes,

> As analysts, our own histories of trauma or loss can feel profoundly shameful. But our fears of being seen as flawed or scarred or still struggling with some aspect of our lives only make us less useful to our patients. Our need to be beyond shame makes us hide from our patients. Ironically, it is in the recognition that we all have areas of shame that the shame itself diminishes. It is our responsibility as analysts to allow ourselves to be vulnerable and to risk our own shame and fragility. Not to do so is to abandon and demean our patients, to sit and look at "them" from afar rather than to join with them on a scary but ultimately hopeful journey. (p. 542)

In treatment, shame often enters the realm of our countertransference reactions when we encounter a particularly complex dynamic. At such moments, the analytic posture can inadvertently provide a way to hide from our own shame and defend against our inadequacies. Yet it serves our patients—and indeed, ourselves—best when we can use it as a beacon to deepen our understanding of our patients and guide them in reaching a more empathic and compassionate attitude toward their own shameful affect.

Clinical vignette: 1

> A colleague told me the following story. He had begun to evaluate a patient whose parents had divorced in the patient's childhood. The patient's uncle was a psychiatrist in a nearby town, and the patient asked the therapist if he knew her uncle. "No, I don't," was the therapist's reply. "That's good," said the patient, "because I really want to keep this very separate from my family. I don't want them to know that I'm even in therapy." The session continued undisturbed.
>
> In the second session, my colleague learned that the patient's parents divorced when she was nine after her father had an affair with a neighbor down the street. The patient learned of the affair when she saw her father downtown, getting into his neighbor's car. She watched her father climb into the car, lean over and embrace the woman who lived four doors down from her own home. The patient, mortified at what she had seen, said nothing to anyone. Months later, when the patient learned that her parents were

separating, she surmised that this was the reason, and she felt a new kind of guilt. Was it her fault, she wondered? Should she have spoken up sooner? Had she told her mother, would her parents still be together?

As the patient continued, she referenced another family member, a cousin, who was the daughter of her mother's brother. To his dismay, my colleague realized that he did know who this cousin was, as he was friendly with a man who worked with the cousin's husband. Surely, my colleague thought to himself, this is a very remote connection, and I will never actually cross paths with the cousin. He did not interrupt the patient to alert her to this new connection. That night, my colleague could not sleep, but found himself tossing and turning all night. He was awakened by the following dream:

> *I was getting into a car, but someone else was already in it, in the driver's seat. I didn't think she belonged there but when I asked her to move, she just laughed. I sensed that she was mocking me, but I thought, "She is not supposed to be there."*

The next day, my colleague consulted with me: Should he tell the patient about the connection he had to the cousin? The connection was so tangential, surely it could pose no problem whatsoever to the treatment. However, it soon became clear that the issue was more complicated. My colleague said, "I feel ashamed, like I was watching a scene I shouldn't be. Should I have told her right then and there? *Did I do something wrong?*"

In the consultation, my colleague came to understand that the issue that had perturbed him had to do not with a potential boundary crossing, that is, knowing someone that the patient knew in a different context, but with the idea of keeping secrets, a theme so central for this particular patient. By not interrupting the patient and letting her know of his tangential connection to her cousin, the therapist felt as though he had somehow recreated a scene that had traumatized—and tantalized—the patient so many years earlier. Like his patient, he had watched and observed, knowing more than he let on, yet not saying anything about it.

This line of reflection, and the ultimate understanding he reached, allowed my colleague to break through the feelings of shame, and identify them as similar to the feelings his patient had experienced years earlier when she discovered her father's affair. He recognized that he needed to tell the patient what he knew and work together to make sense of it. Whether or not the patient would choose to continue the treatment, he couldn't know, but the relief he felt upon deciding to reveal the connection was palpable. The feeling of shame was relieved only when it was possible to make some repair. He understood that informing the patient was clinically necessary. Shame momentarily interfered with the therapist's ability to think like a therapist. Once he came to understand his reaction and could alleviate the painful discomfort of shame, he was able to restore his therapeutic stance.

This clinical moment highlights how, while shame can impair the therapist's ability to carry on with the work, attending carefully to that feeling can restore our therapeutic function. We tend to think of shame as a palpable and immediate response to an overwhelming humiliation, but in fact, it is often a reaction to a small event that occurs in a split second, like a sudden shift in the atmosphere that abruptly raises the temperature of the analyst-patient interaction.

Myriad forms of the analyst's experience of shame

There are countless ways we may feel shame in the consulting room. Here are just a few:

- The shame of forgetting something a patient has told us that they clearly have expected us to remember, or, conversely, "remembering" something that they have not in fact said to us.
- The shame of breaking the frame—whether a real or perceived error—for example, when we are running late, or we are tired, or our clothes are too old, or our desk is messy. We know we are letting something leak into the serenity of the therapeutic milieu, even if our patients do not consciously notice or complain.
- The shame of failing to meet our patient's expectations. For example, a patient once arrived at my office for an initial consultation. When I opened my door, she took one look at me and said, "This won't work. You don't look anything like I thought you would—although your office isn't too bad." Although rationally I knew that there was nothing I could have done differently to prepare for this patient, I was irrationally ashamed of falling short of her expectations.
- The shame of not living up to patients' fantasies about us. For instance, I once had a patient who described in detail what she imagined my

office at home to be: a tranquil space on the third floor of a lovely house, windows all around, sloped ceilings with skylights, and a view of the nearby river. While she described this fantasy, my own smallish, over-packed house where my actual, cluttered desk sits below a half-window in my basement, sharing the space with the family room and the laundry room, flashed in front of my eyes, and I felt my face redden.
- The shame of our own fantasies about our patient, whether wondering if this is someone we wanted to befriend, or imagining being invited to vacation on his family yacht, after hearing about it for many months.
- The shame of seeming "perfect" to our patients, always calm, reflective, measured, never angry or impatient.
- The shame of feeling that we are failing at therapy, that the patient keeps coming even when we don't think we are helping. We uphold our end of the bargain—we listen, we try to understand, we offer our insights—but what if we really can't see our way through the forest at times?
- The shame of feeling overly proud when we are succeeding and our patient appears to be improving. When we think, "I must be better than this patient's prior therapists." When secretly, we want to believe that we are the clinical genius, making gains where others have failed before us.
- The shame of holding onto power in the consulting room—of using it, even out of benevolent authority, to achieve the aim we seek, even when we believe it to be in our patient's best interest—the shame of relishing our power.
- The shame of having curiosity driven by our own self-interest, whether the desire to hear more prurient details, or listening in a self-serving or greedy way. For example, my colleague mentioned a patient who was swinging her feet while talking. The therapist couldn't help but notice and admire her shoes. Every time the patient's foot swung, the therapist tried to catch a glimpse of the sole, to see if she could discern the brand in order to purchase the shoes herself!

In addition to the above-mentioned experiences, there is the shame of being the one to cause discomfort in our patients by asking them to tell us about painful or traumatic events, in an effort to better know and understand them. The shame that our authority as analyst risks inflicting hurt that we may or may not recognize. Bromberg (1998) brings this to light when he writes:

> The reliving with one's therapist of unprocessed traumatic affect from the past, such as fear, is almost always accompanied by a dissociated here-and-now shame experience ... The dissociated shame is triggered by the analyst's inevitable unawareness that his therapeutic "success" in bringing about the reliving is also bringing about, in the relationship with him, a reliving of the hunger for relief and soothing without a way to *directly communicate this hunger*. Why? Because the person whose behavior is creating the distress is also the person most necessary to relieve it, and in the patient's past this was unthinkable. The net result is that the shame of the hunger triggers its own dissociation. ... As long as the patient's dissociated shame caused by this unaddressed and unprocessed aspect of their enactment *continues* to remain unrecognized in the here and now, his dissociative mental structure remains in place and his increased ability to experience and resolve internal conflict is impeded. (pp. 560–561)

At times, moments in which we feel a sense of shame or humiliation briefly capture our attention but then recede into the background, as other affects rise to the foreground. When our attention is even, fluid, and quiet, and is not snagged by shame, we do not stay stuck in one affective state, but rather our thoughts and feelings flow freely from one to the next. We take note of them but generally try to not get sidetracked. In this way, we learn to keep in check our outward display of emotions while maintaining access to the inner dialogue of our own affects, so that they can guide and inform the work we do with our patients. But when we fall victim to our shame, we are trapped, unable to shake free of the discomfort that grips us.

Often, the shameful feelings are those feelings we most need to extrude from ourselves, which can lead to projections and impasses in the work. As Davies (2004) writes,

> I focus not only on the guilt and shame evoked by the analyst's therapeutic and object functions, but on the fate of the analyst's primary areas of shame, guilt, and despair as well [see also Elkind, 1992].

> In this more specific sense, I have not simply evoked a negative transference or become a bad object for my patient. Instead, it is more accurate to state that, at such heightened moments of impasse, something about my current interaction with this patient forces me to become aware of that which is and always has been "bad" within myself, something that I know and have always known to reside squarely within the part of myself I choose to consistently avoid and disown. My point here is to suggest that it can become the passionate mission of such guilty, shame-riddled self states, (whether in patient or analyst) to predict, seek out, and provoke the very worst in the other, in order to literally extrude the badness—to locate and confirm that the badness lies comfortably outside the self. It is I believe in the countertransferential push to extrude these self states of our own, to locate them in the other (in this case, the patient), that the boundary confusion and collapse of self-reflective functioning endemic to moments, of what Stuart Pizer (1998) has termed nonnegotiable therapeutic impasse, may take hold. (p. 718)

If the analyst's self-identity rests particularly on the notion of the self as a good object—helping, nurturing, caring for others, and doing good works—then the inherent impulse to eject "badness" outside of ourselves and onto another—in this instance, our patient—is necessarily at odds with our ideal sense of self. Thus, the analytic process is momentarily blocked, as the analyst struggles with these opposing pulls within him, until he is able to recognize the impasse, work through those conflicts that have been avoided or disavowed, and reemerge with a deeper sense of his capacity to withstand the withering force of shame in favor of a sharper and more nuanced appreciation of his shameful self-states.

A detailed clinical illustration

With some patients, the analyst's sense of shame can be understood as a form of identification with a patient for whom shameful affects are disavowed, poorly metabolized, or inaccessible to the patient. When I recall Letitia, a young patient I saw many years ago, I am reminded of shame's power to disturb the process but, ultimately, to allow for a deepening of the analytic work.

Clinical vignette: 2

Letitia, a young woman of thirty-three, had had multiple surgeries in childhood to correct a genetic anomaly. As a young woman, she thought of herself as ugly and unattractive, someone no one would want. As an adolescent, she grew increasingly resentful and resistant. In reality, she had an attractive and interesting face that was pleasing to look at. Yet she pictured herself to be an object of repulsion to others. She imagined that everyone who met her would scrutinize her and wonder, what's wrong with this picture?

In the early months of the analysis, shame quickly became a central focus in the treatment. She was ashamed of what she perceived to be her incompetence as a mother, ashamed of her anger at her husband, which would emerge as intermittent rages, and ashamed of her sense of failure at her chosen profession. Even Letitia's hesitant speech seemed to tell me she was ashamed of the sound of her voice. I soon learned that the source of her greatest shame lay in her childhood history of her genetic anomaly and the resultant childhood surgeries. As a child, she always felt diminished in relation to the other children, and while she learned to overcome her shyness and make some friends, she had been bullied and mocked at times. The friendships she did have were marked by envy, competition, and idealization.

Feelings of acute self-consciousness became prominent in the analysis. She could not stop wondering what I thought of her. Did I like her appearance? Did I agree with her opinions? Did I think she was too shrill, too severe? Did I judge her to be an incompetent mother, unable to properly care for her active, and at times, difficult toddler? I felt as though I was a distorting mirror she was holding up in front of her face.

Letitia puzzled over her strong resentment about her deformity and the medical treatment and multiple surgeries that ensued. Her family, trying to minimize the impact of her deformity, never spoke about it directly. As a young child, she understood that the timing of the surgeries had to do with the rate at which her bones were growing. She remembers being told when the next surgery was to take place, but feeling as though she had no control over whether or not to continue having the corrective procedures. As an adolescent, she grew increasingly resentful and resistant. Yet a small part of her eagerly anticipated the surgeries, imagining that she would be made "perfect."

Letitia treated me with exaggerated deference. If she arrived a minute or two late for her appointment and my door was open, she never simply entered the room and sat down. Instead, she paused at the threshold hesitantly, peeped her head in, and waited until I invited her to come in, as if I might decide to turn her away at the door or maliciously keep her waiting, just to exercise my power over her. If I started to make a comment, her whole being seemed to spring to alertness, waiting breathlessly for my words, as if I was about to make a prophetic announcement, as if each word I uttered was encased in gold.

The other side of this deference was a profound sensitivity to perceived injury or slights, which were met with taut, wounded silence. Eventually, she would confess, in a voice so low it was practically a whisper, that she was "confused" and she must have been "wrong." Once, she overheard the patient who preceded her give a loud, raucous laugh.

"You've never laughed like that with me," she remarked sadly.

"Perhaps you felt hurt, and couldn't help but be curious about what you may have heard," I ventured in a way I hoped was gentle enough. I became aware of my own frustration, feeling an odd blend of being intruded on, and silently accused.

"No, I'm sure everyone is different in here ... it's just that I thought, 'You must be having fun in here.' I don't know if you ever feel that way with me."

But such exchanges often felt circular and futile to me, with Letitia insisting that she wasn't angry and me trying fruitlessly to help her examine why anger was an emotion she could not allow herself to acknowledge. It felt, to her, like being angry was a sign of a deficient person who was out of control and essentially, fundamentally bad.

Letitia dressed in particularly drab and out-of-style clothes, and tended to wear very plain, flat, unattractive shoes. Spending her days running after her toddler, she probably thought little about her footwear other than being sure it was sturdy and comfortable, but the "clunkiness" of her shoes seemed to worm its way into my mind. Could being drab and colorless, I wondered, be her way of silently rebelling against the world—a world in which she experienced herself as flawed, as damaged goods? Her way of announcing,

"Because I can never be fully mended, I am destined to be Plain Jane, never pretty, never put together"? I found myself bizarrely exasperated with her. Surely, I thought, she could just wear regular sneakers, instead of those black, scuffed, frumpy, lace-up shoes.

She had a habit of removing her shoes before lying down on the couch, which she did with elaborate meticulousness, as if signaling to me, "I wouldn't dream of dirtying your couch." I understood this to be a silent reaction formation against her desire to dump her mess all around my office—and in so doing to besmirch me as well with her rage and envy. I thought of it as masochistic surrender to self-loathing. I joked to myself: "She will be ready to end analysis when she stops wearing such ugly shoes!"

As things turned out, I was right—little by little, as the analysis progressed, she began to dress more attractively and her footwear became more fashionable. From time to time, I even caught a peek of patent leather. But I was unsettled by my private reactions, which felt unnecessarily cruel and judgmental. I felt ill at ease about my vague annoyance at her deference, and my strange inclination to mentally disparage her shoes, her style, and her appearance. Ashamed of myself for my strange irritation, I tried to understand my powerful reaction. I studied my feelings closely, trying to make sense of what they might mean and how they might inform my work with her.

One day, Letitia came in, distraught about something her mother-in-law had said to her. She and her mother-in-law were at dinner with a friend who had recently used Botox. The mother-in-law remarked that the woman's face would just never be perfect, as she was too homely and her nose was too long. Letitia said, "How could she say that in front of me? Doesn't she know how that would make me feel?" She recalled that as a child, she had stood on a chair in her bedroom, gazing at her face in the mirror. "I wanted to see what other people saw in me," she explained. "I was trying to capture the image of my face that I could never see—as if I could catch the expression in someone's eyes when they first look at me, before they politely arrange their smile to hide their disgust." I was reminded of Grealy's (1994) experience of seeing her face for the first time post-surgery, and being astonished at what others had been seeing all along.

As Letitia talked about her subsequent surgery and her disappointment that the outcome had not, in fact, been "perfect," because she still walked with a limp, I asked her for details about the many interventions she had undergone. She had never before allowed herself to describe the painful and frightening aspects of her surgeries. "They had to wrench me away from my mother and strap me to the table, because she wasn't allowed to be in the room with me," she murmured, and started to cry. "I know I'm crying, but I don't know why," she said. I felt sad too, imagining a small, scared child constrained on a hospital gurney. "It must have been frightening to feel so alone," I said to her. "And you endured so much pain and discomfort as well, while you were recovering from the surgery." Letitia seemed startled. "Yes, I guess," she said with some hesitation. "It's strange, I don't think I've ever thought about the pain, about what it really felt like." She began to describe a memory of her weeping mother trying to hold a cold compress to her wounds while she wailed and squirmed away.

Suddenly, I was flooded with a memory of my own. I flashed back in time. There is a wailing, thrashing, screaming toddler, lying on her back in her crib. Her mother is standing over her, crying helplessly. She is trying to jam the child's misshapen feet, curved inward like boomerangs predestined to crash (the effects of metatarsus adductus) into stiff leather shoes, attached to one another with a heavy, metal bar that swiveled when she tried to walk, keeping her misshapen feet evenly spaced apart, with the aim of slowly shifting and straightening the malformed bones. That toddler was me. I still remember the pain, the feeling of constriction, the unbearable frustration of wanting to run and jump but being tied to earth. I would clump angrily around our small apartment, while Mr. Brown, our neighbor in the apartment directly beneath ours, banged on the ceiling with his cane and yelled, "Stop all that noise up there, and shut that child up!" Once, trying to run with my feet bound by this contraption, I slipped on the plastic sheeting that protected my mother's prized oriental rug, banged my head into the wall and split my eyebrow open. When the doctor examined the wound, he told my mother, "The good thing is her eyebrow will hide the scarring." I hated and feared putting on those shoes, and would thrash my legs, making it virtually impossible for my mother to put them on. Mornings and evenings, she would have to go through a rigorous painful exercise regimen with me, which I also resisted.

Because I was young, my recollection of these events are more a series of flashpoints, but the discomfort, the frustration, the rage at being forced to comply and the desire to flee are seared in my memory. As I grew older, I continued to have problems with my feet. All through my childhood and early adolescence, I had to wear flat-soled orthopedic shoes with special inserts that were awkward and uncomfortable. I remember yearly pilgrimages to Harry's Shoe Store, where they would measure my feet, remark on my progress, and fit me once again for the identical pair of lace-up orthopedic shoes, one or two sizes larger than the year before. Oblivious of my disappointment, my mother would feel reassured, patting me on the shoulder as if to say: "See? You're growing just the way you should." But by now, the physical discomfort had waned, and in its place I felt shame.

Inside the shoe store, my eyes would linger longingly over my heart's desire, the coveted slip-on penny loafers. I envisioned myself slipping a shiny new penny into each slot and proudly walking my good luck all the way up Broadway back to our apartment. But each year, "Mr. Harry" would tell me no, those loafers were not for me. "You just can't make the arch for a penny loafer," he would explain earnestly, having no idea how disappointed I was. My mother would shrug and yank my laces tighter.

My ugly shoes, and all the ways that I felt constricted in them, reflected much of how I felt about myself at the time. What is our fascination, sometimes preoccupation, with our shoes and our clothing? There are religious, spiritual, and profoundly personal meanings for how we choose to clothe our bodies. Our clothing is what hides our skin, what covers the parts we consider private, what touches our skin, what marks us, identifies us, shapes others' impressions of who we are. We preen, we admire, we envy, we conceal—clothing is the thin membrane between our selves and the external world, a membrane that simultaneously conceals and reveals something about our truest selves. As Schneider (1987) writes, "... *at its core, shame is intimately linked to the human need to cover that which is exposed*" (p. 199). Buechler (2008) also explores the complex connections among shame, exposure, and daring in her comments on a painting of Adam and Eve by Giotto: "... Adam shields his face while Eve covers her genitals. Perhaps this expresses the exposure that hurts each most" (p. 61). Indeed, when our clothing in some way fails to conceal, or even accentuates, those things of which we feel ashamed, we feel overly exposed, and shame becomes our invisible cloak.

Sitting with Letitia, I recognized in that flash of memory that, with this patient, an old reservoir of shame had opened up in me—one which I had succeeded at pushing to the very back of my mind. My childhood shame had become bound up with my bound feet, my constricted freedom of will and movement, and all that this had come to mean in my own particular set of circumstances. While I had not experienced the profound sort of trauma that my patient Letitia had borne as a child, I still knew something of the struggle for freedom, control, and independence that she had fought throughout her childhood and adolescence.

As though a curtain had lifted from in front of my eyes, I suddenly saw Letitia in a new light. My irritation dropped away from me, and in its place, I felt deep compassion for the suffering she had endured and the scars she could not hope to erase. I saw more clearly what she had been trying to tell me about, verbally and nonverbally, and why I could not fully hear her. I understood that, in a way I had been completely unaware of, my childhood shame of my body and its deformities had recognized hers and joined forces to keep it out of my conscious view. Instead of being able to empathize with her, my mind was pushing it, and Letitia's pain, away, deriding the very experience I could truly understand and yet wanted most to forget.

When I was able to internally unmask my own concealed shame, my capacity to think and feel like her analyst was once again restored. My work with Letitia allowed me to begin to process and unbury my own disavowed childhood shame. With that, I found myself able to respond to her more directly, more fully, and even playfully. A new warmth and lightness began to emerge between us. One day not too long after this session, she entered the room shyly laughing a little. "I thought of you last night," she remarked. "My supervisor at work said something that really bothered me. I thought she was saying that she was angry with me for not getting my proposal to her in time. I felt angry and ashamed. I wanted to tell her, then why did I have to go to that meeting in the first place? It took up all my time. I wondered whether she was telling me that she regretted assigning the proposal to me. Probably

Ellen or Louisa would have done a better job than me. But then, I imagined telling you about this, and suddenly I could hear your voice say, 'That's hogwash!' But you've never even said anything like that to me! Why would I think that?" Then she paused, and continued after a moment, "Maybe I just know you'd take my side. You wouldn't let me get bullied by her! I think it was that I feel like you like me, and then I remembered that my supervisor likes me too. I know she does, it's just that I hate feeling like I've done something wrong." "Maybe," I ventured, "you put words into my mouth that you wished you could say to her yourself: Hogwash!" She laughed, and I went on musingly, "Maybe there are times you'd like to say that to me!" Laughing again, more quietly, she said, "You know, that's probably true. I never thought I'd ever say that to you." When she left her session that day, she commented, "I liked that we laughed together today. That surprised me. It really felt good. I think I even liked how I sounded. I sounded happy, not shrill the way I'm always afraid I'll sound."

Concluding remarks

In the early phase of Letitia's treatment, I had felt stuck and ashamed, unable to understand my critical feelings toward her and unable to feel tenderly toward her or the treatment. This is similar to what Davies (2004) described with a patient whose shame evoked an unnamed, or what Davies refers to as an "extruded" shame in the analyst. Davies writes:

> … particularly toxic impasses can occur when something in the patient's history of extruded self-states engages with something in the analyst's history of extruded self-states. In such instances, the boundary between self and other collapses in the mutual spitfire projections and counterprojections that ensue. The analyst's space for self-reflective processes becomes compromised and potentially shut down when overwhelming shame contributes to his or her rejection of a patient's unconscious communication. The analyst struggles not just to hold a bad object representation for the patient, but also to fend off an intolerable, shame-riddled self-representation of his or her own as part of the formidable effort to co-construct

with the patient a space in which each can feel loved and sane in the same moment. (p. 730)

My deeply buried childhood shame seemed to cast a shadow over my work with this patient and interfere with my capacity to listen and hold the patient's experience in the forefront of my mind. Once I was able to extricate myself from the veil of shame I was able, once again, to work side by side with her. We became partners in uncovering and exploring the layers of physical pain, vulnerability, and exposure that had so long entrapped her in painful feelings of shame. In this way, I helped her turn her gaze away from the face of the imagined shaming other, in whose eyes she sought the "truth" about her appearance. Instead, I became a true "mirror" for her, through which she could begin to see herself as whole, intact, and appealing.

The notion of shame enters the analytic dialogue because the work that unfolds between analyst and patient pulls toward self-exposure and self-revelation. This holds for analyst and patient alike, because each is likely to encounter early fears, wishes, and conflicts that have often become deeply buried beneath the complex strata of each person's psychological development. As Schneider (1987) writes,

> We are called on to maintain a mature sense of shame because we practice in a field marked by the dynamic interplay between covering and uncovering, between the tacit and the explicit .... The proper therapeutic stance is finally one of awe and deep respect, for we stand on holy ground—we engage in an encounter that involves doubleness—the experience of both mystery and revelation, of reticence before the indescribable and of the revelation of that which was concealed. (p. 209).

As analysts, we are compelled to guard the analytic process and to allow our patients to reveal their private thoughts and feelings in a dignified manner. Like Letitia's desire to see her reflection in other people's eyes before their disgust is concealed, it is the work of the analyst to not turn away from shameful moments in our work, whether in our patients or ourselves. Instead, we must reflect the deep sense of care, wonder, and respect for our patients and our work, that will allow such painful feelings to be uncloaked and, ultimately, dissipated in the face of greater self-acceptance and understanding.

REFERENCES

Adichie, C. (2013). *Americanah*. New York: Alfred A. Knopf.
Adler, A. (1927). *Understanding Human Nature*. New York: Greenberg.
Adorno, T. W., Frenkel-Brunswik, E., Levinson, D. J., & Sanford, R. N. (1950). *The Authoritarian Personality*. New York: Harper.
Akhtar, S. (1992). Tethers, orbits, and invisible fences: clinical, developmental, sociocultural, and technical aspects of optimal distance. In: S. Kramer & S. Akhtar (Eds.), *When the Body Speaks: Psychological Meanings in Kinetic Clues* (pp. 21–57). Northvale, NJ: Jason Aronson.
Akhtar, S. (1999). Review of "Internal Objects Revisited" by Joseph and Ann-Marie Sandler. *Psychoanalytic Books, 10*: 532–541.
Akhtar, S. (2000). Mental pain and the cultural ointment of poetry. *International Journal of Psychoanalysis, 81*: 229–243.
Akhtar, S. (2002). Forgiveness: origins, dynamics, psychopathology, and technical relevance. *Psychoanalytic Quarterly, 71*: 175–212.
Akhtar, S. (2009a). *Comprehensive Dictionary of Psychoanalysis*. London: Karnac.
Akhtar, S. (Ed.) (2009b). *Freud and the Far East: Psychoanalytic Perspectives on the People and Culture of China, Japan and Korea*. Lanham, MD: Jason Aronson.
Akhtar, S. (2011). *Matters of Life and Death: Psychoanalytic Reflections*. London: Karnac.

Akhtar, S. (2012a). Fear, phobia, and cowardice. In: S. Akhtar (Ed.), *Fear: A Dark Shadow Across our Life Span* (pp. 3–34). London: Karnac.

Akhtar, S. (2012b). *The Book of Emotions*. New Delhi: Roli.

Akhtar, S. (Ed.) (2013). *Guilt: Origins, Manifestations, and Management*. Lanham, MD: Jason Aronson.

Akhtar, S. (Ed.) (2014b). *Human Goodness: Origins, Manifestations, and Clinical Implications*. Lanham, MD: Rowman & Littlefield.

Akhtar, S. (2015). Some psychoanalytic reflections on the concept of dignity. *American Journal of Psychoanalysis*, 75: 244–266.

Alexander, F. (1938). Remarks about the relation of inferiority feelings to guilt feelings. *International Journal Psychoanalysis*, 19: 41–49.

Allen, S. (1977–1981). *Meeting of Minds*. http://www.steveallen.com/television_pioneer/-meeting_of_minds.htm. Accessed April 3, 2015.

Altman, N. (2006). How psychoanalysis became white in the United States, and how that might change. *Psychoanalytic Perspectives*, 3: 65–72.

Amsterdam, B. (1972). Mirror self-image reactions before age two. *Developmental Psychobiology*, 5: 297–305.

Arblaster, A. (1992). *Viva la Libertà: Politics in Opera*. London: Verso.

Aristotle (c. 350 BCE). *The Art of Rhetoric*. London: Penguin Classics, 1992.

Arlow, J., & Brenner, C. (1964). *Psychoanalytic Concepts and the Structural Theory*. New York: International Universities Press.

Auchincloss, E. L., & Samberg, E. (Eds.) (2012). *Psychoanalytic Terms and Concepts*. New Haven, CT: Yale University Press.

Ayers, M. (2003). *Mother-Infant Attachment and Psychoanalysis*. London: Routledge.

Azzone, P. (2013). *Depression as a Psychoanalytic Problem*. New York: University Press of America.

Baird, J. W. (1990). *To Die For Germany: Heroes in the Nazi Pantheon*. Indianapolis, IN: Indiana University Press.

Barthes, R. (1970). *Empire of Signs*. R. Howard (Trans.). New York: Hill & Wang, 1984.

Benedict, R. (1946). *The Chrysanthemum and the Sword: Patterns of Japanese Culture*. Boston, MA: Houghton Mifflin.

Binion, R. (1973). Hitler's concept of *Lebensraum*: the psychological basis. *History of Childhood Quarterly: The Journal of Psychohistory*, 1: 187–216.

Binion, R. (1991). *Hitler among the Germans*. DeKalb, IL: Northern Illinois University Press.

Bion, W. R. (1959). Attacks on linking. *International Journal of Psychoanalysis*, 40: 308–315.

Bion, W. R. (1962). *Learning from Experience*. London: Karnac, 1984.

Blackman, J. (2003). *101 Defenses: How the Mind Shields Itself*. New York: Routledge.

Blackman, J. (2010). *Get the Diagnosis Right: Assessment and Treatment Selection for Mental Disorders.* New York: Routledge.

Blackman, J. (2013). *The Therapist's Answer Book: Solutions to 101 Tricky Problems in Psychotherapy.* New York: Routledge.

Blatt, S. (1992). The differential effect of psychotherapy and psychoanalysis with anaclitic and introjective patients: the Menninger Psychotherapy Research Project revisited. *Journal of the American Psychoanalytic Association, 40:* 691–724.

Bloch, E. (1994). My patient, Hitler: a memoir of Hitler's Jewish physician. *Journal of Historical Review, 14:* 27–35.

Blos, P. (1960). Comments on the psychological consequences of cryptorchidism. *Psychoanalytic Study of the Child, 15:* 395–429.

Blos, P. (1962). *On Adolescence.* New York: Free Press.

Blum, H. (2005). Psychoanalytic reconstruction and reintegration. *Psychoanalytic Study of the Child, 60:* 295–311.

Blum, L. (2015). Object relations compromise formations during termination. Vamik Volkan Lecture, Virginia Psychoanalytic Society, Charlottesville, Virginia, April.

Bonhoeffer, D. (1955). *Ethics.* New York: Touchstone, 1995.

Boesky, D. (1982). Acting out: a reconsideration of the concept. *International Journal of Psychoanalysis, 63:* 39–55.

Brazelton, T. B., & Als, H. (1979). Four early stages in the development of mother-infant interaction. *Psychoanalytic Study of the Child, 34:* 349–369.

Brenner, C. (1975). Alterations in defenses during psychoanalysis. In: B. Fine & H. Waldhorn (Eds.), *Kris Study Group of the New York Psychoanalytic Institute, Monograph VI* (pp. 1–22). New York: International Universities Press.

Brenner, C. (1982). *The Mind in Conflict.* New York: International Universities Press.

Brenner, C. (2006). *Psychoanalysis: Mind or Meaning.* New York: Psychoanalytic Quarterly Press.

Brenner, I. (1988). Multisensory bridges in response to object loss during the Holocaust. *Psychoanalytic Review, 75:* 573–587.

Brenner, I. (2001). *Dissociation of Trauma: Theory, Phenomenology, and Technique.* Madison, CT: International Universities Press.

Brenner, I. (2004). *Psychic Trauma: Dynamics, Symptoms, and Treatment.* Lanham, MD: Jason Aronson.

Brenner, I. (2009). *Injured Men: Trauma, Healing, and the Masculine Self.* Lanham, MD: Jason Aronson.

Brenner, I. (2014). *Dark Matters: Exploring the Realm of Psychic Devastation.* London: Karnac.

Bretherton, I. (1992). The origins of attachment theory: John Bowlby and Mary Ainsworth. *Developmental Psychology, 28*: 759–775.

Bromberg, P. (1998). *Standing in the Spaces*. Hillsdale, NJ: Analytic Press.

Broucek, F. J. (1982). Shame and its relationship to early narcissistic developments. *International Journal of Psychoanalysis, 63*: 369–378.

Broucek, F. J. (1991). *Shame and the Self*. New York: Guilford Press.

Buechler, S. (2008). *Making a Difference in Patients' Lives*. New York: Routledge.

Caparrotta, L. (1989). Some thoughts about the function of gaze avoidance in early infancy: a mother-baby observation. *Psychoanalytic Psychotherapy, 4*: 23–30.

Chasseguet-Smirgel, J. (1984). *Creativity and Perversion*. New York: W. W. Norton.

Chasseguet-Smirgel, J. (1985). *The Ego Ideal: A Psychoanalytical Essay on the Malady of the Ideal*. New York: W. W. Norton.

Coen, S. J. (1986). The sense of defect. *Journal of the American Psychoanalytic Association, 34*: 47–67.

Cohen, D., & Nisbett, R. E. (1994). Self-protection and culture of honor: explaining Southern violence. *Personality and Social Psychology Bulletin, 20*: 551–567.

Colarusso, C. A., & Nemiroff, R. A. (1979). Some observations and hypotheses about the psychoanalytic theory of adult development. *International Journal of Psychoanalysis, 60*: 59–71.

Coomaraswamy, A. (1945). Understanding and reunion: an oriental perspective. In: A. Christy (Ed.), *The Asian Legacy and American Life* (pp. 229–242). New York: John Day, 1968.

Davies, J. M. (2004). Whose bad objects are we anyway?: repetition and our elusive love affair with evil. *Psychoanalytic Dialogues, 14*: 711–732.

Davoine, F., & Gaudillière, J.-M. (2004). *History beyond Trauma*. S. Fairfield (Trans.). New York: Other Press.

Demopoulos, P. (2014). *Götterdämmerung*: suicide music and the national self as enemy. *www.libraryofsocialscience.com*. Accessed June 7, 2014.

Deutsch, H. (1933). The psychology of manic-depressive states with particular reference to chronic hypomania. In: *Neuroses and Character Types* (pp. 203–217). New York: International Universities Press, 1965.

DeVos, G. A. (1973). *Socialization for Achievement: Essays on the Cultural Psychology of the Japanese*. Berkeley, CA: University of California Press.

Dodds, E. R. (1951). *The Greeks and the Irrational*. Berkeley, CA: University of California Press.

Doi, T. (1973). *The Anatomy of Dependence: The Key Analysis of Japanese Behavior*. Tokyo: Kodansha International, 1990.

Eidelberg, L. (Ed.) (1968). *The Encyclopedia of Psychoanalysis*. New York: Free Press.
Elise, D. (2008). Sex and shame: the inhibition of female desires. *Journal of the American Psychoanalytic Association*, 56: 73–98.
Elkind, S. N. (1992). *Resolving Impasses in Therapeutic Relationships*. New York: Guilford Press.
Emde, R. N. (1983). The pre-representational self and its affective core. *Psychoanalytic Study of the Child*, 38: 165–192.
Emde, R. N. (1991). Positive emotions for psychoanalytic theory: surprises from infancy research and new directions. *Journal of the American Psychoanalytic Association*, 39S: 5–44.
Erikson, E. H. (1950). *Childhood and Society*. New York: W. W. Norton.
Erikson, E. H. (1968). *Identity: Youth and Crisis*. New York: W. W. Norton.
Euripedes (circa 413 BCE). *Medea*. London: Penguin Classics, 1963.
Fenichel, O. (1945). *The Psychoanalytic Theory of Neurosis*. New York: W. W. Norton.
Ferenczi, S. (1911). On obscene words. In: E. Jones (Trans.), *Contributions to Psycho-Analysis* (pp. 112–130). Boston, MA: Richard G. Budger, 1916.
Ferenczi, S. (1933). On the confusion of tongues between adults and the child. In: *Final Contributions to the Problems and Methods of Psychoanalysis* (pp. 155–167). New York: Basic Books, 1955.
Field, T. M., Woodson, R., Greenberg, R., & Cohen, D. (1982). Discrimination and imitation of facial expressions by neonates. *Science*, 218: 179–181.
Fonagy, P., Gergely, G., Jurist, E., & Target, M. (2002). *Affect Regulation, Mentalization and the Development of the Self*. New York: Other Press.
Fonagy, P., Steele, H., Moran, G., & Higgitt, A. (1991). The capacity for understanding mental states: the reflective self in parent and child and its significance for security of attachment. *Infant Mental Health Journal*, 13: 200–217.
Foucault, M. (1975). *Discipline & Punish: The Birth of the Prison* (A. Sheridan, Trans.) (pp. 195–228). New York: Vintage, 1995.
Freud, A. (1956). *Normality and Pathology in Childhood*. New York: International Universities Press.
Freud, S. (1895). Extracts from the Fliess papers. Draft K.: The neuroses of defence (A Christmas fairy tale). *S. E.*, 1: 220–229. London: Hogarth.
Freud, S. (1897). Extracts from the Fliess Papers. Letter 75. November, 1897. *S. E.*, 1: 268–271. London: Hogarth.
Freud, S. (1900a). *The Interpretation of Dreams*. *S. E.*, 4–5: 1–627. London: Hogarth.
Freud, S. (1905d). *Three Essays on the Theory of Sexuality*. *S. E.*, 7: 123–246. London: Hogarth.

Freud, S. (1908b). Character and anal erotism. *S. E.*, *9*: 167–176. London: Hogarth.
Freud, S. (1908e). Creative writers and day-dreaming. *S. E.*, *9*: 141–154. London: Hogarth.
Freud, S. (1911c). Psycho-analytic notes on an autobiographical account of a case of paranoia (dementia paranoides). *S. E.*, *12*: 9–88. London: Hogarth.
Freud, S. (1913c). On beginning the treatment (Further recommendations on the technique of psycho-analysis). *S. E.*, *12*: 121–144. London: Hogarth.
Freud, S. (1914c). On narcissism: an introduction. *S. E.*, *14*: 67–103. London: Hogarth.
Freud, S. (1915b). Thoughts for the times on war and death. *S. E.*, *14*: 273–302. London: Hogarth.
Freud, S. (1916d). Some character-types met with in psycho-analytic work: the exceptions. *S. E.*, *14*: 311–315. London: Hogarth.
Freud, S. (1917e). Mourning and melancholia. *S. E.*, *14*. London: Hogarth.
Freud, S. (1918b). From the history of an infantile neurosis. *S. E.*, *17*: 7–122. London: Hogarth.
Freud, S. (1920g). *Beyond the Pleasure Principle*. *S. E.*, *18*: 1–64. London: Hogarth.
Freud, S. (1923b). *The Ego and the Id*. *S. E.*, *19*: 1–66. London: Hogarth.
Freud, S. (1924d). The dissolution of the Oedipus complex. *S. E.*, *19*: 171–188. London: Hogarth.
Freud, S. (1926d). *Inhibitions, Symptoms and Anxiety*. *S. E.*, *20*: 75–176. London: Hogarth.
Freud, S. (1926e). *The Question of Lay Analysis*. *S. E.*, *20*: 179–250. London: Hogarth.
Freud, S. (1930a). *Civilization and Its Discontents*. *S. E.*, *21*: 59–145. London: Hogarth.
Freud, S. (1932a). The acquisition and control of fire. *S. E.*, *22*: 187–196. London: Hogarth.
Freud, S. (1933a). *New Introductory Lectures on Psycho-analysis*. *S. E.*, *22*: 3–182. London: Hogarth.
Freud, S. (1937c). Analysis terminable and interminable. *S. E.*, *23*: 211–253. London: Hogarth.
Friedländer, S. (2007). *The Years of Extermination: Nazi Germany and the Jews, 1939–1945*. New York: HarperCollins.
Fusella, P. (2014). Hermeneutics versus science in psychoanalysis: a resolution to the controversy over the scientific status of psychoanalysis. *Psychoanalytic Review*, *101*: 871–924.
Gabbard, G. (1989). Two subtypes of narcissistic personality disorder. *Bulletin of the Menninger Clinic*, *53*: 527–532.

Gibbs, P. L. (2004). The struggle to know what is real. *Psychoanalytic Review*, 91: 615–641.
Gibbs, P. L. (2007a). The primacy of psychoanalytic intervention in recovery from the psychoses and schizophrenias. *Journal of the American Academy of Psychoanalysis and Dynamic Psychiatry*, 35: 287–312.
Gibbs, P. L. (2007b). Reality in cyberspace: analysands' use of the internet and ordinary everyday psychosis. *Psychoanalytic Review*, 94: 11–38.
Gibbs, P. L. (2009). Technical challenges in the psychoanalytic treatment of psychotic depression. In: D. Garfield & D. Mackler (Eds.), *Beyond Medication: Therapeutic Engagement and the Recovery from Psychosis* (pp. 107–121). London: Routledge.
Gibbs, P. L. (2009). Denial, mania, and the search for saviors in the fiscal crisis. *Clio's Psyche*, 16: 22–27.
Gill, M. (2000). *Psychoanalysis in Transition: A Personal Perspective*. Hillsdale, NJ: Analytic Press.
Goeschel, C. (2009). *Suicide in Nazi Germany*. Oxford: Oxford University Press.
Goffman, E. (1963). *Stigma: Notes on the Management of Spoiled Identity*. New York: Simon & Schuster.
Goldberg, A. (1987). The place of apology in psychoanalysis and psychotherapy. *International Review of Psycho-Analysis*, 14: 409–422.
Goldberg, C. (1989). The shame of Hamlet and Oedipus. *Psychoanalytic Review*, 76: 581–603.
Grealy, L. (1994). *Autobiography of a Face*. New York: Houghton Mifflin.
Green, M. (1991). *Invisible People: The Depiction of Minorities in Magazine Ads and Catalogues*. New York: City of New York Department of Consumer Affairs, July.
Grinker, R. (1955). Growth inertia and shame: their therapeutic implications and dangers. *International Journal of Psychoanalysis*, 36: 267–276.
Hamann, B. (1999). *Hitler's Vienna: A Portrait of the Tyrant as a Young Man*. New York: Oxford University Press.
Hamann, B. (2008). Hitler's Edeljude. *Das Leben des Armenarztes Eduard Bloch*. (*Hitler's Noble Jew: The Life of Doctor Eduard Bloch*) (pp. 80–103). T. Drevikovsky (Trans.). Munich, Germany: Piper.
Hartmann, H. (1939). *Ego Psychology and the Problem of Adaptation*. New York: International Universities Press.
Heller, Á. (1985). *The Power of Shame: A Rational Perspective*. London: Routledge & Kegan Paul.
Hitler, A. (1936). My Battle (*Mein Kampf*). E. T. S. Dugdale (Trans.). Boston, MA: Houghton Mifflin.
Hoffer, E. (1974). Long live shame: *The New York Times*, D-4, October 18.
Holmes, D. E. (2006). The wrecking effects of race and social class on self and success. *Psychoanalytic Quarterly*, 75: 215–235.

Jacobson, E. (1959). The "exceptions." *Psychoanalytic Study of the Child*, 14: 135–154.
Jacquet, J. (2015). *Is Shame Necessary?: New Uses for an Old Tool*. New York: Pantheon.
James, E. (2012). *Fifty Shades of Grey*. New York: Vintage.
Joiner, T. (2014). *The Perversion of Virtue: Understanding Murder-Suicide*. New York: Oxford University Press.
Joseph, B. (1988). Projective identification—some clinical aspects. In: E. B. Spillius (Ed.), *Melanie Klein Today: Developments in Theory and Practice (Vol. 1)* (pp. 138–150). London: Routledge.
Kafka, J. S. (1995). United States Holocaust Memorial Museum Archives. www.usmm.org. Accessed June 7, 2014.
Kakar, S., & Kakar, K. (2007). *The Indians: Portrait of a People*. New Delhi: Penguin.
Kaufman, G. (1985). *Shame: The Power of Caring*. Rochester, VT: Shenkman.
Kaufman, G. (1989). *The Psychology of Shame: Theory and Treatment of Shame-Based Syndromes*. New York: Springer.
Kernberg, O. F. (1984). *Severe Personality Disorders: Psychotherapeutic Strategies*. New Haven, CT: Yale University Press.
Kernberg, O. F. (1991). Sadomasochism, sexual excitement, and perversion. *Journal of the American Psychoanalytic Association*, 39: 333–362.
Kernberg, O. F. (1994). Aggression, trauma and hatred in the treatment of borderline patients. *Psychiatric Clinics of North America*, 17: 701–714.
Kershaw, I. (2008). *Hitler: A Biography*. New York: W. W. Norton.
Kilborne, B. (2002). *Disappearing Persons: Shame and Appearance*. Albany, NY: State University of New York Press.
Kilborne, B. (2005). Shame conflicts and tragedy in "The Scarlet Letter." *Journal of the American Psychoanalytic Association*, 53: 465–483.
Kinston, W. (1983). A theoretical context for shame. *International Journal of Psychoanalysis*, 64: 213–226.
Kitayama, O. (2004). Cross cultural varieties in experiencing affect. In: S. Akhtar & H. Blum (Eds.), *The Language of Emotions* (pp. 33–48). Northvale, NJ: Jason Aronson.
Kitayama, O. (2007). *Gekitekina Seishinbunseki-Nyuumon: A Dramatic Introduction to Psycho-Analysis*. Tokyo: Misuzu Shobo.
Kitayama, O. (2009). Psychotherapy in the "shame culture" of Japan: a "dramatic" point of view. In: S. Akhtar (Ed.), *Freud and the Far East: Psychoanalytic Perspectives on the People and Culture of China, Japan, and Korea* (pp. 89–104). Lanham, MD: Jason Aronson.
Kitayama, O. (2010). *Prohibition of Don't Look: Living through Psychoanalysis and Culture in Japan*. Tokyo: Iwasaki Gakujutsu Shuppansha.
Kjellqvist, E. (1993). *Red and White: On Shame and Shamelessness*. Stockholm: Carlsson.

Klein, M. (1935). A contribution to the psychogenesis of manic depressive states. In: *Love, Guilt and Reparation and Other Works—1921–1945* (pp. 262–289). New York: Free Press, 1975.
Klein, M. (1940). Mourning and its relation to manic-depressive states. *International Journal of Psychoanalysis*, 21: 125–153.
Klein, M. (1946). Notes on some schizoid mechanisms. *International Journal of Psychoanalysis*, 27: 99–110.
Klein, M. (1952). Some theoretical conclusions regarding the emotional life of the infant. In: *Envy and Gratitude and Other Works—1946–1963* (pp. 61–93). New York: Free Press, 1975.
Kobrin, N. H. (2015). Sadomasochism and the Jihadi death cult: a psychoanalytic look at why people throw themselves into campaigns of murder and suicide. http://tabletmag.com/jewish-news-and-politics/188892/sadomasochism-islamist-death-cult. Accessed February 12, 2015.
Koenigsberg, R. A. (1975). *Hitler's Ideology: A Study in Psychoanalytic Sociology*. New York: Library of Social Science.
Kohut, H. (1966). Forms and transformation of narcissism. *Journal of the American Psychoanalytic Association*, 14: 243–272.
Kohut, H. (1971). *The Analysis of the Self. A Systematic Approach to the Psychoanalytic Treatment of Narcissistic Personality Disorders*. New York: International Universities Press.
Kohut, H. (1972). Thoughts on narcissism and narcissistic rage. *Psychoanalytic Study of the Child*, 27: 360–400.
Kohut, H. (1977). *The Restoration of the Self*. New York: International Universities Press.
Kosawa, H. (1954). Two kinds of guilt feeling: Ajase complex. *Japanese Journal of Psychoanalysis*, 1: 5–9.
Kubie, L. S. (1937). The fantasy of dirt. *Psychoanalytic Quarterly*, 6: 388–425.
Kubizek, A. (2011). *The Young Hitler I Knew: The Definitive Inside Look at the Artist Who Became a Monster*. New York: Arcade.
Lacan, J. (1982). Écrits: A Selection. A. Sheridan (Trans.). New York: W. W. Norton.
Lansky, M. (1991). Shame and the problem of suicide: a family systems perspective. *British Journal of Psychotherapy*, 7: 230–242.
Lansky, M. (1992). *Fathers Who Fail: Shame and Psychopathology in the Family System*. Hillsdale: NJ: Analytic Press.
Lansky, M. (1994). Shame: contemporary psychoanalytic perspectives. *Journal of the American Academy of Psychoanalysis*, 22: 433–441.
Lansky, M. (1995). Shame and the scope of psychoanalytic understanding. *American Behavioral Scientist*, 38: 1067–1090.
Lansky, M. (1999). Shame and the idea of a central affect. *Psychoanalytic Inquiry*, 19: 347–361.

Lansky, M. (2000). Shame dynamics in the psychotherapy of the patient with PTSD: a viewpoint. *Journal of the American Academy of Psychoanalysis*, 28: 133–146.

Lansky, M. (2003a). Shame conflicts as dream instigators: wish fulfilment and the ego ideal in dream dynamics. *American Journal of Psychoanalysis*, 63: 357–364.

Lansky, M. (2003b). The "incompatible idea" revisited: the oft-invisible ego-ideal and shame dynamics. *American Journal of Psychoanalysis*, 63: 365–376.

Lansky, M. (2004). Trigger and screen: shame conflicts and the dynamics of instigation in Freud's dreams. *Journal of the American Psychoanalytic Association*, 32: 441–469.

Lansky, M. (2005). Hidden shame. *Journal of the American Psychoanalytic Association*, 53: 865–890.

Lansky, M. (2007). Unbearable shame, splitting, and forgiveness in the resolution of vengefulness. *Journal of the American Psychoanalytic Association*, 55: 571–593.

Lansky, M., & Morrison, A. (Eds.) (1997). *The Widening Scope of Shame*. Hillsdale, NJ: Analytic Press.

Lapierre, D., & Collins, L. (1975). *Freedom at Midnight*. New York: Simon & Schuster.

Laplanche, J., & Pontalis, J.-B. (1973). *The Language of Psycho-Analysis*. New York: W. W. Norton.

Lasch, C. (1971). *The Culture of Narcissism: American Life in an Age of Diminishing Expectations*. New York: W. W. Norton.

Lax, R. F. (2008). Becoming really old: the indignities. *Psychoanalytic Quarterly*, 77: 835–857.

Leary, K. (1995). Interpreting in the dark: race and ethnicity. *Psychoanalytic Psychotherapy*, 12: 127–140.

Levin, S. (1967). Some metapsychological considerations on the differentiation between shame and guilt. *International Journal of Psychoanalysis*, 48: 267–276.

Levin, S. (1971). The psychoanalysis of shame. *International Journal of Psychoanalysis*, 52: 355–362.

Levy, R. S. (Ed.) (2005). *Anti-Semitism: A Historical Encyclopedia of Prejudice and Persecution*. Santa Barbara, CA: ABC-Clio.

Lewin, B. (1946). Sleep, the mouth, and the dream screen. *Psychoanalytic Quarterly*, 15: 419–434.

Lewin, B. (1952). Phobic symptoms and dream interpretation. *Psychoanalytic Quarterly*, 21: 295–322.

Lewis, D. (2005). *The Man Who Invented Hitler: The Making of the Fuhrer*. London: Bounty.

Lewis, H. B. (1971). *Shame and Guilt in Neurosis.* New York: International Universities Press.
Lewis, M. (1992a). *Shame: The Exposed Self.* New York: Free Press.
Lewis, M. (1992b). Will the real self or selves please stand up? *Psychological Inquiry, 3*: 123–124.
Lichtenberg, J. (1988). Infant research and self psychology. *Progress in Self Psychology, 3*: 59–64.
Loewenstein, R. (1951). The problem of interpretation. *Psychoanalytic Quarterly, 20*: 1–23.
Lowenfeld, H. (1976). Notes on shamelessness. *Psychoanalytic Quarterly, 45*: 62–72.
Lussier, A. (1960). The analysis of a boy with a congenital deformity. *Psychoanalytic Study of the Child, 15*: 430–453.
Lynd, H. M. (1958). *On Shame and the Search for Identity.* New York: Science Editions.
Mahler, M. S., Pine, F., & Bergman, A. (1975). The psychological birth of the human infant: symbiosis and individuation. New York: Basic Books.
Mann, M. (2010). Shame veiled and unveiled: the shame affect and its re-emergence in the clinical setting. *American Journal of Psychoanalysis, 70*: 270–281.
Maranhão-Filho, P., & Silva, C. E. da Rocha (2010). Hitler's hysterical blindness: fact or fiction? *Arquivos de Neuro-Psiquiatria, 68*: 826–830.
Marcus, I. (2013). Marriage, conflict, and loss. Vamik Volkan Lecture, Virginia Psychoanalytic Society, Charlottesville, VA, April 25.
Marcus, I., & Francis, J. (1975). *Masturbation: from Infancy to Senescence.* New York: International Universities Press.
Masson, J. M. (1985). *The Complete Letters of Sigmund Freud to Wilhelm Fliess.* Cambridge, MA: Harvard University Press.
McGinniss, J. (1983). *Fatal Vision.* New York: Penguin.
Menninger, K. (1973). *Whatever Became of Sin.* New York: Hawthorn/Dutton.
Merriam-Webster's Collegiate Dictionary (1998). Baltimore, MD: Williams & Wilkins.
Michaud, E. (2004). *The Cult of Art in Nazi Germany.* J. Lloyd (Trans.). Stanford, CA: Stanford University Press.
Middleton-Moz, J. (1990). *Shame and Guilt: Masters of Disguise.* Deerfield Beach, FL: Health Communications.
Miller, S. B. (1996). *Shame in Context.* Hillsdale, NJ: Analytic Press.
Moore, B., & Fine, B. (Eds.) (1968). *A Glossary of Psychoanalytic Terms and Concepts.* New York: American Psychoanalytic Association.
Moore, B., & Fine, B. (Eds.) (1990). *Psychoanalytic Terms and Concepts.* New Haven, CT: Yale University Press.

Morrison, A. (1983). Shame, ideal self, and narcissism. *Contemporary Psychoanalysis*, 19: 295–318.

Morrison, A. (1989). *Shame: The Underside of Narcissism*. Hillsdale, NJ: Analytic Press.

Morrison, A. (1994). The breadth and boundaries of a self-psychological immersion in shame. *Psychoanalytic Dialogues*, 4: 19–35.

Morton, F. (1980). *A Nervous Splendor: Vienna 1888–1889*. New York: Penguin.

Moss, J. (2005). Shame, pleasure and the divided soul. *Oxford Studies in Ancient Philosophy*, 29: 137–170.

Mosse, G. L. (1964). *The Crisis of German Ideology: Intellectual Origins of the Third Reich*. New York: Grosset & Dunlap.

Mosse, G. L. (1990). *Fallen Soldiers: Reshaping the Memory of the World Wars*. Oxford: Oxford University Press.

Mussen, P. H., & Jones, M. D. (1957). Self conceptions, motivations, and interpersonal attitude of late- and early-maturing boys. *Child Development*, 28: 243–256.

Nathanson, D. (1992). *Shame and Pride: Affect, Sex and the Birth of the Self*. New York: W. W. Norton.

Niederland, W. G. (1965). Narcissistic ego impairment in patients with early physical malformations. *Psychoanalytic Study of the Child*, 20: 518–534.

Obeyesekere, G. (1981). *Medusa's Hair: An Essay on Personal Symbols and Religious Experience*. Chicago, IL: University of Chicago Press.

Obeyesekere, G. (1984). *The Cult of the Goddess Pattini*. Chicago, IL: University of Chicago Press.

O'Connor, A. F., Freeland, A. P., Heal, D. J., & Rossouw, D. S. (1977). Iodoform toxicity following the use of B.I.P.P.: a potential hazard. *Journal of Laryngology and Otology*, 91: 903–907.

O'Donnell, M. (2012). *Dangerous Undercurrent: Death, Sacrifice, and Ruin in Third Reich Germany*. www.libraryofsocialscience.com. Accessed January 7, 2015.

Okano, K. (1998). *Psychoanalysis of Shame and Narcissism*. Tokyo: Isawaki Gakujutsu Shuppansha.

Olson, J. S. (2002). *Bathsheba's Breast: Women, Cancer, and History*. Baltimore, MD: Johns Hopkins University Press.

Parker, I. (2008). *Japan in Analysis: Cultures of the Unconscious*. New York: Palgrave Macmillan.

Petersen, A. C. (1983). Menarche: meaning of measures and measuring meaning. In: S. Golub (Ed.), *Menarche: The Transition from Girl to Woman* (pp. 63–76). Lexington, MA: Lexington.

Piers, G., & Singer, M. (1953). *Shame and Guilt: A Psychoanalytic and a Cultural Study*. New York: W. W. Norton, 1971.

Pine, F. (1997). *Diversity and Direction in Psychoanalytic Technique*. New Haven, CT: Yale University Press.

Pizer, S. A. (1998). *Building Bridges: The Negotiation of Paradox in Psychoanalysis*. Hillsdale, NJ: Analytic Press.

Plato (c. 450-400 BCE). *The Symposium*. W. Hamilton (Trans.). New York: Penguin Classics, 1951.

Plaut, E. A., & Hutchinson, F. L. (1986). The role of puberty in female psychosexual development. *International Journal of Psychoanalysis, 13*: 417–432.

Poland, W. (1975). Tact as a psychoanalytic function. *International Journal of Psychoanalysis, 56*: 155–161.

Post, P., Post, A., Post, L., & Post-Senning, D. (2011). *Emily Post's Etiquette: Manners for a New World, 18th edition*. New York: William Morrow.

Pressman, S. (2014). *50 Children: One Ordinary American Couple's Extraordinary Rescue Mission into the Heart of Nazi Germany*. New York: HarperCollins.

Redfield, R. (1952). The primitive world view. *Proceedings of the American Philosophical Society, 96*: 30–36.

Redlich, F. (1998). *Hitler: Diagnosis of a Destructive Prophet*. New York: Oxford University Press.

Retzinger, S. (1991a). *Shame, Exposure, and Privacy*. New York: W. W. Norton.

Retzinger, S. (1991b). *Violent Emotions: Shame and Rage in Marital Conflicts*. Newbury Park, CA: Sage.

Riviere, J. (1936). A contribution to the analysis of the negative therapeutic reaction. *International Journal of Psychoanalysis, 17*: 304–320.

Riviere, J. (1991). A contribution to the analysis of negative therapeutic reaction. In: *The Inner World and Joan Riviere: Collected Papers: 1920–1958* (pp. 134–153). London: Karnac.

Roland, A. (2011). *Journeys to Foreign Selves: Asians and Asian Americans in a Global Era*. New Delhi: Oxford University Press.

Romane, P. (Ed.) (2007). *The Essential Hitler: Speeches and Commentary*. Wauconda, IL: Bolchazy-Carducci.

Ronson, J. (2015). *So You've Been Publicly Shamed*. New York: Riverhead.

Rushdie, S. (1984). *Shame*. New York: Vintage.

Sandler, J., Holder, A., & Meers, D. (1963). The ego ideal and the ideal self. *Psychoanalytic Study of the Child, 18*: 139–158.

Sandler, J., & Sandler, A.-M. (1998). *Internal Objects Revisited*. London: Karnac.

Sartre, J.-P. (1943). *Being and Nothingness*. H. E. Barnes (Trans.). New York: Washington Square Press, 1993.

Schafer, R. (1981). *A New Language for Psychoanalysis*. New Haven, CT: Yale University Press.

Scheff, T. (1987). The shame-rage spiral: a case study of an interminable quarrel. In: H. B. Lewis (Ed.), *The Role of Shame in Symptom Formation* (pp. 110–142). Hillsdale, NJ: Lawrence Erlbaum Associates.

Scheff, T., & Retzinger, S. (1997). Shame in social theory. In: M. Lansky & A. Morrison (Eds.), *The Widening Scope of Shame*. Hillsdale, NJ: Analytic Press.

Schneider, C. D. (1977). *Shame, Exposure, and Privacy*. New York: W. W. Norton.

Schneider, C. D. (1987). A mature sense of shame. In: D. L. Nathanson (Ed.), *The Many Faces of Shame* (pp. 194–213). New York: Guilford Press.

Schore, A. (1994). The dialogical self and the emergence of consciousness. In: A. Schore (Ed.), *Affect Regulation and the Origin of the Self: The Neurobiology of Emotional Development* (pp. 490–498). Hillsdale, NJ: Lawrence Erlbaum Associates.

Schur, M. (1966). *The Id and the Regulatory Mechanisms of Mental Functioning*. New York: International Universities Press.

Schwab-Stone, M., Cohen, P., & Garcia, M. (1985). The timing of puberty and the occurrence of psychopathology in adolescent girls. Presented at the Annual Meeting of the American Academy of Child Psychiatry, San Antonio, October 12.

Scott, A. O. (2014). Advanced course in diversity: "Dear White People," about racial hypocrisy at a college. *New York Times*, C-1. October 16.

Severino, S. K, McNutt, E. R., & Feder, S. L. (1987). Shame and development of autonomy. *Journal of the American Academy of Psychoanalysis and Dynamic Psychiatry*, 15: 93–106.

Shakespeare, W. (1603). *Hamlet*. New York: Signet Classics, 1998.

Shaw, G. B. (1894). *Arms and the Man*. New York: Dover, 1990.

Silverman, S. (2006). Where we both have lived. *Psychoanalytic Dialogues*, 16: 527–542.

Simmons, R. G., Blyth, D. A., & McKinney, K. L. (1983). The social and psychological effects of puberty on white females. In: J. Brooks-Gunn & A. C. Petersen (Eds.), *Girls at Puberty: Biological and Psychological Perspectives* (pp. 229–272). New York: Plenum.

Snyder, L. L. (1998). *Encyclopedia of the Third Reich*. New York: McGraw-Hill.

Snyder, T. (2012). *Bloodlands: Europe between Stalin and Hitler*. New York: Basic Books.

Sophocles. *Oedipus Trilogy*. F. Storr (Trans.). University Park, PA: Pennsylvania State University Press, 2013.

Spero, M. H. (1984). Shame: an object-relational formulation. *Psychoanalytic Study of the Child*, 39: 259–282.

Spotts, F. (2009). *Hitler and the Power of Aesthetics*. Woodstock, NY: Overlook Press.

St. Exupery, A. (1943). *The Little Prince*. New York: Thorndike Press, 2005.
Steiner, J. (2011). *Seeing and Being Seen*. London: Routledge.
Steiner, J. (2013). The ideal and the real in Klein and Milton: some observations on reading "Paradise Lost". *Psychoanalytic Quarterly, 82*: 897–923.
Steinschein, I. (1973). The experience of separation-individuation through the course of life: maturity, senescence, and sociological implications. Panel report. *Journal of the American Psychoanalytic Association, 21*: 633–645.
Stepien, A. (2014). Understanding male shame. *Masculinities, 1*: 7–27.
Sue, D. W. (2010). *Microaggressions in Everyday Life*. Hoboken, NJ: John Wiley and Sons.
Tanner, J. M. (1962). *Growth at Adolescence*, 2nd ed. Oxford: Blackwell.
Tanner, J. M. (1971). Sequence, tempo, and individual variations in growth and development of boys and girls aged twelve to sixteen. *Daedalus, 100*: 907–908.
Tomkins, S. (1963). *Affect, Imagery, Consciousness. Vol. II: The Negative Affects*. New York: Springer.
Tronick, A., Wise, S., & Brazelton, T. (1978). The infant's response to entrapment between contradictory messages in face-to-face interaction. *Journal of Child Psychiatry, 17*: 1–13.
Twain, M. (1897). *Following the Equator: A Journey around the World*. Mineola, NY: Dover, 2011.
Twitchell, J. (1997). *For Shame: The Loss of Common Decency in American Culture*. New York: St. Martin's Press.
Velleman, J. D. (2001). The genesis of shame. *Philosophy and Public Affairs, 30*: 27–52.
Viereck, P. (2004). *Metapolitics: From Wagner and the German Romantics to Hitler*. New Brunswick, NJ: Transaction.
Volkan, V. D. (1981). *Linking Objects and Linking Phenomena: A Study of the Forms, Symptoms, Metapsychology, and Therapy of Complicated Mourning*. New York: International Universities Press.
Volkan, V. D. (2001). Transgenerational transmissions and chosen traumas: an aspect of large-group identity. *Group Analysis, 34*: 79–97.
Volkan, V. D. (2004). *Blind Trust: Large Groups and Their Leaders in Times of Crisis and Terror*. Charlottesville, VA: Pitchstone.
Volkan, V. D. (2012). *Psychoanalytic Technique Expanded*. Charlottesville, VA: Pitchstone.
Volkan, V. D., Ast, G., & Greer, W. F. (Eds.) (2002). *Third Reich in the Unconscious: Trans-generational Transmission and Its Consequences*. New York: Brunner-Routledge.
Waelder, R. (2007). The principle of multiple function: observations on overdetermination. *Psychoanalytic Quarterly, 76*: 75–92.

Weinberg, G. L. (Ed.) (2006). *Hitler's Second Book—The Unpublished Serial to Mein Kampf by Adolf Hitler*. New York: Enigma.

Weiss, E. (1977). *The Eyewitness*. E. R. W. McKee (Trans.). Boston: Houghton Mifflin.

Wheelis, A. (1975). *On Not Knowing How to Live*. New York: Harper & Row.

White, E. B. (1952). *Charlotte's Web*. New York: Harper & Brothers.

Wieseltier, L. (2015). Among the disrupted: book review of "The Age of the Crisis of Man: Thought and Fiction in America, 1933–1973" by Mark Greif. *Sunday New York Times Book Review*, Section R, pp. 13–15, January 18.

Williams, B. (1993). *Shame and Necessity*. Berkeley, CA: University of California Press.

Winnicott, D. W. (1960). Ego distortion in terms of true and false self. In: *Maturational Processes and the Facilitating Environment* (pp. 140–152). New York: International Universities Press, 1965.

Wu, E. B. M. (2014). *Shame and Guilt: Origins of World Cultures*. North Charleston, SC: Create Space.

Wurmser, L. (1981). *The Mask of Shame*. Northvale, NJ: Jason Aronson, 1994.

Wurmser, L. (2013). *Shame and Its Vicious Cycles*. Lecture delivered at the IPA meeting in Prague, Czech Republic, July 27.

www.census.gov/newsroom/releases/archives/population. Accessed March 21, 2015.

Yanof, J. A. (1986). The specter of genetic illness and its effects on development. *Psychoanalytic Study of the Child*, 41: 561–582.

Yorke, C., Balogh, T., Cohen, P., Davids, J., Garshon, A., & McCutcheon, M. (1990). The development and functioning of the sense of shame. *Psychoanalytic Study of the Child*, 45: 377–409.

Young, H. B. (1971). The physiology of adolescence. In: H. G. Howells (Ed.), *Modern Perspectives in Adolescent Psychiatry* (pp. 271–294). Edinburgh, UK: Oliver & Boyd.

Zalampas, S. O. (1990). *Adolf Hitler: A Psychological Interpretation of His Views on Architecture, Art and Music*. Bowling Green, OH: Bowling Green State University Popular Press.

INDEX

absolute shame 52–53
Action Reconciliation Service for Peace (ASRP) 90
active, being 52
Adichie, C. 146, 155
Adler, A. 28
adolescence
  bodily changes in girls and boys 19
  feeling of shame in 20
  humiliation feeling in 20
  psychological maturation and self-development 20
  puberty 19
  separation-individuation issues 20
  sexuality 40
  threat of falling from expected peer social order 20
adolescent girls
  bodily changes 19–20
  greater risk of depressive and anxiety symptoms 20
  later maturing girls, issues with 20–21
  menarche issues 20–21
Adorno, T. W. 72
adult experience of shame. *see also* shame
  adults' responses to oedipal feelings 40
  anxiety related to difficulties, clinical vignette 37–39
  defensive withdrawal from others, case vignette 42–44
  dynamics of shame and response to later life events, clinical vignette 39–40
  from lack of career success, case vignette 41–42
  in marriage and divorce 40
  relationship between disgust and shame 34
African-American Barbie 142

221

INDEX

Ajase complex 61, 69
Akhtar, S. 51, 58, 77, 89, 93–94, 101, 112, 118–119, 132, 146
Alefeld, E. 80
Alexander, F. 55
Allen, S. 119
Als, H. 22
Altman, N. 50
Amsterdam, B. 23
anal stage of development 4
analyst's sense of shame 187–190.
    see also shame
  clinical vignettes 190–192, 196–202
  forms 192–193
  projections and impasses at work 194–195
apology 131–132
  analyst and 138–139
  in analytic situation, clinical vignettes 132–138
  apologize, failure to 131, 136–138
  shame dynamics and aversion to 139–140
Aristotle 67
Arlow, J. 119, 127
Ast, G. 76
Auchincloss, E. L. 94
authentic German culture 79
autonomy 35
Ayers, M. 52, 56, 68, 145
Azzone, P. 182

Baird, J. W. 80–81
Balogh, T. 21
Barthes, R. 66
Benedict, R. 23, 50, 60
Bentham, J. 70
Bergman, A. 15, 23, 121
Binion, R. 86–87
Bion, W. R. 164, 176–177, 179
Blackman, J. 121–122, 125, 127

Blatt, S. 125
Bloch, E. 85–88
Blos, P. 5
Blum, H. 119–120
Blum, L. 126
Blyth, D. A. 21
Boesky, D. 180
Bonhoeffer, D. 67
Bowlby, J. 119
Braun, E. 74
Brazelton, T. B. 22
Brazelton, T. 21
Brenner, C. 115–116, 118, 124, 127
Brenner, I. 76, 88–90
Bretherton, I. 120
Bromberg, P. 189, 194
Broucek, F. J. 22
Bruckner, A. 78
Buechler, S. 189, 200
bypassed shame 52

Caparrotta, L. 21
careers and career success 40–41
Catay, Z. 63
Chasseguet-Smirgel, J. 97, 100
civilizing property of shame 56
Coen, S. J. 5, 14
Cohen, D. 21, 63
Cohen, P. 20–21
Colarusso, C. A. 36, 39–40, 42
Collins, L. 102
Coomaraswamy, A. 68
Coomaraswamy, R. 68
cultural aspects of shame 68, 106.
    see also racial and ethnic differences; shame
  American consumer culture 57
  cultural influence in therapy, case vignettes 63–68
  Eastern culture 58–63
  Greek culture 56–58
  Indian culture 58–60

Japanese culture 60–62, 106
Sinhalese culture 62–63
Turkish culture 63
Western culture 50, 56–58, 66
cultural hypocrisy 54

Davids, J. 21
Davies, J. M. 194, 202
Davoine, F. 164
debilitating shame 52
defective sense of self 4–5
    case vignette 5–17
    Wilhelm II's narcissistic
        vulnerabilities 5
defense-based shamelessness 103
delophilia 112
Demopoulos, P. 77
destructiveness of shaming 56
Deutsch, H. 165
development
    anal stage of 4
    developmental issues of
        childhood 40
    early affective developmental
        failure, case illustration of
        29–30, 32
    ego 5
    pre-oedipal stage of 4
    relation of self and object in early
        developmental life of infants
        21
development-based shamelessness
    100–101
DeVos, G. A. 61
dharma 59, 69
dignity-based shamelessness
    101–103
disavowed shame 52
discharge-based shamelessness
    104–105
discretionary shame 177
disgrace-shame 177

divorce 40
Dodds, E. R. 50, 56
Doi, T. 50, 60, 67
doubt 96

Eastern culture, shame in 58–63
ego 3–4, 40. *see also* superego
    development 5
    ideal 3–4, 96, 100, 126, 146
Eidelberg, L. 94
Elise, D. 13, 16
Elkind, S. N. 194
Emde, R. N. 22, 100
Erikson, E. H. 4, 35–36, 56, 60, 96,
    100, 116, 164
experienced shame 52
extruded shame 202

fairy tales, use in clinical
    intervention 17
false self 66
Feder, S. L. 4, 14–15
Fenichel, O. 34, 96, 103
Ferenczi, S. 111
Field, T. M. 21
Fine, B. 94
Fonagy, P. 20, 28
Forster, E. R. 82–84, 90
Foucault, M. 70
Francis, J. 119
Freeland, A. P. 86
Frenkel-Brunswik, E. 72
Freud, A. 117
Freud, S. 3–5, 34, 54–55, 66, 101,
    103–105, 112, 118, 121, 146,
    164, 176–178
    development of guilt 3
    perverse sexuality 101, 104
    pleasure principle 115, 118
    on shame 3
    view of narcissism 176
    views on shame 94–95, 146

Friedländer, S. 72, 79
Fusella, P. 182

Gabbard, G. 53
Galenson, E. 119
Garcia, M. 20
Garshon, A. 21
Gaudillière, J.-M. 164
Gergely, G. 20
Ghalib, M. 65
Gibbs, P. L. 166, 169, 179–180
Gill, M. 54
Goebbels, J. 82
Goeschel, C. 82
Goffman, E. 161–162
Goldberg, A. 132
Goldberg, C. 189
Grealy, L. 186–187
   Autobiography of a Face 186
Greek culture and shame 56–58
Green, M. 142
Greenberg, R. 21
Greer, W. F. 76
Greif, M. 182
   Age of the Crisis of Man, The 182
Grinker, R. 93
guilt 3–4, 98
   in Christian theology 57
   implanted 61
   in Indian culture 60
   primary 62
   unconscious 140
   vs shame 51
Guilt (2013) 51
guilt-cultures 50, 62
guilt-ridden person 55

Hamann, B. 87
Hartmann, H. 117
   Ego Psychology and the Problem of Adaptation 117
Heal, D. J. 86

Heidegger, M. 129
Heller, A. 54
Higgitt, A. 28
Hitler, A. 71–73. *see also* Nazi philosophy
   anti-Semitism of 74, 87
   congenital defects of 74
   defenses against shame and humiliation 75–77
   dramatic exit of, and mass suicide 77–79
   fascination for 73–75
   influence of childhood years 74–76
   mother's death and 85–88
   parents and parental behavior towards 74
   superman image of 73
   temporary blindness and feeling of grandiosity 82–85
Hitler, F. 86–87
Hitler, K. 85–86, 89
Hoffer, E. 107
Holder, A. 146
Holmes, D. E. 157–158
Homeric shame 56–57
honor killings 106
Huffington Post 142
Hutchinson, F. L. 12

ideal self 62
identity stages 36
implanted guilt 61
Indian culture and shame 58–60
infantile sexuality 34
infants
   earliest developmental trigger for shame 22
   mirror self-image reactions in 23
   relation of self and object in early developmental life of 21
inferiority feelings 55

interpersonal bridge, rupture of 22
intimacy 36
I-self 56
isolation 36

Jacobson, E. 11
Jacquet, J. 58
James, E. 119
Jane, analysis of self as defective
  background 5–6
  bowel movements and school
    phobia 9–10
  clinical and theoretical analysis
    13–15
  concluding remarks 15–17
  early history 6–7
  fantasy play 9
  fear of menstruation 10–12
  friendships 8
  mother's illness and 7–8, 12
  obsession with Wicca 10–11
  personality 8–9
  relationships with siblings
    8–9
  romantic experience 12
Japanese culture and shame 60–62,
  106
jihadi psychology 66
Joiner, T. 72
Jones, M. D. 19
Joseph, B. 180
Jurist, E. 20

Kafka, J. S. 87
Kakar, K. 59, 67
Kakar, S. 59, 65–67, 69
Kaufman, G. 22, 66, 145
Kernberg, O. F. 103–104, 164
Kershaw, I. 86
Kilborne, B. 20, 52, 93
Kinston, W. 35–36
Kitayama, O. 50, 56, 61–62, 106

Prohibition of Don't Look 61
Kjellqvist, E. 103
Klein, M. 164–165, 176–177
Kobrin, N. 66
Koenigsberg, R. A. 72
Kohut, H. 35, 56, 96–98, 119, 140,
  165, 189
Kosawa, H. 69
Kramer, S. 119
Kroner, K. 83
Kubie, L. 59–60
Kubizek, A. 79

Lacan, J. 72
lajja-baya 63
Lansky, M. 21, 56, 93, 99, 140,
  164–165, 176, 178
Lapierre, D. 102
Laplanche, J. 68, 94
Lasch, C. 107
Lax, R. F. 42
laziness
  compromise formation
    underlying 121–123
  conflicts human beings and,
    clinical vignettes 120
  development and manifestations
    of 116–120
Leary, K. 157
Levin, S. 4, 38, 67, 93
Levinson, D. J. 72
Levy, R. S. 79
Lewin, B. 115
Lewis, D. 82, 84
Lewis, H. B. 3, 15, 32, 35, 52, 56, 132,
  140, 169, 176
Lewis, M. 23, 50, 52
Lichtenberg, J. 21
Loewenstein, R. 158
Lowenfeld, H. 56, 94, 107
Lussier, A. 11
Lynd, H. M. 36

Mahabharata 58–59
Mahler, M. S. 23, 119
Mann, M. 31
Maranhão-Filho, P. 82
Marcus, I. 119, 127
marriage 40
masochism 61
Masson 113
master emotion 50
maturation 19–20
McCutcheon, M. 21
McGinniss, J. 113
McKinney, K. L. 21
McNutt, E. R. 4, 14–15
Meers, D. 146
menarche issues in adolescent girls 20–21
    clinical illustration 26–29, 31–32
Menninger, K. 54
Merriam-Webster's Collegiate Dictionary 100
Michaud, E. 80
Middleton-Moz, J. 52, 66
Miller, S. B. 65
Moore, B. 94
Moran, G. 28
Morrison, A. 3–4, 15, 21–22, 35, 52, 56, 93–94, 98, 145
Morton, F. 116
Moss, J. 56
Mosse, G. L. 79–80
multisensory bridges 89
murderous regimes 71
murder-suicide, phenomenon of 71–72, 115
Mussen, P. H. 19

narcissism 100, 176–177
    narcissistic personality disorder 53
    narcissistic self-esteem 4
    narcissistic self-inflation 52
    self-narcissism 35

Nathanson, D. 65–67, 69
Nazi death camps 71
Nazi philosophy 72–73
    as cult of death 79–82
Nemiroff, R. A. 36, 39–40, 42
Niederland, W. G. 11
Nietzsche 77, 102
Nirvana principle 115
Nisbett, R. E. 63
Nuremberg "Law to Protect German Blood and German Honor," 74

Obama, Barack 144
Obeyesekere, G. 50, 62
    Cult of the Goddess Pattini, The 62
    Medusa's Hair 62
objective self-awareness (OSA) 23, 36
object narcissism 35–36
O'Connor, A. F. 86
O'Donnell, M. 79
oedipal phenomena 40
Oedipus complex 62, 176
Oedipus trilogy
    Oedipus at Colonus 55
    Oedipus the King 55
Okano, K. 106
Olson, J. S. 85, 87
O'Neil, P. 101
online public shaming 58
Other, the, notion of 57, 72

Panopticon 66, 69
paranoid patients, psychoanalytic treatment of 163–181
Parens, H. 119
Parker, I. 50
Petersen, A. C. 21
Petkoff, R. 130
Piers, G. 3–4, 34, 50, 55, 96–97
Pine, F. 15, 23, 111, 121
Pizer, S. 195

Plaut, E. A. 12
pleasure principle 115
Poland, W. 158
Pontalis, J.-B. 68, 94
Post, A. 131
Post, L. 131
Post, P. 131
Post-Senning, D. 131
pre-oedipal stage of development 4
pre-representational self 22
Pressman, S. 73
prohibition 61
psychoanalysis 50, 54
psychoanalytic understanding of shame 161–163. *see also* shame
    clincal vignettes 108–111
    Erikson's views 96
    Fenichel's views 96
    Freud's views 94–96
    issues pertaining to 99
    Klein's views 164
    Kohut's views 96, 98–99
    Piers's views 96–97
    role of shame in treating maniacal triumph and paranoia 163–181
    Singer's views 96–97
psychological colonization 66
psychology of shame 50
puberty. *see also* adolescence
    age of onset 19
    anxiety issues 20
    bodily changes in girls and boys 19–20

racial and ethnic differences. *see also* shame
    in advertisements 142
    analyst's inhibitions in therapeutic sessions 156–159

    being exposed and shame, clinical vignette 151–156
    children of color and feeling of shame 145–146
    clinical understanding of psychological issues with 146–159
    racial identity 141
    sensitivity and 144
    vulnerability to shame and 142–145, 147–151
Ramayana 58–59
Redfield, R. 55
Redlich, F. 73, 75
Retzinger, S. 50, 52, 132, 165, 176, 178–179
Rig Veda 65
Riviere, J. 161, 165, 178
Roiphe, H. 119
Roland, A. 56, 63, 70
role diffusion 36
Romane, P. 81
Ronson, J. 58
Rossouw, D. S. 86
Rudolph, Prince 115–116
Rushdie, S. 59

Samberg, E. 94
Sandler, A.-M. 93
    Internal Objects Revisited 93
Sandler, J. 93, 146
    Internal Objects Revisited 93
Sanford, R. N. 72
Sartre, J.-P. 57
    Being and Nothingness 57
Schafer, R. 54
Scheff, T. 50, 52, 132
Schlageter, A. 80
Schneider, C. D. 165, 176–177, 203
Schopenhauer, A. 77
Schore, A. 22
Schur, M. 115

Schwab-Stone, M. 20
Schwarzchild, L. 85
Scott, A. O. 141
   Dear White People 141
self-acceptance 162
self concept
   defective sense of self 4–5
   earliest self-representation 23
   false self 66
   pre-representational self 22
   self-awareness 22, 36
   somatic self 21
   true self 66
self-doubt 4
self-esteem 4
self-narcissism 35
sensory memories 89
separateness 36
Severino, S. K. 4, 14–15
sexual perversion 101, 104
Shakespear, W. 65
shame. *see also* adult experience of shame; analyst's sense of shame; cultural aspects of shame; racial and ethnic differences
   affective states and 22
   affect of 97, 99
   anal stage of development and 4
   as an inhibitor of hyper-aroused states 22
   as an interpersonal emotion 67
   clinical illustrations of maturational development and 23–31
   as a conflict between ego and ego ideal 3, 34, 51, 96
   defense against 3–4, 52, 96
   definition 51–54
   derivation of word 52
   discretionary 177
   disgrace-shame 177
   earliest experiences of 22
   environmental factors contributing to 145
   experience of being exposed and 35
   exposure of vulnerable aspects and 36
   feelings of inferiority 55
   induction of 23, 98
   intentionality and intersubjectivity 22
   laziness and 118. *see also* laziness
   love withdrawal and 23
   metaphors for 59, 68, 69
   monographs on 97–98
   as a narcissistic response 3
   objective self-awareness and 23, 36
   as a reaction to disapproval 3
   relationship between disgust and 34
   schematization of the experience 53–54
   self concept and 35
   signal 140
   strong reactions of 67
   superego and 59
   threshold of 53
   visual markers of 51
   vs guilt 51
shame-affect 53
shame-anxiety 53
shame-cultures 50
shamelessness 93–94. *see also* shame
   defense-based 103
   definition of 100
   development-based 100–101
   dignity-based 101–103
   discharge-based 104–105
   forms of 100
   sociocultural dimension of 106–108

shame-proneness, understanding of 164–165
shame-prone paranoid patients and maniacal triumph, psychoanalytic treatment of 163–181
  clinical vignettes 166–176
  defenses associated with paranoid-schizoid position 164–166
  expression of violent emotions 166–169, 176–179
  narcissistic vulnerability and masochistic stance 169–176, 180–181
  sense of boundaries 165
  use of Self/Object 177
  working through boundaries 176–181
shame-ridden person 55
shaming others 52
Shaw, G. B. 130–131
  Arms and the Man 130
Shukla, P. 113
signal shame 140
Silva, C. E. da Rocha 82
Silverman, S. 190
Simmons, R. G. 21
Singer, M. 3–4, 34, 50, 55, 96–97
Sinhalese culture and shame 62–63
Sisi, Empress 115
Snyder, L. L. 79
Snyder, T. 71
social anxiety 96
social referencing 100
Socrates 56
somatic self 21
  case of Ted 24–26
Sophocles 54, 56
Speer, A. 77
Spero, M. H. 42, 93
spoiled identity 161

Spotts, F. 80–81
St. Augustine 65
St. Exupery, A.
  Little Prince, The 185
stay-at-home moms 125
Steele, H. 28
Steiner, J. 172, 176
Steinschein, I. 40
Stepien, A. 67
Sue, D. W. 144, 146
superego 3–5, 55, 59, 69, 96, 99, 118–119, 121–122
  development 164

Tanner, J. M. 19
Target, M. 20
temporary shame 52
theatophilia 112
Third Reich 72–73, 77
Tomkins, S. 22
Totenkult monument 79, 81
trauma, intergenerational transmission of 89–90
Tronick, A. 21
trust, sense of 4
Turkish culture and shame 63
Twain, M. 49, 67
Twitchell, J. 52, 57–58, 66

unashamed individual 36
unconscious guilt 140
unconscious shame 52
Urban, K. 85–86

Velleman, J. D. 57
Versailles Treaty 81
Vetsera, M. 115
Viereck, P. 80
Volkan, V. D. 72, 76, 82, 89, 119–120

Waelder, R. 116, 122
Wagner, R. 77–80

Weinberg, G. L. 76
Weiss, E. 84–85
   Eyewitness, The 84
We-self 56
Western culture, shame in 50, 56–58, 66
Wheelis, A. 102
White, E. B. 7
Wieseltier, L. 182
Williams, B. 57
Winnicott, D. W. 109, 145
Wise, S. 21
withdrawal 52
woman, issues surrounding work and 125–126

Woodson, R. 21
workaholic 123
   compromise formation underlying 124–125
   theoretical understanding of 123–124
Wu, E. B. M. 50, 70
Wurmser, L. 53, 93, 97, 101, 103, 105, 112

Yanof, J. A. 5
Yorke, C. 21
Young, H. B. 19

Zalampas, S. O. 86